Holodomor in Uk
The Genocidal Famine,

Learning materials for teachers and students

Valentina Kuryliw

КІУС CIUS

Canadian Institute of Ukrainian Studies Press
Edmonton 2018 Toronto

DEDICATION

To the memory of my beloved parents, Iwan and Nadia Mychajlowskij, who survived the horrors of the Holodomor. My father Iwan was also incarcerated in the notorious Belomor (White Sea) Canal concentration camp in the 1930s.

To the millions of innocent victims who were starved to death and could not speak for themselves.

To the memory of James Mace, whom I had the pleasure of knowing — a man who rekindled the memory of the Holodomor and pioneered its study in Ukraine.

ACKNOWLEDGEMENTS

The following graciously lent their support, permitted use of their materials, or provided recommendations, for which I am grateful:

- The Temerty Foundation for their moral and financial support.
- Halia Sawycky-Dmytryshyn, Oksana Kuryliw, Tamara Kowalczyk, and Roman Serbyn for contributing articles, lessons or other resources.
- Marsha Skrypuch, author of *Kobzar's Children*, for the reprint of the short story "The Rings."
- Roma Franko, for the reprint of her translation of the short story by Olena Zvychayna, "Without Doctors and Priests, without Graves and Crosses," from *A Hunger Most Cruel.*
- Lana Babij, for editing, reorganizing, and updating the resource list found in Part IV.
- Professors Roman Serbyn, Frank Sysyn, Oleh Wolowyna and researchers Andrij Makuch and Bohdan Klid for their suggestions and expertise.
- Morgan Williams for posters from the Holodomor collection, *Through the Eyes of Ukrainian Artists.*
- The National Museum, *Memorial to Holodomor Victims*, in Ukraine for images from the Cardinal Innitzer Holodomor collection and other archival photographs of the period.
- Patriarch Mstyslav Ukrainian Museum, Ukrainian Historical and Educational Center of New Jersey, for the photo of the painting *The Earth (Zemlya).*
- The League of Ukrainian Canadians and the Ucrainica Research Institute for the use of the map *Areas Affected by the Famine*, as well as photos on the Holodomor from the exhibit *Holodomor: The Ukrainian Genocide.*
- The Ukrainian Canadian Congress for the *Five Stalks of Grain* logo, created by Oleh Lesiuk to commemorate the Holodomor.
- Liudmyla Hrynevych for photos of collectivization from the Holodomor Research and Education Centre in Ukraine (HREC in Ukraine).
- Marusia Petryshyn, former director of the Ukrainian Language Education Centre of the Canadian Institute of Ukrainian Studies, University of Alberta and her staff for content editing, supplemental research, supplemental content and for her ongoing encouragement and professional advice in preparing this publication.
- The Holodomor Education Team of the Ukrainian Canadian Congress, Toronto branch.
- The National Holodomor Education Committee, Ukrainian Canadian Congress.
- Members of the Holodomor Research and Education Consortium, University of Alberta, headed by executive director Marta Baziuk, for their support and advice.
- A special thank you goes to Sophia Isajiw for ensuring all the details were completed with care in the final stages.
- My children, Ulyana and Peter, for their patience and support. Ihor Kuryliw, my husband, for his continuous patience and care in bringing this publication to the world.

PREFACE

The Government of Canada officially recognizes five of the genocides that have been committed over the past two hundred years: the Armenian genocide that took place during the First World War, the Ukrainian Holodomor of the 1930s, the Nazi-organized Holocaust of Europe's Jews during World War II, the Rwandan genocide of the early 1990s, and the ethnic cleansing of Bosnians in Srebrenica in the 1990s. Increasingly, Canadian schools are incorporating the study of these events into their curricula.

Holodomor in Ukraine: The Genocidal Famine, 1932-1933 — Learning Materials for Teachers and Students by history specialist Valentina Kuryliw addresses the pressing need for quality materials to teach a difficult subject. The workbook reflects a depth of experience educating generations of Canadian students, enriched by years of teaching educators in Ukraine.

"Holodomor" is a term to describe the famine that inflicted death by starvation on millions of people in Ukraine, a genocide that originated in a series of policies of the Soviet government. Soviet (Bolshevik) rule was finally established in Ukraine after the Russian Revolution (1917) and the period of independent Ukrainian governments (1917-1920). During these years, the large agrarian estates had been broken up, and the position of the peasants as private farmers had strengthened. After initial disastrous attempts to impose control on the peasantry, Soviet authorities relented under the New Economic Policy (1922). Starting in the late 1920s, the Soviet authorities resolved to gain total control over those who worked the land. The peasant farmers were deprived of their property, including agricultural implements and livestock, and forced onto collective farms. The Communist authorities, motivated by a Marxist ideology that declared peasants as backward, embarked on an industrialization campaign that favoured industrial workers at the cost of those in the countryside. By the early 1930s, these policies had wreaked havoc in food production.

Soviet leader Joseph Stalin was increasingly exerting dictatorial control and was indifferent to the consequences of his policies for groups he saw as expendable. Thus, in 1931-1932, the authorities confiscated much of the livestock of the Kazakh nomads in order to feed the Soviet urban centers of Moscow and Leningrad. The Kazakh famine demonstrated not only the disregard of the Communists for groups they considered backward (such as nomads) but also their disdain for peoples peripheral to the Russian political and industrial centres. Some 1.5 million Kazakhs, or 38 percent of the Kazakh people, starved to death.

Ukraine was a focal point in this Soviet war against the peasantry. As a grain-growing region, the Ukrainian Socialist Soviet Republic was central to the Kremlin's plan to extract grain that would be sold abroad in order to provide the hard cash required for funding the Soviet industrialization program. In the minds of Stalin and his associates, Ukraine and its leadership in Kharkiv represented a threat to central authority. In the 1920s, Moscow had embarked on a policy to promote the development of non-Russian cultures in Ukraine and the other republics as a way of gaining local support. The implementation of this policy, known in Ukraine as Ukrainization, was largely a reaction to the difficulty the Bolsheviks had encountered in establishing control in Ukraine in 1917-1921, a period when a series of Ukrainian governments fought for independence. By the early 1930s, Stalin saw the experiment in promoting Ukrainian language, culture, and identity as having gone too far, especially since it had taken hold even among Ukrainians living in the Russian Federated Soviet Republic. He feared that Ukraine and its Communist leaders had the potential to rebel against Moscow's rule.

In the early 1930s, the Soviet leadership was confronted with an agrarian crisis of its own making. As a result of the ruinous Soviet collectivization policy and unrealistic grain procurement quotas, famine struck in many areas of the Soviet Union. In addition to Kazakhstan, the greatest losses of life in the Russian Soviet Federated Socialist Republic occurred in the Volga and Saratov regions as well as the Kuban.

In this period, Communist leaders expressed increasing concern about the potential ramifications of Ukrainian national identity. Seeking to root out expressions of Ukrainian national sentiment, Moscow unleashed campaigns of repression against Ukrainian cultural activists and religious leaders and even against Ukrainian Communist Party officials. Stalin also revoked all cultural rights for Ukrainians in Russia (especially in Kuban, near the Ukrainian border). By late 1932, in a drive to subdue Ukraine, almost all foodstuffs were seized in the rural areas of Ukraine, and the borders of Ukraine and the Kuban and other regions of the North Caucasus were closed. These actions condemned millions to death, the vast majority of them Ukrainians. Members of other national groups in Ukraine also starved to death in large numbers. Those who survived were expected to be pliable instruments of a regime that promoted Russian imperial traditions and the dominance of the Russian language.

For more than fifty years, the Soviet authorities denied that the Famine of 1932-1933 had occurred. It was left to Ukrainian groups in the West, especially survivors, to bear witness. With the fall of the Soviet Union in 1991, researchers gained access to archives that have made it possible to study the Famine comprehensively. Scholars both in and outside Ukraine continue to expand the body of work devoted to the Holodomor. In *Holodomor in Ukraine, The Genocidal Famine, 1932-1933*, educators now have a resource containing the methods and materials not only to teach about the Holodomor but to do so within the broader contexts of genocide and human rights. Valentina Kuryliw has with this publication made a major contribution to the teaching of the Holodomor and to ensuring that the Holodomor be known, understood, and remembered.

Professor Frank E. Sysyn
Holodomor Research and Education Consortium, Canadian Institute of Ukrainian Studies,
University of Alberta

TABLE OF CONTENTS

Part III - Learning Activities 131

PART I
Introduction

IN THIS SECTION

About this Resource

What is the Holodomor?

Why Study the Holodomor?

Curriculum Applications:

Alberta

Manitoba

Ontario

Saskatchewan

"The Earth" (Zemlya) - oil painting by Bohdan Pevny. The Patriarch Mstyslav Museum of the Ukrainian Historical and Educational Center of New Jersey.

The introduction provides information about how the topic of the Holodomor enhances the teaching of genocide and the study of history. It brings out the unique aspects of the genocidal Famine that for decades had been denied, ignored and covered up and examines the Famine's significance and influence on events in present-day Europe.

The approach of this publication is generic, providing basic information and activities that encourage the development of critical and historical thinking skills, which are major expectations in history and social studies curricula across Canada. The variety of materials gives teachers the opportunity to select the best suited to their students' needs from the lesson plans, assignments and projects enclosed.

A separate section on suggested applications for specific courses of study in the provinces of Alberta, Manitoba, Ontario, and Saskatchewan is included, based on curriculum guidelines of 2014.

Holodomor = death inflicted by starvation.

Orphans wandered the countryside and cities looking for food.

Laws passed that led to the human-made famine in Ukraine.

OGPU = Soviet secret police in the 1930s used to enforce government decrees.

Death and **Destruction** in the countryside.

Oats, wheat and barley - taken away by the Soviet authorities.

Millions were starved to death.

Old and young died.

Remember the victims of the Holodomor on the 4th Saturday in November.

HOLODOMOR – Holod No More

Since 1933, the Holodomor was known by various names: the Famine, the Terror-Famine, the Great Famine, the Famine-Genocide, the Genocidal Famine and now the Holodomor. These terms may appear in some of the resources but the contemporary usage preferred is the Holodomor.

About this Resource

This resource was originally created by Valentina Kuryliw for the workshop "The Unknown Genocide: The Holodomor in Ukraine 1932–33" for the Ontario History and Social Studies Teachers' Association (OHASSTA) Conference in 2008. This workbook is not a narrative or comprehensive account of all aspects of the Holodomor. It is a collection of stand-alone items for teachers to use in the classroom. In addition to timelines, background information, lesson plans, and learning activities, it also provides primary resources such as documents, eyewitness accounts, and excerpts from literature. This resource takes a cross-curricular approach, making it possible to adapt sections to the expectations of school jurisdictions across Canada, the United States, and elsewhere. In this workbook, the terms "peasants" and "farmers" are used interchangeably to identify villagers in Ukraine.

Increasingly, the Holodomor is included in units of study on abuse of human rights and courses on genocide that are now being introduced into curricula from kindergarten to grade 12 by ministries of education and school boards. This revised edition has added resources and lesson plans with contributions from educators Roman Serbyn, Oksana Kuryliw, Halia Dmytryshyn and Tamara Kowalczyk, and researchers Nicole Loroff, Jordan Vincent and Orest Zakydalsky.

The materials in this learning resource are divided into four sections:

PART I contains the introduction, information about this resource, rationale for studying the Holodomor, as well as the identification of history and social studies curricula applications for the provinces of Alberta, Manitoba, Ontario and Saskatchewan.

PART II consists of learning resources such as essays, maps, newspaper articles, primary documents, survivor accounts and excerpts from historical fiction. It also includes resources for lessons and identifies additional materials available online.

PART III contains lesson plans and learning activities for teachers to use with students from grades 5 through high school. Some lessons are suggested for the grade 10 level Ontario Civics course on Human Rights Abuse; others requiring more advanced critical thinking skills are for senior history, geography and social studies students.

PART IV is the Appendix, which includes an extensive bibliography and resource list of print, online and multi-media resources, plus selected materials on the Holodomor for teachers to use in the classroom.

The **HOLODOMOR TEACHING KIT**, created by Kuryliw, is available through the Holodomor Research and Education Consortium (HREC) of the Canadian Institute of Ukrainian Studies (CIUS). The kit contains this publication, pamphlets, a DVD of the documentary *Harvest of Despair*, the booklet *Holodomor Ukrainian Genocide in the Early 1930s* and the book *Holodomor of 1932-33 in Ukraine: Documents and Materials.* To acquire the kit contact HREC at **hreced@ualberta.ca**.

What is the Holodomor?

During the twentieth century, colossal human tragedies occurred — among them the Armenian Genocide, the Ukrainian Holodomor, the Holocaust, the Rwandan Genocide, the Bosnian Genocide and most recently, the Genocide of the Yazidis.[1] This resource focuses on the genocidal famine known as the "Holodomor," which in the Ukrainian language means "death inflicted by starvation." Millions of men, women and children were starved to death in the early 1930s through the implementation of a Soviet policy that destroyed a large segment of the Ukrainian population. The Holodomor encompasses the starvation of the farmers as well as a broader assault on Ukraine as a whole. The forced famine was coupled with an attack on the cultural, religious and political leadership of Ukraine.[2] Thus, a significant part of the largest minority national group within the Soviet Union, the Ukrainians, was destroyed, and their aspirations for autonomy and independence was crushed for decades.

The Soviet regime that conducted this genocide denied its occurence and terrorized its own population into silence for generations in order to minimize global awareness of the crime. Since the demise of the Soviet Union in 1991, archives in Russia and Ukraine, which for decades had been closed to scholars, were opened. Researchers identified previously inaccessible documents and materials that clarify the motivations of the Soviet leadership in the 1930s regarding Ukraine and the conduct of its regional leaders during the Holodomor. This research has led to major changes in understanding this tragedy and its historical significance, including its far-reaching consequences for present-day Ukraine.

Holodomor monument in Edmonton, Alberta, created by Ludmilla Temertey, 1983.

---

1 The UN declared in June 2016 that the Yazidis, a non-Islamic community in Iraq and Syria, have been targeted by Islamist militants "to erase their identity."

2 From the speech "Soviet Genocide in the Ukraine" by Raphael Lemkin, 1953. See Appendix in this resource to read Lemkin's full speech.

Why Study the Holodomor?

1. To prevent future genocides

a) The UN Convention on the Prevention and Punishment of the Crime of Genocide, ratified by 143 countries, recognized that genocide is one of the gravest crimes against humanity. Yet since the Convention's declaration in 1948, the world has failed to prevent a number of genocides. The prevention of genocides remains a challenge for a global citizenry. Studying the processes by which genocides are implemented allows people to recognize the behavioural patterns of discrimination and bullying. The first step toward prevention is understanding the phenomenon so that the potential for genocide can be recognized and action can be taken to halt its occurrence.

The prevention of genocides remains a challenge for a global citizenry.

b) An informed citizenry can put pressure on elected officials to respond to events leading to genocides. The genocides of the twentieth century were often met with ignorance and inaction by foreign governments that had little incentive to act. The principle of non-interference in the actions of a sovereign state is still a powerful factor that can complicate the response of the world community to genocide and embolden perpetrators who have not been held to account.

c) The Holodomor is a prime example of using "food as a weapon;" it was perpetrated by depriving nourishment from the very people who were the producers of food. This practice has since occurred in other parts of the world.

Use of food as a weapon.

2. To reduce prejudice and bullying

The study of genocide involves critical thinking that assists students to understand:

- how extreme beliefs or fundamentalist ideologies can foster and later unleash discriminatory and violent actions;
- the incremental nature of prejudice, stereotyping, bullying and discrimination and how these can evolve into genocide;
- how ordinary men and women can participate in ethnic violence;
- how power relations impact decisions regarding discrimination and exploitation;
- how extreme actions may lead to legislation to reduce prejudice and to foster a more humane and informed citizenry.

Prejudice and bullying as precursors to genocide.

3. To increase vigilance against encroachments on human rights

a) History shows that a stepped-up "legally-enforced" erosion of human rights is often a precursor to genocide. Vigilance is required to monitor the actions of both democratic and authoritarian governments with respect to human rights abuses and genocide. The study of the Holodomor and genocide in general helps students understand the importance of protecting individual rights in the Canadian Charter of Rights and Freedoms. These rights are not the birthright of the few, but the birthright of all.

b) Genocides are often viewed in the context of "war crimes." The Holodomor, however, was a genocide committed in a time of peace, in the 1930s. That said, it could be viewed within the context of a *de facto* war on independent farmers in Ukraine.

Holodomor - a genocide committed in a time of peace.

c) Yale history professor Timothy Snyder explains in his book *Bloodlands* that the Holodomor can be viewed as an example of the escalation of genocidal activities by an authoritarian regime, that was not confronted for its crimes against people under its authority.

Escalation of genocide due to inaction.

4. **To examine Canada's response to crimes against humanity**

a) Canada has played an important role in international peacekeeping and in establishing the International Criminal Court to address crimes against humanity. To further Canada's international role in these areas, citizens must be prepared to study these questions in depth, to find solutions that prevent genocides, and to ensure redress when crimes against humanity do occur.

The importance of the International Criminal Court.

b) For the most part, genocides and other crimes perpetrated by Communist powers have yet to be dealt with and condemned by the global community. The Holodomor is a prime example of such inaction.

Condemnation of Communist crimes of genocide.

5. **To set the UN's response to genocide in perspective**

The study of the Holodomor provides an opportunity to examine the origin of the term "genocide" and the views of Raphael Lemkin, the primary author of the UN Convention on the Prevention and Punishment of the Crime of Genocide. His story demonstrates the difficulties and the devotion required to bring about international justice. Familiar with the Armenian genocide and the situation in Soviet Ukraine prior to World War II, he pursued the question of how to prevent and redress such crimes through international law. Ultimately, he came up with the legal concept of genocide. Lemkin referred to the Soviet Ukrainian case as "a classic example of genocide." Due to his perseverance, today we have legal means to redress this horrific crime.

Holodomor as a classic example of genocide.

6. **To review critically media coverage of the Holodomor**

An examination of media treatment and cover-up of the Holodomor provides an excellent opportunity for teaching students about the use and abuse of media to sway world opinion.

The role of media in creating public opinion.

7. To understand totalitarian communist regimes

The study of the Holodomor not only teaches us about the destruction of humanity that took place in the Soviet Union, but it also provides a learning opportunity to examine how a totalitarian society functions.

a) The Holodomor is a horrific example of peacetime social engineering gone wrong, which killed millions not for what they had done, but for who they were.

A case of social engineering gone wrong.

b) The Soviet Union was a particularly ruthless and powerful state with a history that spanned most of the twentieth century, lasting much longer than Nazi Germany, with dire consequences for millions of people.

Soviet history spans a period of over 70 years.

c) Historians have tended to overlook the nationalities policy of the Soviet Union and the subjugation of its minorities, too often treating the history of the Soviet Union as "Russian" and its nationalities as a homogeneous "Soviet people" or as Russians.

The nationalities policy of the Soviet Union needs to be addressed.

d) Hitler learned many lessons from Stalin. Timothy Snyder *(Bloodlands)* writes that Stalin's strategy was well thought out, even methodical, and was likely a template for the crimes by the Nazis. Some experts question whether Hitler would have been so bold with his genocidal plans had the perpetrators of the Ukrainian genocide been held accountable internationally.

Stalin's actions – were a template for Hitler.

8. To become familiar with today's Ukraine

Today, Ukraine is both a post-genocidal and post-colonial society that is still coming to terms with its history, including the devastation of its culture, the physical destruction of its people, and the denial by some of its separate identity. The study of the Holodomor is crucial to understanding political processes in Ukraine and Eastern Europe in general, as well as Ukraine's struggle with Russia for the right to national self-determination.

Current problems in Ukraine are tied to the past. For example, the Holodomor.

9. To make connections to Canadian history

a) At the end of World War II Canadian soldiers encountered thousands of refugees of Ukrainian background in camps for displaced persons in Europe and in German concentration camps. Many of these Ukrainians were also survivors of Soviet concentration camps and the Holodomor. They still faced the threat of forced repatriation to the Soviet Union, with dire consequences, because of an agreement between the Western powers and the Soviet Union to return displaced persons to their states of origin. Many of

Survivors of the Holodomor serve as eyewitnesses.

the Holodomor survivors who managed to avoid repatriation made their home in Canada and have given testimonies of their ordeal during the 1930s.

b) More than 1,300,000 Canadians are of Ukrainian ancestry, among them survivors of the Holodomor, their children and grandchildren. Canadians of Ukrainian ancestry across the country expect that significant events in Ukraine's history be included in the curriculum taught to their children and the general public.

10. To consider the consequences of historical injustice

a) The Holodomor was denied, ignored, and covered up for about 50 years. The Holodomor is still denied in some circles. The Holodomor raises the question of historical justice. Should the victims be acknowledged and the perpetrators brought to light?

Denial of the Holodomor still a concern.

b) In contrast to international criminal proceedings, historical justice may involve restitution, reparation, rehabilitation, truth commissions, official apologies, and material or symbolic rectification. Studying the Holodomor provides an opportunity to examine appropriate responses to genocide.

Acknowledgement will lead to historical justice and closure.

Genocide is the destruction of an ethnic or religious group or nation.

Elimination of identified undesirable elements in society.

No more genocide.

Operational and intentional decrees carried out by perpetrators: individuals or governments.

Commemoration of victims of the Holodomor and other genocides.

Identity may lead to genocide: national, ethnic, racial, or religious.

Destruction of a people, nation, culture, religion, or identity.

Everyone is affected; both the victims and survivors, as well as perpetrators and bystanders.

The Holodomor in Canadian Curricula

Alberta, Manitoba, Ontario, Saskatchewan

This section provides the curriculum applications as of August 2014 for the topic of the Holodomor and the expectations of programs of study for the provinces of Alberta, Manitoba, Ontario and Saskatchewan. Included are additional recommended resources on the Holodomor for classroom use. Part IV provides a listing of resources.

ALBERTA CURRICULUM CONNECTIONS

Social Studies 10-1 and Social Studies 10-2
Social Studies 20-1 and Social Studies 20-2
Social Studies 30-1 and Social Studies 30-2

In keeping with the overall goals of Alberta's social studies program, the study of the Holodomor provides students with a case study that exemplifies the differences between Canada's democratic institutions and those of a totalitarian regime. Through this program, students will gain a greater appreciation and understanding of citizenship and identity in a Canadian context, these being the ultimate learning objectives of Alberta's social studies curriculum. A case study of the Holodomor meets many of the curriculum's overall criteria in the following areas: values and attitudes, knowledge and understanding, skills and processes, core concepts of citizenship and identity, and finally pluralism: diversity and cohesion.[3]

Social Studies 10-1: Perspectives on Globalization
Social Studies 10-2: Living in a Globalizing World

Although many consider globalization a recent phenomenon, the Soviet Union had as its primary goal the spreading of Communism across the world. To prove that Communism was superior to capitalism, the USSR implemented ambitious industrialization and educational targets. The USSR attempted to integrate all of its republics linguistically, culturally and economically. The Holodomor is a prime example of how the USSR responded to any serious threats to its vision. Study of the Holodomor addresses Key Outcomes of Social 10-1 and 10-2 curriculum as students will better understand the complexities of globalization. The Holodomor also enables students to assess the impact of globalization on indigenous peoples and what the individual can do to influence globalization.[4]

Social Studies 20-1: Perspectives on Nationalism
Social Studies 20-2: Understandings of Nationalism

---

3 Alberta, Alberta Education, *Social Studies 20-1 and 20-2.* [Alberta, Canada], 2007, pp. 1-9. https://education.alberta.ca/social-studies-10-12/programs-of-study/everyone/programs-of-study/. Note: Each of the PDFs provided on Alberta Education's web page begin with the same preamble on the program rationale and philosophy.

4 Alberta, Alberta Education, *Social Studies 10-1.* [Alberta, Canada], 2007, pp. 13-25, https://education.alberta.ca/media/160209/program-of-study-grade-10.pdf; Alberta, Alberta Education, *Social Studies 10-2.* [Alberta, Canada], 2007, pp. 27-28, https://education.alberta.ca/media/160209/program-of-study-grade-10.pdf.

The Holodomor was in many ways the result of the conflict between national, ultranational and supranational identities. As such, it lends itself well to the key and general outcomes of the Social 20 curriculum. In terms of Key Outcomes, it enables students to understand the complexity of nationalism as one people struggles for self-determination while another tries to build a multi-national state. In terms of General Outcomes, the Holodomor is useful in demonstrating the impact that the pursuit of nationalism has on national interests.[5]

Social Studies 30-1: Perspectives on Ideology
Social Studies 30-2: Understandings of Ideology

The USSR was a revolutionary state founded on the principles of Marxism-Leninism, an ideology radically different from that of liberalism. In fact, much of the twentieth century may be characterized as a decades-long struggle between these two belief systems. The Holodomor represents the pinnacle of an ideology overstepping respect for human life. Moreover, the genocidal actions of the Soviets provide a stark example of the differences between Stalinism and liberalism. Through the examination of the Holodomor, students will gain skills in assessing ideologies — the differences between words and actions — thus meeting the Key Outcomes for Social 30-1 and 2. The Holodomor best meets the General Outcome criteria as it identifies the link between identity and ideology.[6]

For an overview of the contents of Alberta's Social Studies programs of study, go to: **http://www.education.alberta.ca/teachers/program/socialstudies/programs.aspx**

MANITOBA CURRICULUM CONNECTIONS

Social Studies: Grade 9, Canada in the Contemporary World: A Foundation for Implementation
Social Studies: Grade 11, History of Canada (30F)
Social Studies: Grade 12, Global Issues: Citizenship and Sustainability (40S)

- The Holodomor, the history of Ukraine and the history of Ukrainian-Canadians are particularly relevant to the above-listed elements of the Manitoba Social Studies curriculum. This learning resource is particularly useful for exploring *World Issues: Unit 3, Topic 2: Quality of Life in the USSR* and *Unit 4, Topic 2: The Famine in the Ukraine 1932–1933.*

- The Holodomor is well suited for highlighting the major goals of this soon to be revised course in order to "...help students gain a better understanding of quality

5 Alberta, Alberta Education, *Social Studies 20-1 and 20-2.* [Alberta, Canada], 2007, pp. 13, 25.

6 Alberta, Alberta Education, *Social Studies 20-1 and 20-2.* [Alberta, Canada], 2007, pp. 13, 25, https://education.alberta.ca/media/160210/program-of-study-grade-11.pdf .

of life in various parts of the world..."[7] Although Unit 4, Topic 2 (which is optional) is devoted solely to the Holodomor, study of this Famine can still be incorporated into Unit 3, Topic 2, as it speaks volumes about the priorities of the Soviet regime and its attitude toward the welfare of its citizens.

Manitoba Education's rationale for Holodomor study can be found at:
http://www.edu.gov.mb.ca/k12/cur/multic/holodomor.html

For access to Manitoba's available online curricula, follow the links available on:
http://www.edu.gov.mb.ca/k12/cur/socstud/index.html

ONTARIO CURRICULUM CONNECTIONS

Newly revised curricula for *Canadian and World Studies* (2013) for grades 9 and 10, *Social Sciences and the Humanities* (2013) for grades 11 and 12, *Canadian and World Studies* (fall of 2015) for grades 11 and 12 have been established by the Ontario Ministry of Education.

Grade 10: Civics, Open (CHV2O)
Grade 10: Canadian History since WWI, Academic (CHC2D), Applied (CHC2P)
Grade 11: Equity, Diversity and Social Justice, Workplace Preparation (HSG3M)
Grade 11: Understanding Canadian Law, University/College Preparation (CLU3M)
Grade 11: Politics in Action: Making Change, Open (CPO3O)
Grade 11: World History since 1900: Global and Regional Interactions (CHT3O)
Grade 12: Equity and Social Justice: From Theory to Practice, University/College Preparation (HSE4M)
Grade 12: Adventures in World History, Workplace Preparation (CHM4E)
Grade 12: World History since the Fifteenth Century, University Preparation (CHY4U)
Grade 12: World History since the Fifteenth Century, College Preparation (CHY4C)
Grade 12: Canadian and International Politics, University Preparation (CPW4U)
Grade 12: Canadian and International Law, University Preparation (CLN4U)

The Ontario curriculum offers a variety of courses in which teaching the history of the Holodomor has a strong connection to the overall expectations of the curriculum, particularly its focus on the creation of responsible and informed citizens who understand

7 Manitoba, Manitoba Education, Citizenship and Education, *Grade 12 World Issues* (1990). [Manitoba, Canada], 1990, p. 1, http://www.edu.gov.mb.ca/k12/cur/socstud/global_issues/index.html

the interactions of their social, cultural, historical, and environmental worlds. Study of the Holodomor can be implemented in the following courses:

Grade 10: Civics, Open (CHV2O)
The Genocidal Famine is suggested as a case study to highlight the differences between authoritarian and democratic states. Furthermore, it provides students with opportunities to better understand their responsibilities as informed, purposeful and active citizens, supporting the three strands used for establishing the course's overall expectations.[8] Expectation: C.2 Inclusion and Participation.

Grade 10: Canadian History since World War I, Academic (CHC2D), Applied (CHC2P)
Study of the Holodomor will meet the course's overall expectations in the area of: C.3.2: Identity, Citizenship and Heritage as an international event with significant influences on Canadian identity and heritage (pp. 117, 134) as well as in E3.3 and E3.4: Identity, Citizenship and Heritage, as an event acknowledged and commemorated in Canada (pp. 124, 139-140).

Grade 11: Equity, Diversity and Social Justice, Workplace Preparation (HSG3M).
Study of the Holodomor strongly complements this newly created course, addressing the issues of equity, diversity, identity, empathy, power relations and social actions through the study of "historical and contemporary issues." This is best done in A1: Exploring, as an example of "social injustice," A1.2: concept of genocide in which "food was a weapon," B2: Power Relations, B2.3: examining systemic forms of discrimination and oppression towards Ukraine's farmers, eliminating them along with their cultural and religious identity, B2.4: effects of discrimination, B3: Social Awareness and the Individual, and B3.3: role of media and education in raising awareness and commemorating Holodomor Memorial Day.

Grade 11: World History since 1900: Global and Regional Perspectives, Open (CHT3O)
Since the aim of this course is for students to "...investigate the causes and effects of global and regional conflicts and the responses of individuals and governments to social, economic and political change," the Holodomor is well suited for highlighting these points. The Holodomor also meets many of the course's General and Specific outcomes.

Grade 12: Equity, and Social Justice, Theory and Practice, University and College Preparation (HSE4M)
Study of the Holodomor strongly complements this newly created social justice course, addressing the issues of equity, diversity, identity, empathy, power relations and social actions through the study of "historical and contemporary issues." The Holodomor is a prime example of ethnic, cultural and religious discrimination. Topics could include the manipulation of media, propaganda (B3.2), denial, recognition, and commemoration, denial of Ukrainian identity through the suppression of Ukrainian culture and religion. The examination of primary and secondary sources (government decrees, eyewitness reports

8 Ontario, Ontario Ministry of Education, *The Ontario Curriculum Grades 9 and 10: Canadian and World Studies, Revised.* [Ontario, Canada], 2005, p. 63, http://www.edu.gov.on.ca/eng/curriculum/secondary/canworld910curr2013.pdf

and correspondence of survivors), fosters critical thinking skills in students and creates historical context, while at the same time, meets the general and specific expectations of the course. Research: (A1) Why haven't international courts condemned the perpetrators of the Ukrainian Genocide?

A1 and A1.2: identify key concepts - genocide, food as a weapon, origin of the term Holodomor and its significance. B1.3: the use of systemic factors such as government decrees and discriminatory actions against the farmers of Ukraine to destroy them and their culture. The policy of dehumanization of the peasants/farmers is studied through an examination of eyewitness accounts by survivors in Ukraine (B2.4).

Grade 12: World History since the Fifteenth Century, University Preparation (CHY4U)
With this course's emphasis on the historical and intellectual developments that have created the modern world, teaching the Holodomor integrates well with the course's Overall Expectations. It also meshes well with the Specific Expectations located under Conflict and Cooperation, Western Beliefs, Ideologies and Philosophies, Citizenship and Human Rights, Economic Structures and Political Organization.[9]

The Holodomor as an outcome and example of Soviet policy could be dealt with under "Change and Continuity" (B3.3) by including the concept of "internationalism vs. national identity," the creation of a new society, a new "Soviet man" in which Ukrainian national identity conflicted with Soviet internationalism as it did in Ukraine in the 1930s. The Soviet solution was the deliberate destruction of millions of inhabitants of Ukraine, the largest non-Russian republic of the Soviet Union, most especially affecting ethnic Ukrainians.

Grade 12: World History since the Fifteenth Century, College Preparation (CHY4C)
Just as in its university-preparation sister course, this course's Overall Expectations align well with the study of the Holodomor. Unlike the University Prep course (CH4YU), this College Prep course makes specific reference to the Holodomor under its Specific Expectations for Conflict and Cooperation.[10]

Grade 12: Adventures in World History, Workplace Preparation (CHM4E)
The General Outcome of this course that best lends itself to the Holodomor is the section pertaining to Social, Economic and Political Structures. The Holodomor also fits into the Specific Expectations of the Power and Authority, International Conflict, and Human Rights sections.[11]

Grade 12: Canadian and World Politics. University Preparation (CPW4U)
This course lends itself to the study of diverse political systems. The Holodomor is an example of the kind of actions taken by authoritarian regimes to quell dissent and opposition to their policies, by adopting decrees that aim to eliminate and punish their own citizens,

9 Ontario, Ontario Ministry of Education, *The Ontario Curriculum Grades 11 and 12: Canadian and World Studies, Revised.* [Ontario, Canada], 2005, pp. 193–201, http://www.edu.gov.on.ca/eng/curriculum/secondary/2015cws11and12.pdf

10 Ibid., p. 206.

11 Ibid., pp. 215–220.

even in a time of peace. Political Processes, Political Procedures (B4.1) includes genocide as a means to an end, a tool for dealing with conflicts. The Soviet government through its decrees used "food as a weapon" to destroy a large segment of the Ukrainian nation. The use of primary documents, correspondence and eyewitness accounts lend themselves to the development of critical and historical thinking skills.

Access the Ontario Ministry of Education's online curricula and follow links: **http://www.edu.gov.on.ca/eng/curriculum/secondary/grades.html**

SASKATCHEWAN CURRICULUM CONNECTIONS
Saskatchewan is undergoing a review of its present social studies curriculum.

According to the Ukrainian Education's Virtual Resource Portal of the Saskatchewan Ministry of Education, the Holodomor can be taught between grades 7–12. It is best suited for Saskatchewan's History 20 course.[12]

Grade 11: History 20: World Issues. Unit Two: The Totalitarian State

Grade 11 history and social studies are the most applicable areas for the study of the Holodomor. Specifically, the Holodomor meets three out of four main points of examination offered by this course, namely, how totalitarian regimes affect the rights of their citizens, how they use violence to achieve their ends, and how the West's inability to confront these regimes can have profound consequences.

For access to the Social Science courses offered by the Saskatchewan Ministry of Education, visit: **https://www.edonline.sk.ca/bbcswebdav/library/curricula/English/Social_Studies/History_20_1994.pdf**

12 Saskatchewan, Saskatchewan Ministry of Education, *Ukrainian Famine Genocide: Holodomor 1932–33.* [Saskatchewan, Canada], 2009, http://www.spiritsd.ca/ukrainian/eng_high_holodomor.htm

PART II

Learning Resources

IN THIS SECTION

Background to Ukraine

The Holodomor, 1932-1933

Timeline of Events

Holodomor Victims and Losses

Cover-Up and Denial

Raphael Lemkin's Contribution to Historical Justice

Eyewitness Accounts

Historical Documents

Quotes and Excerpts from Literature

Commemorating the Holodomor

"Mother of the Year '33" by Nina Marchenko. From the collection "Holodomor: Through the Eyes of Ukrainian Artists." Founder & trustee Morgan Williams.

This section contains background information on Ukraine and the Holodomor, maps, a brief description of the Holodomor, an extensive timeline, explanatory notes on the cover-up and denial, the aftermath and a glossary.

Specific stand-alone items include an essay, the text of the UN Convention on Genocide and Raphael Lemkin's "Soviet Genocide in the Ukraine." Quotations about the Famine, primary documents, newspaper articles, and selected segments from literature, as well as excerpts from government decrees on the recognition of the Holodomor are provided as learning resources.

These resources are suitable for introducing, teaching, or organizing activities for students on the topic of the Holodomor, the Ukrainian genocide, at the high school level. An additional resource with a prolific amount of original documents, memoirs, eyewitness accounts, and essays is available in *The Holodomor Reader* (Bohdan Klid and Alexander Motyl, ed. Edmonton: CIUS Press, 2012.)

"Aside from certain Don and Volga regions, only Ukrainian agricultural areas faced complete confiscation of foodstuffs, only Ukrainian agricultural areas were sealed off from the rest of the world, only Ukrainian villages were blacklisted for failing to fulfill their grain delivery quotas and only Ukrainians were denied the possibility of leaving their impacted regions. As a result of this, within just a six month period in 1933 more than 4 million Ukrainians died."

Professor Andrea Graziosi, historian, University of Naples
Quoted in Peter T. Woloschuk, *The Ukrainian Weekly*, July 25, 2010, No. 30, p. 4.

"As a nation we were subject to destruction. The remnants of the Ukrainian people were to become material for forming a 'new historical society - the Soviet People,' with the Russian population, language and culture at its core."

Vasyl Ovsiienko, "Antyradianska knyzhka" (The Anti-Soviet Book) in *Svitlo liudei. Memuary ta publikatsiya*. Knyha II. Kharkiv: Prava liudyny, 2007, pp. 157-158.

Background to Ukraine

Orest Zakydalsky

Ukraine lies at the crossroads between Europe and Asia, at 49 degrees north latitude and 32 degrees east longitude. Its neighbours to the north are Belarus and Russia; to the west, Poland, Slovakia, and Hungary; to the southwest, Romania; and to the east, Russia. Ukraine covers 603,550 sq. km and is the second largest country in Europe, roughly the size of France or the province of Manitoba. The capital of Ukraine is Kyiv. Ukraine is made up of 24 oblasts (provinces) and the Autonomous Republic of Crimea on the Black Sea.

Map of Ukraine within Europe, 2015.

> *In 2014 the Russian Federation invaded Crimea in violation of international law.*

The borders of Ukraine changed several times in the twentieth century. In 1922, after the First World War, the Ukrainian Soviet Socialist Republic was established within the Soviet Union from parts of Ukraine that had been under the Russian Empire. The western regions of Ukraine, which were divided among Poland, Romania and Czechoslovakia, were incorporated into the Ukrainian SSR during and after the Second World War. Crimea became a part of Ukraine in 1954. The Russian Federation invaded Crimea in 2014 and illegally annexed it.

Map of Ukraine's changing borders in the 20th century. City names given as they appeared in 1991.

Most of the terrain of Ukraine consists of vast plains known as steppes, where the black earth *(chornozem)* is extraordinarily rich and fertile. Ukraine became known as the "Breadbasket of Europe" because *chornozem* is ideal for growing wheat and other grain crops as well as certain vegetables such as sugar beets. Ukraine is also a land rich in minerals — particularly iron ore, coal, manganese and salt.

Population

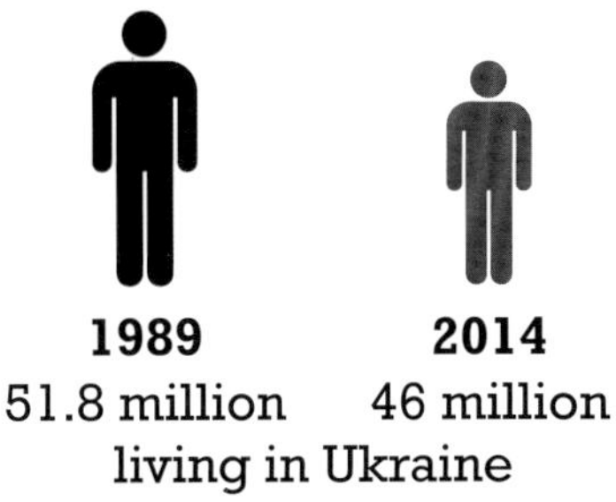

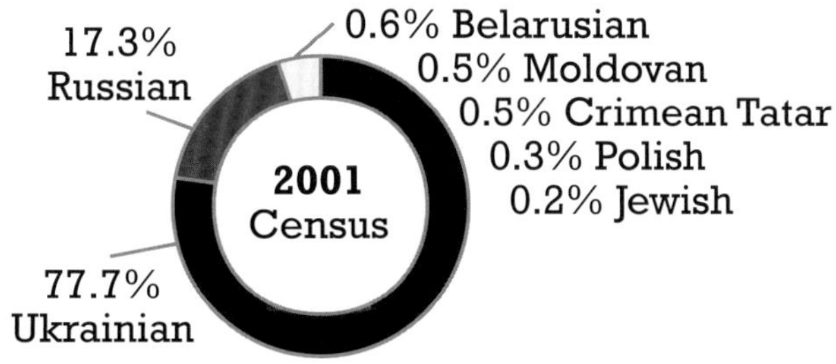

In 2014 there were 46 million people living in Ukraine. The ethnic breakdown, according to the 2001 census, was: 77.7% Ukrainian, 17.3% Russian, 0.6% Belarusian, 0.5% Moldavan, 0.5% Crimean Tatar, 0.3% Polish, and 0.2% Jewish.

The population in 1989 was 51.8 million, with 69% of the people living in cities while 31% lived in rural areas. The demographic decline from 1989 to 2014 is due mainly to a low birthrate (related to difficult economic conditions within the country), a relatively low life expectancy, and emigration. The rights of minorities are respected in Ukraine. The literacy rate is almost 100%, with comparatively high levels of enrollment in higher education.

Ukraine under Foreign Rule

The lack of natural geographic barriers, coupled with its richness in both natural resources and agriculture, and its strategic location as a crossroads between Europe and Asia, have made Ukraine a land coveted by its neighbours throughout history. Both European (Polish-Lithuanian Commonwealth, Austro-Hungarian Empire, Russian Empire, Soviet Union, Nazi Germany) and Asian (Golden Horde, Ottoman Empire) forces invaded, fought over, and ruled Ukrainian territory. For more than two hundred years (from the late 18th to the 20th centuries) most of Ukraine's territory was ruled by the Russian Empire and later the Soviet Union.

In 1918, Ukraine became independent but independence was brief. The Red Army invaded and most of Ukraine's territory became part of the Soviet Union (USSR). In 1922 the Ukrainian Soviet Socialist Republic became a part of the USSR and the republic was governed from Moscow until 1991. According to the Soviet census of 1926, Ukraine had a population of 29 million people (about 20% of the total Soviet population). Ukrainians were the largest national group within the USSR after the Russians. Ukraine regained its independence in 1991, leading to the dissolution of the Soviet Union.

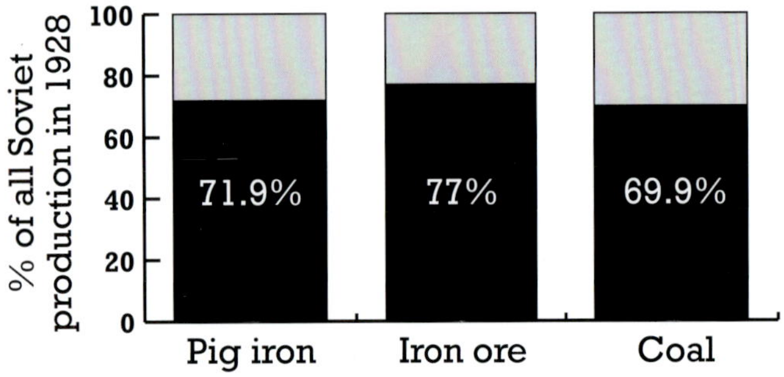

The Soviet Union depleted and plundered Ukraine's riches. Much of its grain was exported. Its minerals fed the industrial machine of the Soviet Union: Ukraine provided the Soviet Union with 71.9% of its pig iron, 77% of its iron ore, and 69.9% of its coal in 1928. Under Soviet rule, Ukraine saw a period of massive industrialization and urbanization. While this period led to economic growth, the ecological and environmental consequences were disastrous. Air, water and soil pollution continues to be a massive problem. In 1986, Ukraine suffered the worst nuclear disaster in history at the Chornobyl Atomic Energy Station, the consequences of which are still felt today.

Chornobyl Atomic Energy Station, reactor #4 with enclosing sarcophagus, 2007.

SOURCES:

- http://www.ukrstat.gov.ua/operativ/operativ2007/ds/nas_rik/nas_e/nas_rik_e.html
- United Nations statistics Division. http://unstats.un.org/unsd/demographic/products/socind/
- http://www.ukrstat.gov.ua/operativ2011/ds/kn/kn_e/kn0911_e.html

The Holodomor, 1932–1933

Valentina Kuryliw

> *The word Holodomor is used to describe death inflicted by starvation. It comes from two Ukrainian words: "holod," meaning starvation and "moryty," to cause death.*

One of the most devastating events of the twentieth century occurred in Ukraine after it was incorporated into the Union of Soviet Socialist Republics (USSR) in 1922. A genocide was carried out against the Ukrainian population in 1932–1933, which subsequently was denied, dismissed and hidden from world scrutiny for more than five decades. Although Ukrainians in the West had long maintained that millions had died as a result of the Soviet state's policies, the true nature of the Holodomor came to light only when archives in Moscow and Ukraine were opened following the collapse of the Soviet Union in 1991. In addition to those who died of starvation, countless numbers of Ukrainians were executed by firing squads, deported to Siberia or sent to the Gulag. The word *Holodomor* is used to describe death inflicted by starvation. It comes from two Ukrainian words: *holod*, meaning starvation, and *moryty*, to cause death. For generations, the very mention of the Famine was forbidden in Ukraine, and the Holodomor was often a bitter secret guarded by survivors, hidden even from their own children. In the West, this great human tragedy was little known or acknowledged. How and why did this happen and who was responsible for the death of these millions?

Historical Background

After 250 years of Russian Tsarist rule, Ukrainians declared independence from Russia in January 1918 in the midst of war and revolution. Ravaged by war, revolution and invasion by various armies, Ukraine lost the battle for independence. By 1921, Ukraine was partitioned, with the central and eastern regions controlled by Bolshevik forces and the western regions annexed by Poland, Romania, and Czechoslovakia. Ukrainians became the largest non-Russian nationality within the newly formed USSR. To stabilize and rebuild the economy within the Soviet Union, the Soviet leadership launched a New Economic Policy in 1921 that provided greater economic freedom and permitted private enterprise, mainly independent farms and small businesses. To increase support for the Communist regime, a policy of indigenization *(korenizatsiia)* was introduced in 1923, which sought to develop the non-Russian Soviet republics culturally. Throughout much of the 1920s, Ukrainian village populations flourished — socially, politically, educationally and demographically, bringing about an increase in the number of successful independent farmers on the black soil *(chornozem)* of Ukraine. The Ukrainian SSR also experienced a notable cultural rebirth, with writers, artists and intellectuals creating innovative new works in the Ukrainian language.

Lead-up to the Genocidal Famine

By 1928 Joseph Stalin won the power struggle within the Communist Party and became the dominant and undisputed leader of the USSR. His rule was characterized by the ruthless elimination of anyone and anything he perceived as a threat to his power. For Stalin, the independent-minded farmers and cultural freedoms in Ukraine constituted a threat. Starting in 1929, Ukraine's writers, artists, educators, intellectuals and cultural elites were repressed for being too Ukrainian and not Soviet enough. In 1930 Stalin destroyed Ukraine's independent church, the Ukrainian Autocephalous (independent from the Russian) Orthodox Church, and its clergy. Following the attack on the intellectuals and the church, the Ukrainian farmers, who made up 80 percent of Ukraine's population and thus were carriers of the language and culture, were next to be dealt a mortal blow.

Joseph Stalin

"Zdaiut khlib" (Giving up grain), Kyiv Oblast, 1932.

In 1928 the first Five-Year Plan of the Soviet Union was put in place, which had as its aim the rapid industrialization of the USSR at any cost. As part of the Five-Year Plan of 1928–1933, the Soviet leaders conducted a massive reorganization of privately owned farms into collective (state-controlled) farms and imposed high crop requisition quotas. It was the sale of grain that was to pay for industrialization. Independent farmers were forced to give their private land, livestock and equipment to the collective farm without compensation. They became simply workers on state-controlled collective farms, paid only if the collective farm handed over the quota in crops set by Moscow.

The opposition of Ukrainian farmers to collectivization was fierce and revolts were widespread. The Soviet state reacted quickly and ruthlessly. First, the more well-to-do farmers and their families were labelled by the state as *kurkuls* in Ukrainian or *kulaks* in Russian, and these village leaders were targeted and demonized in the press by the Soviet government as "anti-Soviet, unwanted elements." Beginning in 1929, so-called *kurkuls/kulaks* and their families, about half a million in Ukraine, were executed by firing squads or deported, many to Siberian concentration camps. Anyone opposed to collectivization was conveniently labelled a *kurkul/kulak* and dealt with accordingly.

"Small amount of goods a kurkul was allowed to take," Donetsk Oblast, in the early 1930s.

Implementing the Holodomor

Having disposed of the leaders and successful farmers in Ukraine, the Soviet regime continued with the forced collectivization of agriculture, and the remaining farmers became the target. Several measures were implemented. The state imposed huge quotas for wheat, which were especially severe in Ukraine. Any opposition to collectivization was met with brutal force. Secret police (OGPU) and Red Army units were sent to villages to collect the very last bit of grain by force. The state then implemented policies that aimed not just at the collection of quotas, but also caused the death of millions of farmers in Ukrainian villages. Communist brigades were sent out to search the homes of individual farmers, supposedly for hidden grain and seed, but they also confiscated all kinds of foodstuffs — onions, pumpkins, vegetables pickled in jars for the winter — anything the families might use to survive. A law enacted in August 1932, The Law of Five Stalks of Grain, stated that anyone, even a child, caught taking any produce from a collective field could be shot or imprisoned for stealing "socialist property." A decree in January 1933 sealed the borders of Ukraine. The Soviet government also started a system of internal passports, which made it more difficult for farmers to leave their villages to seek food elsewhere, and to travel or obtain a train ticket without permission. Those caught attempting to flee to the cities or beyond Ukraine's borders, where conditions were better, were imprisoned or sent home to die. Over one-third of the villages in Ukraine and the Kuban (an area in the Russian republic adjacent to Ukraine where the population was mostly Ukrainian) were put on a blacklist (*chorna doshka*) and blockaded for failing to meet grain quotas and were forbidden from receiving any supplies. This was essentially a collective death sentence for these villages. Settlers

"Young girl," Kharkiv Oblast, 1933.

With permission of the League of Ukrainian Canadians and the Ucrainica Research Institute from the exhibit/CD "Holodomor: The Ukrainian Genocide."

from Russia and Belarus were later brought in to resettle some of these depopulated areas, but not all remained.

In the meantime, the wheat stored in government warehouses was often sold abroad for export, rotted due to mismanagement or used for the production of alcohol. In fact, in 1932, Soviet wheat from Ukraine — confiscated from Ukrainian farmers by Red Army troops and secret police — was dumped on world markets at exceedingly low prices. Even Canadian farmers suffered because they could not match the low prices set for Soviet grain. Many could not believe that the people who had grown the wheat were being starved to death.

To minimize possible sympathy for the suffering of the local population, Stalin also attacked political leaders in Ukraine, imprisoning many and putting others to death. Some committed suicide. Some of these Ukrainian Communists were replaced with Party members from outside the Ukrainian SSR. Having brought the Ukrainian farmers to their knees and eliminated the political leadership that might harbour Ukrainian national awareness, there was little open opposition to Soviet rule. On the collective farms, those who survived became little better than slave labourers on land cultivated by their ancestors, which had served as the breadbasket of Europe for centuries. In the summer of 1933, after the Soviet state opened the granaries the famine subsided. The nation was devastated and defeated and had lost millions of its citizens.

"Village scene (starving women)," Kharkiv Oblast, 1933.

Causes

Why did this happen? This remains a very important question for historians. For decades, the USSR denied outright that the Famine had taken place, to say nothing of the charge that it was human-made. One group of historians attributes the loss of life to "excesses" or difficulties in the process of collectivization. There is no question that the disruption of agricultural life through the reorganization of land ownership and cultivation methods led to food shortages and deaths. However, this point of view does not account for the disproportionate, massive starvation that occurred in Ukraine and the Kuban.

"Confiscation of hidden grain," Donestk Oblast, early 1930s.

Another school of historians has concluded that the Famine was deliberate and linked to a broader Soviet policy to subjugate the Ukrainian people. With the fall of the Soviet Union and opening of Soviet-era archives, researchers have been able to demonstrate that Soviet authorities undertook measures in Ukraine with the knowledge that the result would be the deaths of millions of Ukrainians by starvation. The most recent research leaves little doubt that the Holodomor was an act of genocide.

Nationalities Policy

As can be expected, the economy was not the only concern of the newly created state — establishing Soviet power over the different nationalities was also a major concern. In 1923 the Soviets launched a policy called indigenization *(korenizatsiia)*, which was aimed at attracting members of non-Russian nationalities into the Communist Party. In Ukraine this policy was called Ukrainization. It led to a cultural renaissance, growth in Ukrainian national identity, and also a more favourable view of the USSR. Many Ukrainians were conscious of their national identity, valued their language and culture, and considered themselves a separate and distinct group equal to the Russians. However, the resistance to collectivization and to forced grain requisitions in Ukraine were in Stalin's mind related to a growing Ukrainian nationalism that could lead to the separation of Ukraine from the USSR. In August 1932, at a critical time in the events leading to the Holodomor, Stalin expressed his concern that "if we do not correct the situation ... we could lose Ukraine."

"...if we do not correct the situation ... we could lose Ukraine."

"That explains the fact that the peasantry constitutes the main army of the national movement, that there is no powerful national movement without the peasant army, nor can there be. That is what is meant when it is said that, in essence, the national question is a peasant question."

Stalin, J. V. *Concerning The National Question in Yugoslavia.* Speech delivered at the Yugoslav Commission of the E.C.C.I., March 30, 1925, from the collected archives *J.V. Stalin Works.* Moscow: Foreign Languages Publishing House, 1954, Vol. 7, pp. 71-72.

http://www.marx2mao.com/Stalin/CNQY25.html

Reaction to the Ukrainian Genocidal Famine

Some foreign journalists stationed inside the USSR largely ignored the Holodomor in the 1930s, or did not accurately report on it, while most governments whose countries were going through the Great Depression knew, but did nothing about it.

The journalist, Walter Duranty, of the *The New York Times*, who was awarded a Pulitzer Prize for his articles about the USSR, wrote that:

> ***"There is no actual starvation or deaths from starvation, but there is widespread mortality from disease due to malnutrition... conditions are bad. But there is no famine."***

There were a few journalists who wrote about starvation in Ukraine. Two such journalists were the Welshman Gareth Jones, who wrote for the *New York American* and *Los Angeles Examiner*, and Malcolm Muggeridge, a British foreign correspondent. In his article "War on the Peasants" in the *Fortnightly Review*, May 1, 1933, Muggeridge wrote:

> ***"On one side, millions of starving peasants, their bellies often swollen from lack of food; on the other, soldiers, members of the GPU (secret police) carrying out the instructions of the dictatorship of the proletariat. They had gone over the country like a swarm of locusts and taken away everything edible, they had shot or exiled thousands of peasants, sometimes whole villages, they had reduced some of the most fertile land in the world to a melancholy desert."***

In Ukraine, it was impossible to mention publicly, teach about or to discuss the Holodomor openly until the late 1980s. Information about the Famine was only available in the West, mostly from eyewitness testimonies of refugees who had survived the event and escaped from the Soviet Union during World War Two.

A succession of Soviet governments formally denied that the Holodomor had taken place. Even today, authorities of the Russian Federation will admit that there were famines in the 1930s in the USSR, although they refuse to acknowledge that Ukraine and Ukrainians were singled out in decrees that led to disproportionate deaths. The truth about the Holodomor started to become openly available to the citizens of Ukraine only on the eve of the break-up of the USSR. Eyewitness accounts and documentary evidence emerged that showed that Ukraine was indeed targeted for starvation in the wake of a shift in Soviet nationality policy. There are many ways of bringing about the destruction of a nation or its parts — starvation was just one of these methods, and it was used against the Ukrainians in the twentieth century.

Until recently, the Holodomor was denied, covered up and ignored. Today, the Holodomor is commemorated worldwide each year on the fourth Saturday in November. Canada and numerous other countries have recognized the Holodomor as genocide. Across Canada, many school boards commemorate Holodomor Memorial Day each year on the fourth Friday in November. We remember and honour its victims and resolve to prevent such crimes from occurring again.

> ***They are just too many to forget.***

Conquest, Robert. *Harvest of Sorrow: Soviet Collectivization and the Terror Famine.* New York, NY: Oxford University Press, 1986.

teacher tip

To futher explore the above section, a student worksheet is available in Part III, pp. 231-232.

"Armed guard guarding wheat," Kharkiv Oblast, 1933.

Timeline of Events

Valentina Kuryliw, Nicole Loroff, Jordan Vincent

teacher tip

A two-page shortened timeline is available for students in Part IV, pp. 267-268. For additional reading on certain events in the timeline, see the next section, "Read More."

1914

JULY - The First World War began. Ukrainians were conscripted for both the Russian and Austro-Hungarian empires and their homeland became a battleground between these powers.

1915

APRIL 24 - The Armenian Genocide, which claimed one and a half million lives, took place in the Ottoman (Turkish) Empire.

1917

MARCH - The first Russian Revolution led to the break-up of the Russian Empire. Ukraine established the **Central Rada** (*Read More #1*) in Kyiv as a provisional government, autonomous from Russia *(Read More #2)*. The Russian Tsar abdicated and Russia set up a Provisional Government.

NOVEMBER 7 - The **Bolsheviks** (Communists) (*Read More #4*), led by **Vladimir Lenin**, overthrew the Provisional Government in Petrograd and assumed control of Russia. The Central Rada in Ukraine, in turn, proclaimed the establishment of the Ukrainian People's Republic.

1918

JANUARY 22 - The Central Rada declared the independence of the Ukrainian People's Republic through a decree called the Fourth Universal. This would be one of three independent Ukrainian governments in this period, the others being the Hetman government under Pavlo Skoropadsky and the Directory under **Symon Petliura** *(Read More #6 and #7)*.

MARCH 3 - The **Treaty of Brest-Litovsk** (*Read More #5*) ended the First World War on the Eastern Front. It was a peace treaty signed by the Central Rada of Ukraine, Bolshevik Russia and imperial Germany, recognizing Ukrainian territorial integrity and Ukraine as a separate country.

1919

1919-1921 - The Ukrainian struggle for independence continued for several chaotic years until 1921, with the Red Army, White Army (Russian monarchists), anarchists and German, Polish and Romanian forces fighting on Ukrainian soil *(Read More #11)*.

Negotiations about the self-determination of nations and the **Treaty of Versailles** (*Read More 9#*) were held. Ukraine was excluded and was not recognized as a separate country by the victors of World War I. The renewed Polish state established its control over much of Western Ukraine.

Photos: (L) Central Rada, Symon Petliura; (R) V. Lenin, Signing of Treaty, *Daily Mirror* placard.

1920

The Bolsheviks established political and military control over central and eastern Ukraine with the aid of the **Red Army** *(Read More #11)*.

1921

1921-1923 - **Famine** occurred in Soviet-controlled Ukrainian lands from 1921 to 1923 as a result of poor crop yields, worsened by huge grain requisitions that were sent to Russia. Soviet authorities accepted foreign aid in this famine, although initially the assistance was sent only to the Volga region of Russia, but not Ukraine. Over 700,000 Ukrainians starved to death.

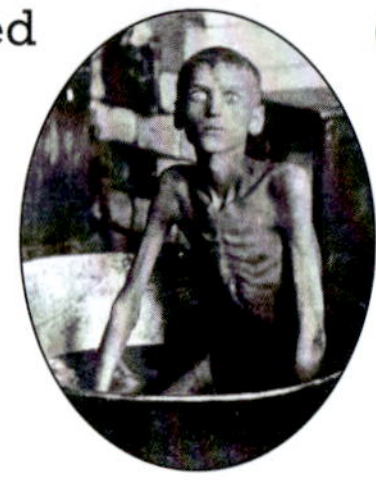

1921-1928 -
The **New Economic Policy** (NEP) was introduced by the Bolsheviks to revive the economy after the Civil War (*Read More #12*). It allowed for a mixed economy, permitting farmers to continue working their private land plots and the operation of small businesses in Soviet-controlled Ukraine.

1922

The **Ukrainian Soviet Socialist Republic** was formally incorporated into the Soviet Union in late December, with Kharkiv as its capital. The most important political and administrative decisions within the USSR, however, were made by the Kremlin in Moscow.

1923

The Soviet Union launched an indigenization policy (aimed at winning the support of local peoples and increasing their low numbers within Communist Party ranks). In Ukraine this took the form of **Ukrainization** (*Read More #13*), a policy that included promoting Ukrainian language and culture. A cultural renaissance of Ukrainian artists, writers and film directors followed. Some Ukrainian intellectuals joined the Communist Party of Ukraine and some who had fled returned to Ukraine.

1924

Vladimir Lenin died and a power struggle emerged within the Communist Party between Joseph Stalin and **Leon Trotsky** (*Read More #8*).

1926

The census for 1926 indicated a population of about 29 million in Soviet Ukraine.

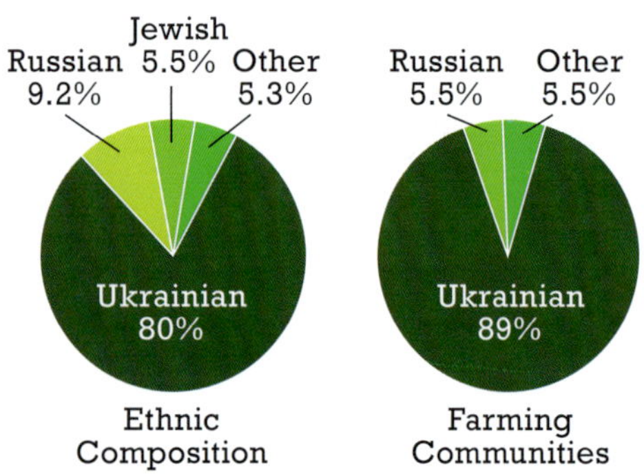

Photos: (L) Red Army poster, famine in Ukraine in 1921, Ukrainian SSR flag map, Trotsky in Leningrad; (R) Ukrainization poster.

1928

Stalin consolidated his power over the Soviet Union and became the General Secretary of the All-Union Communist Party. He abolished the NEP and introduced the first **Five-Year Plan** (1928–1933), which focused on rapid industrialization and collectivization with the goal of turning the USSR into a major and modern economic power. Key to the Plan was the selling of grain abroad in order to pay for industrialization and the military *(Read More #23).*

1929

The Soviet secret police, the **OGPU** (*Read More #14*), launched an attack on independent Ukraine's government and old political parties, scholars, writers and others. A show trial, held in the Kharkiv Opera House from March 9 to April 19, 1930, accused the arrestees of being members of a fictitious **Union for the Liberation of Ukraine (SVU)** (*Read More #16*) that were allegedly plotting to establish an independent Ukraine in collaboration with farmers and Ukrainian church leaders.

NOVEMBER - Forced collectivization on a massive scale was imposed by the Stalinist leadership. At the same time, Soviet leaders introduced policies to liquidate successful farmers (***kurkuli/kulaks***, *Read More #15*), who were believed to be potential leaders of resistance to the state collectivization effort. Dekulakization resulted in more than half a million farmers and their families being executed, deported to Siberia, or sent to the **Gulag** (*Read More #17*), often with their families. The property of "rich farmers" was confiscated and transferred to collective farms. Uprisings against the government were widespread.

1930

JANUARY - An attack was launched on the **Ukrainian Autocephalous Orthodox Church** based on a false charge that it had collaborated with the SVU. Clergy were arrested and the Church was liquidated *(Read More # 3).*

FALL - The above average **grain yield** in Ukraine was used to set quotas for future harvests. Collectivization continued with very harsh economic penalties and discriminatory policies for those who chose to remain independent farmers.

1931

Despite a harvest that was poorer than in 1930, the Soviet leadership insisted on fulfillment of the high grain procurement quota, forcing the **collective farms** in Ukraine to hand over seed grain reserves. Some Ukrainian farmers slaughtered their livestock rather than give them over to collective farms *(Read More #21).*

Photos: (L) OGPU insignia, Ukrainian Orthodox Church in Kyiv; (R) wheat field in Ukraine, grain collection point.

1932

JANUARY - **Ukrainian farmers** in substantial numbers began to flee their villages to cities and towns in search of food.

JUNE 10 - Ukrainian officials sent letters to **Viacheslav Molotov** and **Joseph Stalin** regarding food shortages in Ukraine. Stalin was not only unsympathetic but questioned where other Ukrainian officials stood on this issue.

JULY 6-9 - At the Third Party Conference of the Communist Party of Ukraine, **Lazar Kaganovich** and **Viacheslav Molotov** pressured the Ukrainian Communist Party leadership into accepting the directives of Moscow and agreeing to unrealistically high grain quotas.

AUGUST 7 - The decree on safeguarding of state property, known as the **"Law of Five Stalks of Grain,"** (*Read More #28*) came into effect, which ordered harsh penalties—even death — for anyone caught stealing grain or other "socialist property" from fields and elsewhere.

AUGUST 11 - In a letter to **Kaganovich**, Stalin bluntly expressed his views on the situation in the Ukrainian SSR, describing the CP(b)U leaders and membership who had been questioning the grain procurement campaign as unreliable and ultimately dangerous. He twice cited the possibility of losing Ukraine and stressed the need to "correct" the situation by using harsher methods. He also insisted that changes in the republic's leadership were required.

OCTOBER 22 - Molotov (for Ukraine), and Kaganovich (for Northern Caucasus, Kuban) were put in charge of special teams to ensure that Party and state officials continued the grain procurement drive. The effort was assisted by thousands of **Communist activists** sent from the cities, including from Russia, into the countryside to search for and seize hidden grain stores (*Read More #18*).

NOVEMBER 18 - New fines were introduced that stipulated that villages and collective farms thought to be "sabotaging" requisition efforts were to be placed on a blacklist (***chorna doshka***, *Read More #24*). These would subject them to blockades so that no food or other goods could enter or leave the settlements. More than one-third of Ukrainian villages were put on this list, and often all food, not only grain, was removed by force from these villages, condemning people to starvation.

DECEMBER 31 - An **internal passport** (*Read More #25*) system was introduced to prevent starving Ukrainian farmers from moving into the cities or across the border into Russia, where the chances of finding food were much better.

Photos: (L) migrating farmers, blacklisting village; (R) V. Molotov, Law logo by Oleh Lesiuk, confiscating wheat.

1933

JANUARY 22 - A secret directive from Moscow directed local officials in Ukraine and the North Caucasus to prevent the mass flight of peasants from their territories to other parts of the USSR looking "for bread"—in effect, closing the borders of Ukraine.

JANUARY 24 - The **Politburo** of the **CC AUCP(B)** (*Read More #23*) passed a resolution addressing the failure of Ukraine's Party to carry out the tasks demanded of it, appointing **Pavel Postyshev** to Ukraine's Party leadership. He quickly launched a campaign of repression against cultural figures in Ukraine, overseeing a large-scale purge of the middle and lower levels of Ukraine's Party structures, and presided over the worst phase of the Holodomor. In response to the growing terror unleashed upon the population in Ukraine, prominent leaders such as Mykola Khvylovy and Mykola Skrypnyk committed suicide.

MARCH - The **Kuban** (*Read More #27*), an area in the Caucasus adjacent to Ukraine where some 60 percent of the population was Ukrainian, also experienced widespread starvation.

APRIL - Some grain was rationed (selectively) to villagers. Mortality rates remained abnormally high.

MAY - A crash effort for the 1933 sowing season began. **Starving farmers**, too weak to work to full capacity, died of exertion. Factory workers and other urban dwellers were brought in to work the fields.

JUNE - At the height of the Holodomor, about 28,000 people per day were dying of starvation.[14] About 117,000 Russians and Belarusians were sent to resettle areas emptied by the death of Ukraine farmers.

The harvest was substantially less than that of 1932 and 1933. Although conditions had improved, many people continued to die of starvation.[13] The USSR was invited to join the **League of Nations** (*Read More #26*).

LEAGUE OF NATIONS

SOCIETE DES NATIONS

1934

1937

1937-38 - The Holodomor was followed by the **Great Terror**. It was a period of arrests and executions of intellectuals, military officials, and political leaders suspected of disloyalty to Joseph Stalin. Victims continued to be executed and sent to Siberia. Many who had been labelled *kulaks* and sent into exile were simply shot upon their return.

Census figures indicate shockingly high mortality rates in Ukraine. Stalin had the leading census takers shot or imprisoned and suppressed the census results.

1948

The UN Convention on the Prevention and Punishment of the Crime of Genocide was ratified, the culmination of **Raphael Lemkin**'s long and lonely struggle to have genocide recognized as a crime by the United Nations.

1930-80

At a Ukrainian-American rally in New York in 1953, Raphael Lemkin described the Famine in Ukraine as "a classic example of Soviet genocide," explaining how it fit his "four-pronged theory."

The Soviet Union denied any Famine had taken place and maintained that position until the late 1980s.

Photos: (L) starving family, League emblem, Lemkin; (R) P. Postyshev.

13. Subtelny, 1988.
14. Wolowyna, 2013.

Read More

Valentina Kuryliw, Nicole Loroff, Jordan Vincent

Combine "Read More" with the "Timeline of Events" on preceding pages for discussion, reading or writing activities.

1. **Central Rada** became Ukraine's first parliamentary body in April 1917. It was a council uniting various political and civic organizations and groups. The Central Rada established the Ukrainian People's Republic in November 1917, first as an autonomous republic within Russia, and then declared independence as a separate country on January 22, 1918. *Rada* is Ukrainian for council.

2. **Mykhailo Hrushevsky** (1866–1934) was independent Ukraine's first president, or head of the Central Rada. A prominent scholar, Hrushevsky was the first historian to write a history of Ukraine from prehistoric times to the mid-seventeenth century, emphasizing the continuity of the Ukrainian people throughout history. After the Central Rada was removed from power in a military coup headed by General Pavlo Skoropadsky, Hrushevsky went into exile. He returned to Soviet Ukraine in 1924 during a period of cultural renaissance called Ukrainization. He, like many other Ukrainian intellectuals, was persecuted by Soviet authorities in the early 1930s. He was exiled to Moscow. He died under mysterious circumstances in 1934.

3. **Ukrainian Autocephalous Orthodox Church, UAOC** (1921-1930). An independent national church that used the Ukrainian language for its liturgy and was forced to self-liquidate under pressure from the Soviet regime. Its clergy and parishioners, along with its Metropolitan Vasyl Lypkivsky, were persecuted and many were liquidated in attempts to destroy elements of Ukrainian culture and identity.

4. **Bolsheviks** were a radical Marxist offshoot of the Russian Social-Democratic Labour Party, which split in 1903 into two factions, the Bolsheviks and Mensheviks. Following their takeover of power in November 1917, the name of the Bolshevik wing of the party was changed to the Russian Communist Party (RKP[b]). In 1925 this became the All-Union Communist Party (AUCP[b]). In 1952 the name of the party was again changed to the Communist Party of the Soviet Union (CPSU). The Bolsheviks also established Bolshevik parties for each of the republics within the USSR, subordinated to the All-Union (central) Party authority in Moscow.

5. **Treaty of Brest-Litovsk** was a peace treaty signed in Brest (now in Belarus) on March 3, 1918, between the Central Powers (Germany, Austria-Hungary, Bulgaria, and Turkey) and the Bolshevik government. The treaty ended World War I on the Eastern Front. The terms of the treaty forced the Soviet government to recognize Ukraine as an

independent country. In return for military protection, Ukraine's Central Rada agreed to supply grain to Germany and the Austro-Hungarian Empire.

6. **The Hetman government** was established by General Pavlo Skoropadsky, following a military coup in April 1918. Skoropadsky, from a prominent Cossack family, was then proclaimed hetman of the Ukrainian state. (In the 17th and 18th centuries, the hetman had been a military-political leader who led Cossack armies and headed the state known as the Hetmanate.) Skoropadsky alienated some Ukrainians by restoring wealthy landowners to their estates and allowing Germans to requisition food. When he was overthrown in late 1918, Skoropadsky fled to Germany, where he died during the Second World War.

7. **The Directory** - With the defeat and collapse of the German Empire in November 1918, German forces supporting the Skoropadsky regime withdrew. At this point, the **Directory**, a committee of five political leaders formed in opposition to the Hetman government, headed a rebellion that overthrew Skoropadsky, and restored the Ukrainian People's Republic. The Directory was headed by **Symon Petliura**, a political and military leader. By January 1919, the Directory was at war at first with the White Army and then the Bolsheviks (Red Army). Driven out of much of eastern Ukraine by the Bolshevik armies, Petliura sought an alliance with Poland. Together, Polish and Ukrainian forces recaptured Kyiv in the spring of 1920, but the Red Army forced them out and began to consolidate their control over Ukraine.

8. **Leon Trotsky** was a leading Bolshevik who played a critically important role during the Russian Revolution, the Russian Civil War and the early years of the Soviet Union. He was the commander of the Red Army during the Civil War and was responsible for much of its successes and brutal excesses. A brilliant ideologue and orator, he nevertheless alienated many of his colleagues and lost the power struggle for the Soviet leadership against Stalin. Stalin eventually expelled him from the Communist Party and exiled him from the USSR. A Soviet agent assassinated him in 1940 in Mexico City.

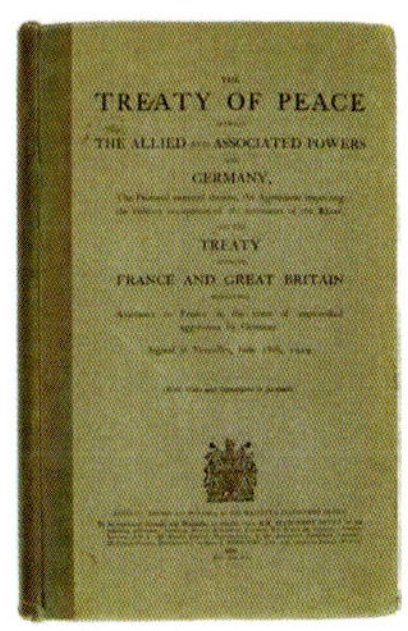

9. **Treaty of Versailles** (June 1919) formally ended the state of war between Germany and the victorious Entente Powers. By signing this treaty, Germany accepted responsibility for starting the First World War and was forced to pay reparations. US president Woodrow Wilson, one of the three chief negotiators (known as the Big Three) of the treaty, supported the concept of national self-determination during the negotiations. Poland, Czechoslovakia, Lithuania, Latvia and Estonia were successful in establishing independent countries following the First World War. Ukraine, on the other hand, despite sending representatives to the negotiations, was not recognized as a separate nation state by the victorious powers.

10. **Soviet-Polish War** of 1920–1921 saw Bolshevik leaders strive to regain the lands of the former Russian Empire lost in the Treaty of Brest-Litovsk. At the same time, Poland's leadership hoped to consolidate control over western Ukraine, which had been incorporated into Poland, and drive the Bolsheviks from central-eastern Ukraine in alliance with the forces of the Ukrainian People's Republic. Central-eastern Ukrainian lands were to be part of an independent Ukrainian state. The joint Polish-Ukrainian armies occupied Kyiv in May 1920, but were soon driven back by the Red Army. Hostilities ended with the signing of the **Treaty of Riga** in March 1921, which divided most Ukrainian lands between Soviet Russia and Poland.

11. **White Army**, or the Whites, were one of the two main fighting forces in the Russian Civil War (along with the Bolsheviks, or the Reds). The Whites were an assortment of monarchists, republicans, and Russian nationalists who opposed Bolshevik rule. They were also in favour of restoring a greater Russia based on the old Russian Empire and avoiding its break-up into separate states. Their armies fought battles on Ukrainian soil and thus weakened Ukrainian forces. The most prominent White general to operate on Ukrainian soil was Anton Denikin.

12. **The New Economic Policy (NEP)**, launched by Lenin in 1921 in order to revive the economy and pacify the peasants (small-scale or subsistence farmers) after the devastation of the economy during the Civil War. Seen as a retreat towards capitalism, it was nevertheless hoped by Bolshevik leaders that the NEP could buy time before bringing in collectivization. Under NEP, the state retained control of banking, communications, heavy industry and military production, but private small and medium-sized businesses were allowed to operate. In the countryside, farmers were permitted to work their own land and sell their produce on the open market after paying a tax to the state. It was a time of prosperity in Ukraine.

Village girls in Ukraine.

13. ***Korenizatsiia*** (indigenization) was a policy introduced by the Bolsheviks in 1923 in the non-Russian republics, including Ukraine. The policy called for the recruitment of non-Russians into the Communist Party and the government, for Soviet officials in the republics to use the national languages, and for support of cultural and social development of the nationalities of the USSR. The Ukrainian version of this policy was called **Ukrainization**. By the late 1920s, Ukrainization had achieved some impressive results. Government employees were required to know and speak Ukrainian, and the

"Anti-religious lesson," Kharkiv, 1932. Chalkboard translation: "Religion is opium, down with priests."

reported overall percentage of state business conducted in Ukrainian rose from 20% in 1925 to 70% in 1927. By 1929 over 97% of Ukrainian schoolchildren were enrolled in Ukrainian-language schools. Overall literacy rates in Ukraine rose dramatically during the 1920s. The success of the policy was due not only to state support but to the enthusiasm and hard work of thousands of Ukrainian activists, intellectuals and teachers, who were finally allowed to promote their native language and culture. The policy of Ukrainization was rolled back at the time of the Famine in a decree issued by the Soviet Communist Party and government authorities on December 14, 1932.

14. **OGPU**: The Russian acronym for "Unified State Political Directorate," which served as the Soviet regime's secret police; the GPU was the acronym for the Ukrainian republic's secret police. Originally founded as the Cheka during the Civil War, it was renamed the OGPU in 1922. The OGPU became the NKVD in 1934. Finally, the NKVD was renamed the KGB in 1954. Given sweeping powers, the Soviet secret police subjected those suspected of opposing the Soviet regime to surveillance, arrests, torture and executions. Their troops policed forced labour camps and were responsible for running what came to be called the Gulag system. In the run-up to and during the Holodomor, secret police troops were used to suppress protests and revolts by farmers. They also arrested members of the Party who were suspected of defying or not complying with orders to confiscate grain and other foodstuffs from farmers. The OGPU (and later NKVD) was Stalin's main instrument for carrying out the Great Terror and other repressions, deportations and executions of Soviet citizens.

"Kurkul's house being emptied," Kharkiv Oblast, 1932.

15. ***Kulak*** in Russian or ***kurkul*** in Ukrainian refers to a prosperous farmer. (The word *kulak* means "fist," used as a derogatory and dehumanizing term in Soviet society.) The Bolsheviks considered the kulaks to be ideological enemies because they were assumed to be the strongest supporters of free enterprise amongst the villagers. In order to divide the farmers, intimidate them and help create support for collectivization, Soviet authorities split them into three sub-groups, according to their overall income and wealth: kurkuls/kulaks or the most prosperous farmers, middle-income farmers (*seredniaky*) and the poor (*bidniaky*). With collectivization came a dekulakization campaign, during which so-called prosperous farmers and their entire families were rounded up, stripped of their property and subjected to arrest and deportation. Some kulaks were executed. As the incomes and overall wealth of the more well-off farmers were in reality not much different than that of the middle-income farmers, officials could apply the term *kulak* to a wide range of farmers in order to intimidate them. Many arrestees were middle-income and poorer farmers. A *troika* (or group of three people), in this case a Party

member, an OGPU agent and a local representative of the village council could review an individual's file and determine whether or not someone was a *kulak*.

16. **The Union for the Liberation of Ukraine**, or SVU *(Spilka Vyzvolennia Ukrainy)*, was a fictitious Ukrainian organization that was concocted by and then "uncovered" by OGPU agents in 1929. The show trials of the accused (largely Ukrainian scholars, intellectuals, priests and students) took place in the Kharkiv Opera House in March and April of 1930. The accused were charged with seeking to create an independent Ukraine and of trying to make the Ukrainian language as linguistically distinct as possible from Russian. The arrests and show trials provided justification for expanding the search for opponents to the Soviet regime and resulted in the removal of many low-level Ukrainian Communists and teachers from their posts. The SVU affair was a major setback for Ukrainization. Beginning in 1933, during the height of the Famine, the persecution of those in favour of Ukrainian cultural rights was extended to include the Ukrainian Communist intelligentsia and political elite.

Trial of the Union for the Liberation of Ukraine.

17. **Gulag** is the Russian acronym for the "Main Administration for Corrective Labour Camps" founded under Lenin for reeducating political enemies. During his rule, Stalin drastically increased the size and scale of the Gulag system of concentration camps. Millions of Soviet citizens were sentenced to these labour camps, often for fictitious crimes against the state. Many died during their internment and transportation to the camps. Soviet citizens (including *kulaks*, priests and Ukrainian "nationalists") not sent to the Gulag were sometimes executed or deported to the far reaches of the Soviet Union. The majority of the Gulag camps were located in the Soviet Arctic, Far East or Siberia, where inmates often worked on major construction projects under horrific conditions. Among the most notorious projects was the building of the White Sea Canal (Belomor Kanal), completed between 1931 and 1933 at the cost of the lives of many camp inmates.

White Sea Canal concentration camp, 1933.

18. **The 25,000ers** were Communist Party or Komsomol (Communist Youth League) members from the cities, including from Russia, who were assigned to the countryside to ensure the success of the collectivization policy. Unlike Communist Party activists sent to villages to requisition grain and then move on, the 25,000ers were permanently settled in the villages. Initially 27,000 were sent to the countryside, who were soon joined by thousands more volunteers comprised of demobilized soldiers, accountants

and former industrial workers. Angry farmers passively and actively resisted the 25,000ers. This resistance included riots by groups of village women.

19. ***Pravda*** was the official newspaper of the Communist Party of the Soviet Union. *Pravda* means truth in both Russian and Ukrainian. Stalin once served as its chief editor. Founded prior to the First World War, it remained an organ of the Communist Party until the collapse of the USSR in 1991.

20. **"Dizzy with Success"** was the title of an article by Stalin published in *Pravda* in March 1930 in which he called off his crash collectivization campaign. The chaos in the countryside, he wrote, was not due to collectivization but rather to the excesses of those activists sent out to implement it. What he failed to mention was that there was wide-scale resistance and even rebellion in the countryside that had to be put down by force. The OGPU reported Ukraine as a centre of resistance to the collectivization campaign, with more than a million acts of resistance during the collectivization process.[15]

21. **Seed grain** is that part of the grain crop put aside by farmers at the end of the harvest to be used as seed when planting the next year's crop. In 1932 and early 1933, Soviet authorities confiscated even the seed grain to meet the unrealistic quotas that had been imposed on the farmers. This policy not only affected future planting but also deprived farmers and their families of a food source that could have maintained them after all food stores were gone. Some of the seed crop collected during the grain requisition campaigns ended up being exported by the Soviet state to fulfill export contracts and to earn hard currency to finance industrialization.

22. **Kazakhstan** was not yet a full union republic of the Soviet Union (as were Ukraine, Russia and Belarus) in 1931 at the time of collectivization, and Kazakhs were predominately a nomadic people who lived by herding. In a program referred to as "sedenterization," roughly 38 percent of Kazakhstan's population (about 1.45 million) died from starvation because their livestock and other foodstuffs were taken from them.

23. **Ukrainian Party officials** were those who worked within the bureaucracy of the Communist Party (Bolshevik) of Ukraine (CP[b]U). The USSR was comprised of individual republics, each representing a particular nation or nationality, and each had its own Communist Party. It is important to note that the republican parties were subordinate to the All-Union (or federal) Communist Party.

The seat of the Soviet and Russian Governments, The Kremlin, Moscow.

15 Snyder, *Bloodlands*, p. 29.

The leader of the Communist Party of each republic, the first secretary, was chosen by Stalin, ensuring his control throughout the USSR. The USSR also established autonomous republics of the less numerous peoples and nations within union republics.

At Communist Party congresses (conventions), members would elect a Central Committee. The Central Committee would then elect a Politburo (political bureau) for times when it could not meet. At the head of the Communist Party was the General Secretary. The congress gatherings and elections were meant to look democratic. In reality, the congresses hardly ever met, and the Soviet Union was run by the Politburo. If a decision was reached by the Party leadership, all of its members accepted it without question. The General Secretary, as head of the party, had enormous power and could appoint members to key positions.

Running parallel to the Communist Party were the institutions of the Soviet state. "Soviet" is the Russian word for council, and each administrative-territorial unit or area in the USSR had its own soviet. From this soviet, a delegate would be elected (in reality appointed by higher authorities) to represent the area at higher administrative-territorial levels. Theoretically, the highest level of government authority in Ukraine was the Ukrainian Congress of Soviets.

The All-Union (federal) Congress of Soviets was a quasi-parliamentary body that essentially rubber-stamped decisions already made by the Communist Party. The Congress of Soviets would elect the Council of People's Commissars (cabinet) to head the USSR's various commissariats (ministries). The head of the government was titled the Premier of the Soviet Union. Those elected to head a commissariat, or even those elected to the soviets, were always Communist Party members. Thus, the Communist Party controlled the government and all of its functions. For this reason, the USSR was referred to as a "party-state." Although the USSR tried to present itself as a democracy, the country was actually controlled by the Politburo and the General Secretary of the Communist Party from Moscow. The institutions of the Soviet state were essentially copied at the republic level. Thus, in Ukraine, the republican Congress of Soviets elected a Council of People's Commissars.

24. **Blacklist:** Villages and collective farms that failed to meet quotas were put on a **blacklist**, which meant they were cut off from all trade and contact with the outside world and subject to additional searches and penalties. Procurement brigades would sometimes take all of a blacklisted area's remaining livestock and poultry and all other food they could find. These additional confiscations often meant the difference between life and death for a family during the Famine. In Ukrainian the term for blacklist is ***chorna doshka***, meaning "blackboard." More than one-third of the villages in Ukraine were thus blacklisted and subjected to starvation.

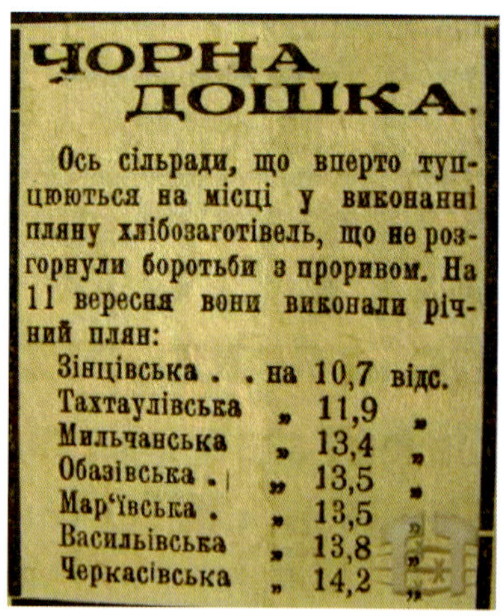

ЧОРНА ДОШКА.

Ось сільради, що вперто тупцюються на місці у виконанні пляну хлібозаготівель, що не розгорнули боротьби з проривом. На 11 вересня вони виконали річний плян:

Зінцівська . .	на	10,7	відс.
Тахтаулівська	„	11,9	„
Мильчанська	„	13,4	„
Обазівська .	„	13,5	„
Мар'ївська .	„	13,5	„
Васильівська	„	13,8	„
Черкасівська	„	14,2	„

25. **Internal passport system:** It was introduced by the Soviet government in late 1932. Farmers were denied passports and could be prosecuted if found beyond their villages or in urban areas. The borders of Ukraine were closed on January 22, 1933 and farmers who had left their villages in search of food were arrested and sent back to their villages to starve. Passports in this case served as a means of identifying residency and also of restricting freedom of movement. It was impossible to buy a railway ticket without a passport. The passport also made note of one's nationality. Agricultural workers were granted passports only in 1953, although their freedom of movement was still severely restricted. The internal passport system lasted until the collapse of the USSR in 1991.

26. **The League of Nations** was established in 1919 following the end of the First World War. The League served as a precursor to the United Nations. It was hoped that diplomatic efforts mediated by the League would serve to stop future conflicts. However, by the 1930s, it was apparent that the League of Nations lacked the means to enforce its mandate and ensure peace. Efforts were also severely hampered by the fact that the United States never joined the League, even though its creation was the brainchild of US president Woodrow Wilson.

LEAGUE OF NATIONS

SOCIETE DES NATIONS

27. **The Kuban** was a region within the Russian Soviet Federated Socialist Republic (today, in the Russian Federation), adjacent to southeastern Ukraine. At the time of the 1932–1933 Famine, some 60% of the population in the Kuban were ethnic Ukrainians, mostly descendants of Cossack forces from Ukraine settled there from the late 18th century. Like Ukraine, the Kuban suffered brutal requisitions of grain, and poor crop procurement results were blamed on the Ukrainian nationalism of local officials and Cossacks. Stalin's trusted lieutenant, Lazar Kaganovich, was sent to the Kuban in the fall of 1932 to oversee the grain requisition drive, which he did, using repressions and striking fear among the local population. Kaganovich ordered the deportation of entire Cossack settlements as punishment for non-fulfillment of the state grain collection quotas. The Famine in the Kuban region as a result was exceptionally acute, with the rate of death in this predominately ethnic Ukrainian area considerably higher than that in other parts of the Russian republic, except the lower Volga region.

28. **Five Stalks of Grain Law**: On August 7, 1932, Joseph Stalin issued a law that established a sentence of death or ten years imprisonment for the theft of collective farm "socialist property." This law led to mass arrests, deportations and some executions. Even children caught picking handfuls of grain from fields could be convicted or shot on the spot.

Holodomor Victims and Losses

After eighty years, it has been established beyond a doubt that millions died in the forced Famine of 1932-33 in Ukraine, known as the Holodomor (death inflicted by starvation). Estimates of the number of victims have ranged from 2.6 million to 10 million. Recent findings indicate that about 4 million people were starved to death in Ukraine.

Here are some reasons for these variations in the numbers of mortality:

a) Until the late 1980s, the Soviet Union systematically denied the existence of the Holodomor in the USSR during the 1930s.
   - A successful denial campaign was carried out both inside the Soviet Union and in the West until the late 1980s.
   - The gradual opening of Soviet archives in the late 1980s allowed scholars to document the 1932-33 Famine and its consequences.
   - After the Orange Revolution in 2004 in Ukraine, the government of Ukrainian President Viktor Yushchenko recognized the Holodomor as genocide and the Institute of Demography and Social Studies of the National Academy of Sciences of Ukraine established a preliminary figure of 3.9 million unnatural deaths.

b) Accurate records of deaths were not kept during the Famine, not only because the Soviet authorities denied any famine was taking place but also because there were just too many dead. Victims were often put in common graves. People died in forests, on the streets, and in their homes. Many of the starving wandered the countryside looking for food and perished far from their homes, and so their deaths were never registered.

   In some cases, those entering information in vital statistic registries avoided noting "starvation" or related maladies as a cause of death. Instead, the records registered the cause of death as "unknown" or "not identified."

c) Numerous records related to the Famine in Ukraine were destroyed by Soviet officials. Thus, the paper trail was significantly diminished, although not completely eliminated, as copies of many of these records survived in Moscow archives.

d) A recent study published in the journal *Canadian Studies in Population* shows that there were 3.9 million ***unnatural deaths*** attributed to starvation within the borders of Soviet Ukraine during 1932 - 1934, and about 600 thousand births were lost due to the Famine during this period. These figures, derived by a working group at the Institute of Demography of the National Academy of Sciences of Ukraine and an American demographer, are based on the most complete set of statistics and documents from Ukrainian and Russian archives.

THE DATA: ESTABLISHING THE NUMBER OF VICTIMS

1. Census

- According to the first Soviet census in 1926, the population of Soviet Ukraine was 28,994,980, with 23,218,860 Ukrainians and 2,677,166 Russians.

- The second Soviet census took place in 1937. The census director I. Kravel was awarded the Order of Lenin for his meticulous work. After the results of the 1937 census were submitted to the government, Stalin declared the census "subversive," access to census data was closed, and the top census officials were shot. Once the data became accessible, it was established that the census figures were credible.

- Another census was held in 1939, and the drastic population losses due to the Famine were to some degree hidden, thanks to a sophisticated program of falsification of the census data. However, according to growth rates from previous records, the number of Ukrainians should have been 37,246,000 in 1939.

	1926	1939	GROWTH RATE
Population of the USSR	147,028,000	170,557,000	+16%
Ukrainians in USSR	31,195,000	28,111,000	-11%
Russians in USSR	77,791,000	99,591,000	+28%
Source: Palij, 2010.			

2. Demographics

- The figure of 3.9 million "excessive deaths" in Soviet Ukraine is the one presented by demographers for the period 1932-1934. Nearly a third of those who died during the Famine were children under 10 years of age, or one out of five children in Ukrainian villages and one out of every 13 children in the cities.

- The elderly were another group that suffered great losses during the Holodomor, with at least 20% perishing.

UNNATURAL CAUSES OF DEATH BY AGE	PERCENTAGE
Children under 10 years	31%
Youth 11-15 years of age	7%
Men and women 16-60 years of age	42%
Elderly (over 60)	20%

- By June 1933, at the height of the Famine, people in Ukraine were dying at the following rate:

Ukraine villager deaths from Famine

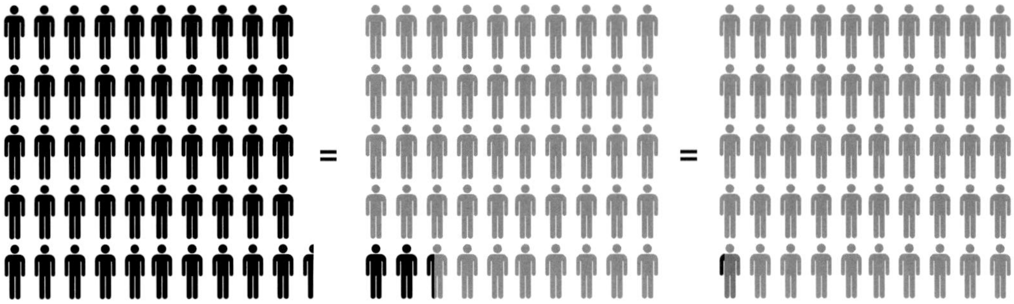

28,000 per day = **1,167** per hour = **19** per minute

Allied soldier deaths during Battle of Verdun

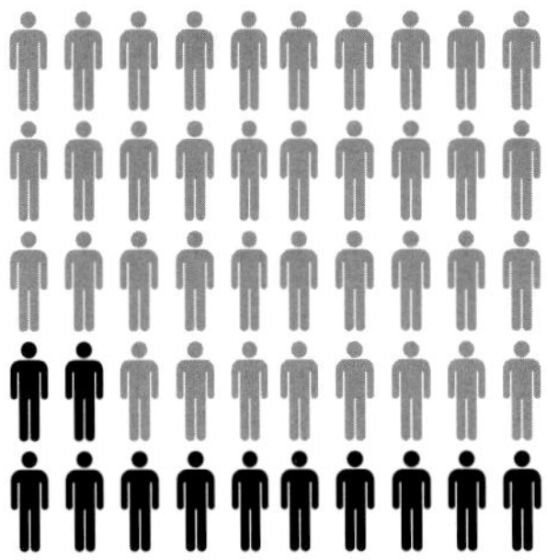

6,000 per day

***Note:** Compare the above rates of mortality to the mortality rate of allied soldiers during the Battle of Verdun (WWI): 6,000 per day.*

Number of direct losses of deaths for urban and rural areas in Ukraine by month in 1933

MONTH	URBAN	RURAL	TOTAL
January	9,422	78,755	88,177
February	11,905	111,168	123,073
March	19,358	260,641	279,999
April	19,787	367,059	386,846
May	20,775	581,477	602,251
June	25,188	815,853	841,041
July	25,649	607,627	633,276
August	21,024	199,302	220,326
September	14,406	115,237	129,643
October	10,152	78,702	88,854
November	8,375	57,292	65,668
December	7.885	62,157	70,043
Between January and June the number of deaths increased ten times. | Reference: Wolowyna, 2013.			

3. Additional Considerations

Soviet officials first denied there had been any Famine. When they could not sustain that lie, they claimed that the Famine was due to crop failure or climatic conditions. However, the harvest in the Ukrainian SSR in this period could, in fact, readily have fed its entire population.

- The Soviet policy of excessive requisitioning/quotas and the removal of vast quantities of grain from Ukrainian villages under the policy of collectivization led to starvation. Additional Soviet government decrees led to the removal of almost all food from over a third of the villages in both Ukraine and the Kuban region inhabited largely by Ukrainians. This is what led to the mass starvation in 1933.

- At the same time, the Soviet regime, desperate for hard currency, dumped 1.7 million tons of grain on western markets at the height of the Famine. Ukrainian butter was exported by the Soviet Union to Great Britain in 1933.

- Even prior to 1932, starting in 1929, as a result of collectivization in Ukraine, people were dying from starvation, were shot for opposing collectivization, and were deported to Siberia or to the Gulag with their families where many perished.

- More than one thousand uprisings against collectivization were brutally suppressed by the GPU (Soviet secret police) and Red Army troops, who executed many of the farmers who dared to protest prior to 1932. Half of all uprisings were in Ukraine.

- The Kuban, an area within the Russian Soviet Federated Socialist Republic (RSFSR) adjacent to Ukraine in the southeast, in which the majority of the people were ethnic Ukrainians was also subjected to the same decrees as Ukraine in 1932-1933 and suffered horrific loss of life. These numbers are not included in the 3.9 million Ukrainian deaths cited by demographers.

- Minority groups of various ethnic backgrounds (Russians, Poles, Mennonites, Jews, and others) living in Ukraine also suffered as a result of the Holodomor. Research on this subject is currently being undertaken in Ukraine.

4. Government policies led to legally sanctioned atrocities

Official Soviet government policies in the USSR and the Ukrainian SSR were key in creating the legal, oppressive conditions that caused the escalation of the Holodomor in 1932. These decrees and laws included:

Law of Five Stalks of Grain (7 August 1932) stipulated death or imprisonment for ten years, even for children, for taking even a few stalks of grain.

"Blacklisting" (initiated 6 December 1932) punished villages in Ukraine and the Kuban by removing foodstuffs and blocking all supplies. Over one third of villages in Ukraine were blacklisted, leading to mass starvation.

Ukrainian SSR borders were closed (22 January 1933) and its isolation was enforced by military patrols. Villagers caught searching for food in Russia were either imprisoned or sent back to their villages to die.

An internal passport system was introduced for urban dwellers and denied to rural villagers, preventing them from travelling and moving to cities.

Below are two accounts regarding the views of two prominent figures who denied the existence of the Famine, as recalled by others.

- Joseph Stalin, as related by Winston Churchill:

> ***"Tell me,"* I [Churchill] asked, *"have the stresses of war been as bad to you personally as carrying through the policy of the collective farms?"***
> **This subject immediately roused the Marshal [Stalin].**
> ***"Oh, no," he said, "the Collective Farm policy was a terrible struggle."***
> ***"I thought you would have found it bad "* said I, *"because you were not dealing with a few score thousands of aristocrats or big landowners, but with millions of small men."***
> ***"Ten millions,"* he said, holding up his hands. *"It was fearful. Four years it lasted. It was absolutely necessary for Russia..."***

Winston S. Churchill and the editors of *Life, The Second World War* (Vol. 1). New York, NY: Time Incorporated, 1959. Fom the chapter, "Moscow: A Relationship" (pp. 271-272).

- Walter Duranty, who denied the Famine in his articles in the *New York Times,* as retold from a private conversation:

> ***"Mr. Duranty thinks it is quite possible that as many as 10 million people may have died directly or indirectly from lack of food in the Soviet Union during the past year."***

Statement by William Strang, British Foreign Office Correspondent, British Embassy Dispatch, 30 September, 1933. *The Foreign Office and the Famine*, ed. M. Carynnyk, L. Luciuk and B. Kordan. Kingston, ON: Limestone Press, 1988, p. 313.

- Recent research has established that there were considerable variations in Holodomor deaths by oblasts, or provinces, in Ukraine. The greatest losses occurred in the swath of territory including what was then Kyiv and Kharkiv *oblasts* (provinces). Some were initially resettled by Belarusian and Russian peasants and army officers in the recent depopulated lands of Ukraine that had been devastated by Famine. Official records show that within one year a large number of these peasants returned to where they came from or moved somewhere else. *(Refer to the map on the next page.)*

Reference: This map is from The Great Famine Project, MAPA: Digital Atlas of Ukraine program, undertaken by the Harvard Ukrainian Research Institute. It visualizes data based on estimates of deaths during the Holodomor period, derived from "Estimation of Regional Losses of the 1932 - 1934 Famine in Ukraine," a project conducted by Oleh Wolowyna (University of North Carolina at Chapel Hill) and Omelian Rudnytskyi, Natalia Levchuk, Pavlo Shevchuk, and Alla Kovbasiuk (Institute of Demography and Social Studies in Kyiv).

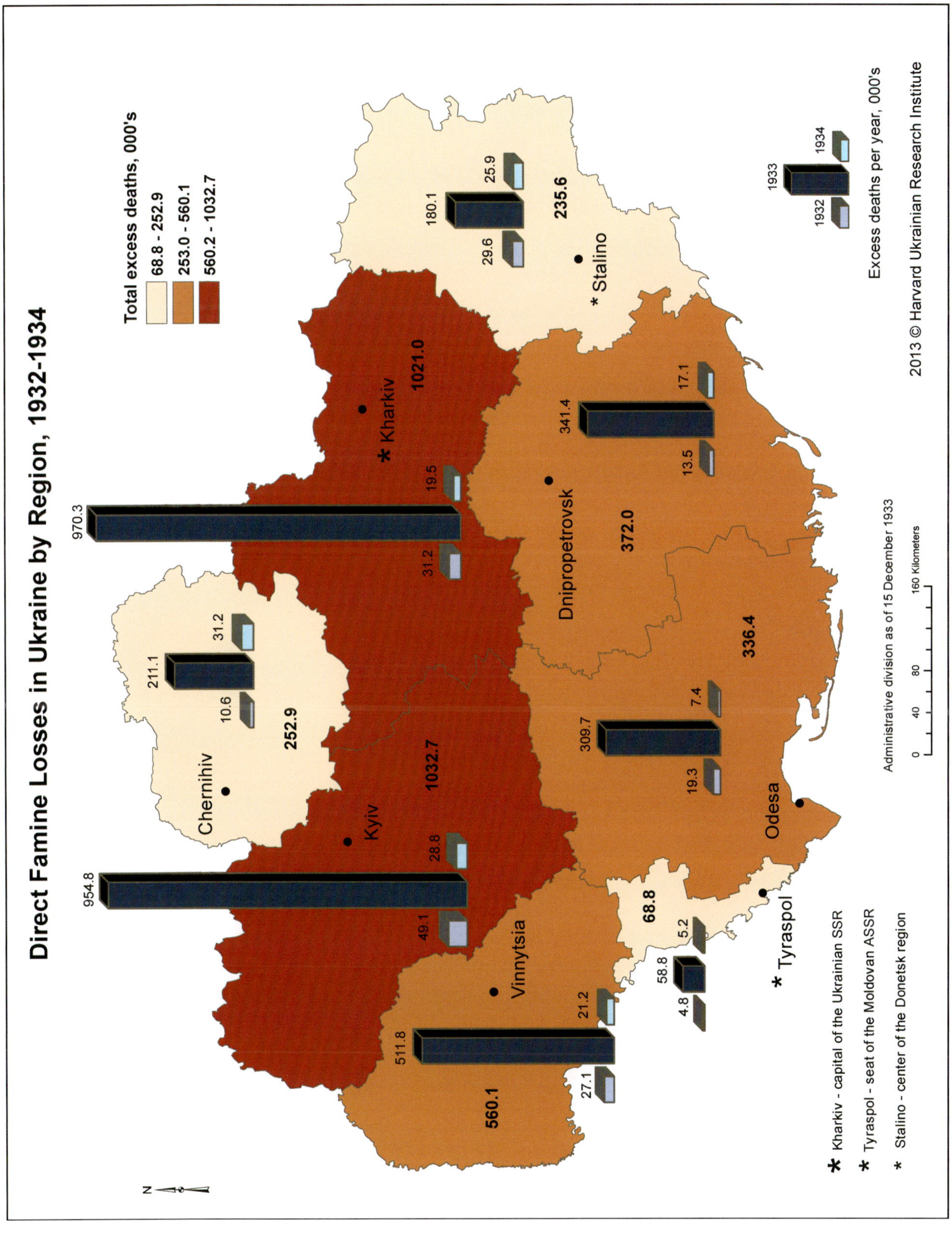

The Great Famine Project, MAPA: Digital Atlas of Ukraine

For information on the Holodomor presented in a unique visual form, see the *Atlas of the Holodomor* of the Ukrainian Research Institute at Harvard University (HURI). The Atlas is an interactive Geographic Information Systems-based (GIS) series of maps drawing upon the latest innovations of information technology. Its main goal is to present various types of data in graphic and map form to better understand the nature and effects of the Holodomor. This is done in a coherent and comprehensive manner using all of the advantages of a cartographic interface to deal with chronological, spatial and other kinds of relationships not obvious from the data alone.

The mapping of the Great Famine will help answer important questions such as: which areas of Ukraine were affected most severely? How did deaths vary by gender? What was the ethnicity of victims? This data analysis is poised to make a pioneering contribution to studies of the Stalinist era, as it is the first such project. *The Atlas of the Holodomor* is an invaluable teaching tool for teachers and students researching the Holodomor. One of the maps, "Direct Famine Losses in Ukraine by Region, 1932-1934," is found on the previous page of this publication.

The link to the The Great Famine Project: **http://gis.huri.harvard.edu/**

"The Ukrainian Famine was the crime of the century that nobody ever heard of."

James Mace, historian

In Conclusion

While the genocidal Famine was undoubtedly the most horrific Soviet crime against the Ukrainian population and claimed the most victims, it should be seen as a part of an ongoing campaign of repression that lasted from the Bolshevik Revolution in 1917 until the breakup of the Soviet Union in 1991. These cycles of repression targeted different social groups in Ukraine at different times, and viewed in full, were a concerted attempt to destroy resistance to Soviet rule and the desire for an independent Ukraine. Those targeted included intellectuals and cultural leaders, representatives of Ukrainian churches, ethnic minorities within Ukraine and members of the Communist Party of Ukraine, who were ruthlessly purged throughout the 1930s. Many see in recent events (the Euromaidan and the Revolution of Dignity, annexation of Crimea, and Russian aggression in Ukraine's eastern provinces of Donetsk and Luhansk) the continued legacy of past repressions and the ongoing struggle of the Ukrainian people to determine their own future.

Q. "Why is the Holodomor unique among genocides and great crimes against humanity?"
A. "Because its last chapter has not yet been written."

Walter Zaryckyj, Center for US Ukrainian Relations, 2014

SOURCES:

Conquest, Robert, *The Harvest of Sorrow. Soviet Collectivization and the Terror-Famine.* New York, NY: Oxford Press, 1986.

Dolot, Miron, *Execution by Hunger: The Hidden Holocaust.* New York: W. W. Norton, 1985.

Klid, Bohdan and Alexander Motyl, eds. *The Holodomor Reader: A Sourcebook on the Famine of 1932-33 in Ukraine.* Edmonton: Canadian Institute of Ukrainian Studies Press, 2012.

Maksudov, M. "Ukraine's Demographic Losses 1927-1938," in *Famine in Ukraine 1932-33*, edited by Roman Serbyn and Bohdan Krawchenko, pp. 27-43. Edmonton: Canadian Institute of Ukrainian Studies Press, 1986.

Rudnytskyi, O., N. Levchuk, O. Wolowyna, P. Shevchuk, and A. Kovbasiuk. "Demography of a man-made human catastrophe: The case of massive famine in Ukraine 1932–1933". *Canadian Studies in Population,* 42 no. 1–2 (2015): 53–80. http://ejournals.library.ualberta.ca/index.php/csp/article/view/21772

Serbyn, Roman and Bohdan Krawchenko, eds. *Famine in Ukraine 1932-1933.* Edmonton: Canadian Institute of Ukrainian Studies Press, 1986.

Census Data

Palij, Olexandr, "23 reasons for the Holodomor to be considered a genocide with no qualifications" (Ukrainian language), UNIAN, Nov. 27, 2010. http://www.unian.ua/ukr/print/40

Demographics Data

Wolowyna, Oleh. 2013. "Monthly distribution of demographic losses in 1933 related to the 1932-1934 famine in Ukraine. (1921-1923, 1932-1933, 1946-1947)" in "Famines in Ukraine during the first half of the XX century: causes and consequences (1921-1923, 1932-1933, 1946-1947)" Paper presented at the Proceedings of International Scholarly Conference, Kyiv, 2013, pp. 233-242.

"The corpses in the streets of Kharkiv," Kharkiv, 1933.

How the Genocide Was Organized

Isolation of villages by imposing a system of blacklists

The blacklisted villages would be surrounded by armed detachments. All food and seed supplies would be removed, and deliveries of any kind of goods were prohibited. Trade was prohibited. Adding an inhabited location or territory to the blacklists was equivalent to placing a death sentence on its population.

Reprinted with persmission of the League of Ukrainian Canadians and Ucrainica Research Institute from the exhibit/CD "Holodomor: The Ukrainian Genocide." 2008 poster.

Cover-Up and Denial

Nicole Loroff, Jordan Vincent and Valentina Kuryliw

There are numerous factors in explaining the lack of public awareness about the Holodomor and why this genocidal Famine remained relatively little known until the late 1980s.

Soviet cover-up during and after Stalin

A) OUTRIGHT DENIAL

Maxim Litvinov

The Soviet government in the 1930s refused offers of international aid from the Red Cross and other groups on the grounds that there was no famine. Soviet Foreign Minister Maxim Litvinov publicly denied the existence of a famine in the USSR in 1933. Discussion of the Famine or its causes was forbidden in the Soviet press, and once the Famine was over, no references were made to it in Soviet historical accounts. Moreover, citizens of the USSR could not discuss the Holodomor openly for more than half a century.

B) DISINFORMATION

In camouflaging the extent of the Ukrainian Famine by admitting to some "food difficulties," Soviet authorities mixed small amounts of truth into their denial, thus making it more difficult to discern what had actually happened. The Soviet media attacked any reporter or foreign dignitary who spoke out on this issue, drowning those voices in a sea of criticism. The Soviet cover-up extended into the 1980s. In April 1983, for instance, the Soviet embassy in Canada issued a statement denouncing public statements on the occasion of the 50th commemoration of the Holodomor as "slanders against the USSR."

C) POTEMKIN VILLAGES

Model villages were used by the Soviets for duping foreign visitors touring the USSR into believing that all was well. A showcase village would be set up with items and food brought in for the occasion, making the village look prosperous. Destitute villagers were removed and replaced by well-fed loyal Party members and/or performing artists. In short, these Potemkin villages were a façade. Touring westerners were easily fooled and reported on this false reality to the world, and were labelled "useful idiots."

D) REVOKING PRESS PRIVILEGES

The Soviet government could cancel a journalist's visa if it felt that the reporter's work was not regime-friendly. If the journalist's reporting painted the USSR in a positive light, he or she could be given extra privileges, such as a luxurious place of residence or preferred access. Journalists feared losing their visas because it would threaten their livelihood. Likewise, western workers or businessmen operating in the USSR could lose their commercial contracts if they were critical of the Soviet state.

Western Press Coverage

- Foreign correspondents were strongly advised by the press department of the Soviet Commissariat for Foreign Affairs to remain in Moscow, and in 1933 were formally barred from entering Ukraine and the North Caucuses (where the Kuban is located). Even prior to this ban, Western journalists could only travel outside of Moscow if accompanied by Soviet officials.

- Not a single newspaper in the West or press agency protested publicly against the confinement of its correspondents to Moscow or investigated the reason for this extraordinary measure. The majority of reporters complied, fearing possible expulsion and loss of their privileges.

- However, Walter Duranty of the *New York Times* was permitted into Ukraine. He reported that there was no famine, admitting only some "partial crop failures." Duranty set the tone for a good deal of western press coverage with what seemed to be authoritative denials of starvation. He referred to the Famine as the alleged man-made famine of 1933. However, according to a British diplomatic report, Duranty conceded off the record that "as many as 10 million" may have perished in the Soviet Union and that "Ukraine had been bled white."

Walter Duranty

- A number of other reporters, such as Malcolm Muggeridge and Gareth Jones ignored the travel ban and reported on the Famine. Nonetheless, articles by such men as Duranty overshadowed the work of these honest journalists.

Gareth Jones

- In 1932 Walter Duranty received the Pulitzer Prize for his reporting on the Soviet Union. Despite a public campaign to have the award revoked, a Pulitzer review board in 2003 determined to let the award stand given that "there was not clear and convincing evidence [in his earlier writing for which he received the prize] of deliberate deception." The *New York Times* did issue a public acknowledgement of Duranty's failures as a journalist.

- Commenting on the failure of journalists in the West to cover the Ukrainian Famine accurately, thoroughly and with the vigour it deserved, Eugene Lyons, a correspondent for United Press International, concluded in 1937 that, The Kremlin, in short, "had gotten away with it."

The Kremlin, in short, "had gotten away with it."

- Recently, information about the reporting of Canadian journalist Rhea Clyman has surfaced. Her articles about the Holodomor appeared in the Canadian press in the 1930s and provide vivid descriptions of the Famine in Ukraine.

Indifference of Western Governments

- Archival evidence (reports sent in diplomatic pouches, as well as press coverage) indicates that Western governments, notably Great Britain, Canada, the United States, Germany, Italy and Poland, were informed about the Famine in Ukraine. However, they chose to adopt a policy of non-interference in the internal affairs of a foreign sovereign state.

- The US State Department was well aware of what was occurring in Ukraine but did nothing because the republic was not vital to American interests. Franklin Delano Roosevelt, the American president at the time, was aiming to establish formal diplomatic relations with the USSR and did not wish to compromise negotiations. Diplomatic ties were established between the two countries in November 1933 just after the height of the Famine.

Franklin D. Roosevelt

- France's former Premier Edouard Herriot visited the USSR and Soviet Ukraine in August and September of 1933, near the height of the Famine. In Kyiv, Ukraine's historic capital, Herriot was impressed by its cleanliness and abundance of goods, either unaware of or ignoring the fact that Soviet authorities had staged this display; moreover, the citizens of Kyiv were forbidden from shopping or appearing in public during his stay. The September 13, 1933 issue of the official Soviet newspaper *Pravda* stated that Herriot "categorically denied the lies of the bourgeois press about a famine in the Soviet Union." Herriot's words had a considerable effect on European public opinion.

Edouard Herriot

- Even though Ukraine's borders were sealed in early 1933, some Ukrainians managed to escape into Poland and reported to authorities about the extent of the Famine. However, Poland had signed a non-aggression pact with the USSR in July 1932 and did not want to antagonize its neighbour to the east.

- During the 1930s, Canada had only just begun conducting its own foreign affairs and in many ways still followed the actions of Great Britain. Canada's primary interest at the time was to have a healthy trading relationship with the USSR and to prevent the Soviet Union from becoming the British Commonwealth's primary supplier of grain. So, the Canadian press focused more on covering harvest conditions and grain yields than on the Famine itself. Although the province of Saskatchewan lobbied the federal government to protest what was happening in Ukraine, there was ultimately no official Canadian response.

Richard B. Bennett

Western Historians and Intellectuals

Sidney & Beatrice Webb

- Sidney and Beatrice Webb, British founders of the prestigious London School of Economics and Political Science, visited the USSR in 1932-33. Their 1935 book *Soviet Communism, a New Civilization?* praised the USSR's developments in economics and education. The Webbs viewed *kulaks* as lazy usurpers who did not want to contribute to society. As for the Famine issue, they believed that only partial crop failures occurred and that these shortages were not enough to cause mass starvation.

George Bernard Shaw

- The writer George Bernard Shaw, a co-founder of the London School of Economics, favourably compared the USSR to the West and noted that during his visits (to Potemkin villages), he did not see a single undernourished person. Shaw was typical of many Western socialists who refused to believe that the world's first workers' state had a dreadful dark side. Shaw's uncritical assessment of the USSR presented a rosy, idealized image of the USSR to the West.

- In contrast, George Orwell, the British author of the dystopian novel *1984*, noted that "huge events like the Ukrainian Famine of 1933, involving the deaths of millions of people, have actually escaped the attention of the majority of English Russophiles" (*Notes on Nationalism*, 1945). While fighting in the Spanish Civil War, he became convinced that the USSR was a tyrannical dictatorship. He wrote his novel *Animal Farm* as a biting commentary on the totalitarian Soviet system and the Ukrainian Famine. His introduction to an early Ukrainian translation of *Animal Farm* is the most extensive essay on his reasons for writing the novel.

- A prime example of Holodomor denial is the book *Fraud, Famine, and Fascism: The Ukrainian Genocide Myth from Hitler to Harvard*, by Douglas Tottle, which was published in 1987 by a printing house affiliated with the Communist Party of Canada. It contends that the whole notion of the Famine was fabricated by Ukrainian nationalists. "The book was likely compiled in the Soviet Union" according to University of Alberta historian Frank Sysyn. The book has been viewed time and time again as an example of Soviet disinformation and propaganda to discredit the Ukrainian diaspora on the Holodomor.

- Robert Conquest was a renowned scholar of the Soviet Union. His ground-breaking *Harvest of Sorrow: Soviet Collectivization and the Terror-Famine*, published in 1986, was the first academic book in the West on the Holodomor. Conquest's book brought long overdue attention to the Ukrainian Famine, both to academics and the general public.

- Key recent works include: Timothy Snyder's *Bloodlands* (2011), Norman Naimark's *Stalin's Genocides* (2012), editors Bohdan Klid and Alexander Motyl's *The Holodomor Reader* (2012), George O. Liber's *Total Wars and the Making of Modern Ukraine* (2016) and Anne Applebaum's *Red Famine: Stalin's War on Ukraine* (2017).

Ukraine's Position

Viktor Yuschenko, 3rd President, 2005-2010.

- Following independence in 1991, the first two presidents (Leonid Kravchuk and Leonid Kuchma) recognized the Famine as genocide. In 2003, a resolution by the Ukrainian Parliament stated that, "the Holodomor of 1932-33 was deliberately organized by the Stalin regime and should be condemned by Ukrainian society and the international community as one of the largest genocides in world history by virtue of the number of its victims." Viktor Yushchenko, the third president, strongly backed efforts to have the Famine recognized as an act of genocide. Under his presidency, Ukraine's Parliament passed a law on November 28, 2006, declaring that, "the Holodomor of 1932-33 was a genocide of the Ukrainian people." This provoked a reaction in the Russian parliament, which on April 2, 2008, passed a resolution in which it stressed that victims of the Famine constituted "millions of citizens of the USSR representing different peoples and nationalities living largely in agricultural areas of the country." Today, the Russian Federation still denies that the 1932-33 Famine in Ukraine was a genocide.

"The Holodomor of 1932-33 was a genocide of the Ukrainian people."

Viktor Yanukovych, 4th President, 2010-2014.

- Ukraine's fourth president, Viktor Yanukovych, emphasized that the Famine was a tragedy of the Soviet people as a whole and did not acknowledge it as a genocide of the Ukrainian people. On November 23, 2013, the 80th anniversary of the Holodomor was widely commemorated in Ukraine by civil society groups and by numerous other countries that recognized the Holodomor as genocide. It was then that the Revolution of Diginity evolved. Demonstrators in Kyiv took to the streets protesting against the corrupt government of Yanukovych and his decision not to sign an association agreement with the European Union because of pressure from Moscow. It was events like the Holodomor that brought out thousands more to demonstrate and defend their right to determine their own future and not have foreign powers control their fate.

- In 2013-2014 a massive number of people in Ukraine rose in protest against Viktor Yanukovych's sudden refusal to sign the agreement with the European Union. Their protest was dubbed the "Euromaidan" Revolution. Police violently attacked the protestors and the pro-Russian government supporters fled to Russia. That same year, Petro Poroshenko was elected president by a majority of voters in Ukraine and he spent the next years defending Ukraine and its territory from Russian aggression. He also brought back the memory of Ukraine's historic past, including the Holodomor. The Famine became the symbol of what happens to a people under the rule of a foreign oppressive neighbour that has not yet accepted the breakup of its empire.

Petro Poroshenko, President since 2014.

- The UN General Assembly passed a Joint Statement on the Famine on November 10, 2003, recognizing it as a "national tragedy" for Ukraine.

- As of September 2017, countries that have recognized the Famine as an act of genocide or atrocity, include:

Australia	Brazil	Canada	Poland	U.S.A.	
Andorra	Azerbaijan	Argentina	Belgium	Colombia	Czech Rep.
Ecuador	Estonia	Georgia	Hungary	Italy	Latvia
Lithuania	Mexico	Moldova	Paraguay	Peru	Slovakia
Spain	Vatican City	Portugal			

Child lighting a candle on Holodomor Memorial Day in Seattle, Washington, USA, 2014.

Raphael Lemkin

Genocide Defined

Raphael Lemkin is the person who coined the term "genocide." He spent most of his life working to develop effective means of addressing this crime against humanity. Lemkin was educated in Belarus, Poland and Western Ukraine, an area that experienced genocide during his lifetime.

Raphael Lemkin

From a young age, he was interested in the shadow part of inter-cultural relations — ethnic and religious hatred, in particular when it resulted in the massacre or genocide of an ethnic or religious group. This interest motivated his transfer from linguistics to legal studies at the university in Lviv (now in Ukraine, then part of Poland). He did graduate work in Heidelberg, Berlin and Paris and completed a doctorate in law. His areas of specialty were criminal law and criminal fiscal law. He became very influential in Polish legal circles and was on friendly terms with the highest judicial authorities and leading intellectuals of Western Europe.

Lemkin was a prominent member of both Polish society and the Jewish community. Keenly aware of Hitler's anti-Jewish policies, he left Poland after it had been invaded by the Germans and the Soviets in 1939. Lemkin's international legal friends assisted him in fleeing, first to Sweden and then to the United States.

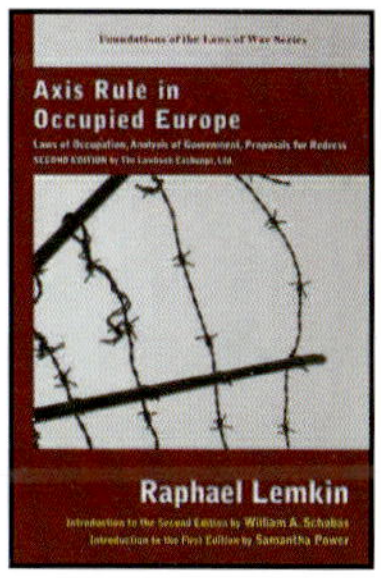

He collected all the legal acts and regulations promulgated by the Nazis to support their rule in occupied territories. This legal scholarship was published in 1944 as *Axis Rule in Occupied Europe: Laws of Occupation, Analysis of Government, Proposals for Redress*. In this publication he showed how the law was used to subjugate populations. He included in this book a chapter about his new concept of genocide — the destruction of a nation or an ethnic group.

Appointed to the War Crimes Office of the Judge Advocate General's Office in the USA, he drafted indictments and otherwise worked on the Nuremberg trials of Nazi war criminals. Disappointed that his concept of genocide was not accepted as a major part of the Nuremberg judgment, he continued in his efforts to elaborate this category of crime and to have it accepted in international law. This struggle was neither quick nor easy, nor in any way profitable.

With the creation of the United Nations, Lemkin lobbied to have genocide declared as an international crime.

On December 9, 1948, the UN Convention on the Prevention and Punishment of the Crime of Genocide was passed. Twenty-four countries ratified the convention by October 16, 1950. Lemkin was convinced that the implementation of this convention internationally would require the support of a superpower, and thus began his efforts in the USA. In the face of American and British reluctance to ratify the Genocide Convention, Lemkin turned to other writing projects in 1948 — the history of genocide and his memoirs. As a result of of irregular funding, Lemkin did not finish his book, but sections of it as well as his memoirs are available to scholars. He died in 1959 without the USA ratifying the convention. Excerpts from his case study of the Ukrainian Famine appear further in this section.

Ratification Agreement, UN Convention on the Prevention and Punishment of the Crime of Genocide, 1950.

SOURCES

- John Cooper. *Raphael Lemkin and the Struggle for the Genocide Convention.* New York: Palgrave Macmillan, 2008, pp. 7-191.
- Samantha Power. "A Problem from Hell" in *America and the Age of Genocide.* New York: Harper Perennial, 2002, pp. 17-78.

Lemkin and the UN Convention on the Prevention and Punishment of the Crime of Genocide

Roman Serbyn, Ph.D.

Roman Serbyn, Ph.D., a scholar of the Ukrainian famines, has argued that the Holodomor was the largest but not the only Stalinist assault against Ukrainians. He stresses that a range of acts by the Stalinist regime in Ukraine were aimed at the destruction of the Ukrainian people and that this catastrophe meets the criteria set out in the 1948 UN Convention on the Prevention and Punishment of the Crime of Genocide.

Serbyn bases his argument on the work of Raphael Lemkin, the father of the UN Convention. The following pages include excerpts from Lemkin's analysis of Ukraine in the 1930s.

Professor Roman Serbyn.

Raphael Lemkin (1900-1959) was an expert in international criminal law, with a particular interest in the prevention of mass human extermination. It was he who coined the term "genocide," and many of his ideas were incorporated into the United Nations Convention on the Prevention and Punishment of the Crime of Genocide in 1948.

In Article 2 of the present Convention, "genocide" is defined as any of the following acts committed with intent to destroy, in whole or in part, a national, ethnical, racial or religious group as such:

- killing members of a group
- causing bodily or mental harm to members of a group
- deliberately inflicting on the group conditions of life calculated to bring about its physical destruction in whole or in part
- forcibly transferring children of the group to another group

It should be noted that Lemkin applied the term "genocide" to attempts at destroying the Ukrainian nation. Ukrainian farmers were targeted as integral components of one genocidal process.

Lemkin speaks of the genocidal process as having four prongs:

- the decimation of the Ukrainian national elites
- the destruction of the Ukrainian Orthodox Church
- the starvation of the Ukrainian farming population and
- its replacement with non-Ukrainians from the RSFSR and elsewhere

The only dimension missing in Lemkin's analysis is the destruction of the ethnic Ukrainians living outside of Ukraine, of which there were eight million on the eve of the genocide.

NOTES

- Lemkin's full text on "Soviet Genocide in the Ukraine" may be found in Part IV of this resource, pp. 262-266.
- The Kyiv-based Ukrainian journal *Suchasnist* printed a Ukrainian translation in November 2008 (Rafael Lemkin, "Sovietskyi henotsyd v Ukraini," *Suchasnist* 11 (2008), pp. 40-45) and the English original was published in Luciuk, ed., *Holodomor: Reflections on the Great Famine*, Kingston, Ontario: Kashtan Press, 2008. pp. 235-42.

"Starving children rummaging for food in the rubble," Kharkiv, 1933.

Lemkin: "Soviet Genocide in the Ukraine" (Excerpts)

In his unpublished work History of Genocide, *Raphael Lemkin, a Polish-Jewish scholar, writes about the Soviet genocide in Ukraine. The following are excerpts from "Soviet Genocide in the Ukraine." Excerpts compiled by Professor Roman Serbyn.*

> ***What I want to speak about is perhaps the classic example of Soviet genocide, its longest and broadest experiment in Russification – the destruction of the Ukrainian nation.***

"As long as Ukraine retains its national unity, as long as its people continue to think of themselves as Ukrainians and to seek independence, so long Ukraine poses a serious threat to the very heart of Sovietism. It is no wonder that the Communist leaders have attached the greatest importance to the Russification of this independent [-minded] member of their 'Union of Republics,' have determined to remake it to fit their pattern of one Russian nation. For the Ukrainian is not and has never been, a Russian. His culture, his temperament, his language, his religion – all are different."

"Ukraine is highly susceptible to racial murder by select parts and so the Communist tactics there have not followed the pattern taken by the German attacks against the Jews. The nation is too populous to be exterminated completely with any efficiency. However, its leadership, religious, intellectual, political, its select and determining parts, are quite small and therefore easily eliminated, and so it is upon these groups particularly that the full force of the Soviet axe has fallen, with its familiar tools of mass murder, deportation and forced labor, exile and starvation."

"The attack has manifested a systematic pattern, with the whole process repeated again and again to meet fresh outbursts of national spirit. The first blow is aimed at the intelligentsia, the national brain, so as to paralyze the rest of the body."

"Going along with this attack on the intelligentsia was an offensive against the churches, priests and hierarchy, the *soul* of Ukraine. Between 1926 and 1932, the Ukrainian Orthodox Autocephalous Church, its Metropolitan [Lypkivsky] and 10,000 clergy were liquidated."

"The third prong of the Soviet plan was aimed at the farmers, the large mass of independent peasants who are the repository of the tradition, folklore and music, the national language and literature, the national spirit, of Ukraine. The weapon used against this body is perhaps the most terrible of all – starvation. Between 1932 and 1933, five million Ukrainians starved to death, an inhumanity that the 73rd Congress decried on May 28, 1934. There has been an attempt to dismiss this highpoint of Soviet cruelty as an economic policy connected with the collectivization of the wheat lands, and the elimination of the kulaks, the independent farmers, was therefore necessary. The fact is, however, that large-scale farmers in Ukraine were few and far-between. As a Soviet writer Kossior [error: Kosior was party boss of Ukraine – R.S.] declared in *Izvestiia* on December 2, 1933, "Ukrainian nationalism is our chief danger," and it was to eliminate that nationalism, to establish the horrifying uniformity of the Soviet state that the Ukrainian peasantry was sacrificed. The method used in this part of the plan was not at all restricted to any particular group. All suffered – men, women, children. The crop that year was ample to feed the people and livestock of Ukraine, though it had fallen off somewhat from the previous year, a decrease probably due in large measure to the struggle over collectivization. But a famine was necessary for the Soviet[s] and so they got one to order, by plan, through an unusually high grain allotment to the state as taxes. To add to this, thousands of acres of wheat were never harvested, were left to rot in the fields. The rest was sent to government granaries to be stored there until the authorities had decided how to allocate it. Much of this crop, so vital to the lives of the Ukrainian people, ended up as exports for the creation of credits abroad."

"In the face of famine on the farms, thousands abandoned the rural areas and moved into the towns to beg [for] food. Caught there and sent back to the country, they abandoned their children in the hope that they at least might survive. In this way, 18,000 children were abandoned in Kharkiv alone. Villages of a thousand had a surviving population of a hundred; in others, half the populace was gone, and deaths in these towns ranged from 20 to 30 per day. Cannibalism became commonplace."

"The fourth step in the process consisted in the fragmentation of the Ukrainian people at once by the addition to the Ukraine of foreign peoples and by the dispersion of the Ukrainians throughout Eastern Europe. In this way, ethnic unity would be destroyed and nationalities mixed."

"These have been the chief steps in the systematic destruction of the Ukrainian nation. Notably, there have been no attempts at complete annihilation, such as was the method of the German attack on the Jews. And yet, if the Soviet program succeeds completely, if the intelligentsia, the priests and the peasants can be eliminated, Ukraine will be as dead as if every Ukrainian were killed, for it will have lost that part of it which has kept and developed its culture, its beliefs, its common ideas, which have guided it and given it a soul, which, in short, made it a nation rather than a mass of people. The mass, indiscriminate murders have not, however, been lacking – they have simply not been integral parts of the plan, but only chance variations. Thousands have been executed, untold thousands have disappeared into the certain death of Siberian labor camps."

"This is not simply a case of mass murder. It is a case of genocide, of destruction, not of individuals only, but of a culture and a nation. Soviet national unity is being created, not by any union of ideas and of cultures, but by the complete destruction of all cultures and of all ideas save one – the Soviet."

See activity on excerpts of Lemkin's speech in Part III, pp. 191-192.

The Holodomor and Article II of the UN Convention
Roman Serbyn, Ph.D.

NOTE: Article II of the UN Convention on the Prevention and Punishment of the Crime of Genocide defines the term genocide.

CONVENTION TEXT	COMMENTARY
In the current Convention, genocide means any of the following acts committed with intent to destroy, in whole or in part, a national, ethnical, racial or religious group, as such:	• A key element in the definition of genocide is the "intent to destroy, in whole or in part, a national, ethnical, racial or religious group." Stalin's "intent to destroy" is clear from documents including the "Five Stalks of Grain Law," the forcible return by government forces of Ukrainian farmers fleeing famine to Russia in search of food, and the results: millions of famine victims; export of grain during the famine; denial of the famine; and rejection of foreign aid. Stalin's intent to destroy is now generally accepted. • The definition of genocide, according to the Convention, is acts committed with intent to destroy "in whole or in part." As Stalin still needed Ukrainian farmers to work on the collective farms, he destroyed the Ukrainian nation "in part." • The question of target groups: Ukrainians formed a distinct group in both the national and ethnic sense — "national" refers to civic identity (citizens of the UkrSSR) and "ethnic," to their identity as Ukrainians; there were eight million ethnic Ukrainians in the RSFSR and 23 million ethnic Ukrainians in the Ukrainian SSR (81% of the republic). At the time, the overwhelming majority of Ukrainians were farmers. • The expression "as such" means that the group was targeted for destruction as an entity, in the physical and/ or spiritual sense. The specific forms of destruction listed by the Convention show that the destruction did not necessarily have to be physical. Forcing a group to change from one nationality to another or one religion to another is tantamount to the annihilation of that group (as such), and fits the Convention's definition.
(a) Killing members of the group;	• Most of the Ukrainians were farmers who perished from starvation, but some urban residents also died from hunger, and many others (intellectuals, workers) were executed or died from exposure during deportation or in the Gulag.

CONVENTION TEXT	COMMENTARY
(b) Causing serious bodily or mental harm to members of the group	• The Holodomor obviously caused serious bodily and mental harm; it should be noted that the clause does not specify complete physical destruction.
(c) Deliberately inflicting on the group conditions of life calculated to bring about its physical destruction in whole or in part	• Deliberate acts of commission and omission. • Confiscation of the fruits of farmers' work. • Export of food necessary for survival. • Refusal to accept foreign aid.
(d) Imposing measures intended to prevent births within the group	• Separation of families (husband sent to one camp and wife to another) • Starvation is an impediment to procreation.
(e) Forcibly transferring children of the group to another group	• The sense of this clause is that the children are not physically destroyed but become lost to the group of origin by change of nationality, ethnicity, or religion. • The subjection of whole families to the same transfer certainly falls under this category: in other words, the deprivation of an ethnic group of those conditions which allow it to live and develop as an ethnic entity. • In the Ukrainian case: deportation from Ukraine to Russia, where Ukrainians must integrate into the Russian milieu. • The abolition of Ukrainization in the Russian Republic (RSFSR) in 1932 and forced Russification of all public life was one way of transferring the ethnically Ukrainian population to the Russian ethnos. • The result of this decree can be seen in the census of 1937, which shows 3 to 4 million ethnic Ukrainians in the RSFSR, compared to the 8 million recorded in the 1926 census.

The question of motive

The UN Convention does not require the establishment of motive, only proof of intention. However, the understanding of motive helps us to better assess intention. Did Stalin have any reason to destroy the Ukrainian nation as such?

To destroy the whole Ukrainian population in the physical sense would have been folly; after all, the Ukrainian SSR had almost 30 million people (23 million Ukrainian farmers), out of a total of about 150 million Soviet citizens. Ukrainians were also known for being good farmers. Such a loss of manpower would have been most detrimental to the power status that Stalin was seeking for his empire. On the other hand, he did want to destroy the separate identity of Ukrainians.

Stalin feared that the Ukrainian elites would unite with Ukrainian farmers, the mainstay of the Ukrainian nation, against Moscow. This was the reason for the elimination of the Ukrainian elites in 1929-1930 (SVU and *kulaks*), and then, in 1932-1933, the purges within the Communist Party of Ukraine and state administration.

Stalin wrote in the summer of 1932 that the Ukrainian Communist Party of 500,000 was full of rotten elements, infiltrated by Petliurites and Polish agents, and that "we can lose Ukraine" unless we take steps to transform it into a "Soviet fortress." This was his motivation for attacking the farmers ("the nation's army") and its elites (the intelligentsia and the cultural, religious and political leadership) — to decimate the Ukrainian nation. Ukrainians perished because they stood in the way of Stalin's ambitions.

"Starvation in Ukraine 1933," painting by William Kurelek, 1977.

Quotations on the Holodomor

Quotations are a wonderful tool for educators to use in the classroom. They may be used to introduce a topic, encourage a discussion on a specific aspect or concern, or as a starter statement for an essay topic for students to research and analyze. Below are a number of appropriate quotations.

On genocide

> ***"A genocide begins with the killing of one man – not for what he has done, but because of who he is."***
>
> Kofi Annan, Nobel lecture, Oslo, December 10, 2001.
> (Annan was the Secretary General of the United Nations.)

> ***"The intrusion of history is not just theoretical. It is also the legacy of being an accomplice or a victim, or just an onlooker. In each case, history entails the uncomfortable presence of earlier unresolved roles."***
>
> Maier, Charles S. *The Unmasterable Past: History, Holocaust, and German National Identity.* Cambridge, MA: Harvard University Press, 1998, p. 160.

Genocide in Ukraine

> ***"This was the first instance of a peacetime genocide in history. It took the extraordinary form of an artificial famine deliberately created by the ruling powers. This savage combination of words for the designation of a crime — "an artificial, deliberately planned famine" — is still incredible to many people throughout the world, but indicates the uniqueness of the tragedy of 1933, which is unparalleled, for a time of peace, in the number of victims it claimed."***
>
> Hryshko, Wasyl. *The Ukrainian Holocaust of 1933.* Toronto: Bahriany Foundation, Suzhero, Dobrus, 1983, p. 107.
> (Hryshko was a survivor of the Holodomor).

"Here, the genocide of a 'class' may well be tantamount to the genocide of a 'race' — the deliberate starvation of a child of a Ukrainian kulak as a result of the famine caused by Stalin's regime is equal to the starvation of a Jewish child in the Warsaw ghetto as a result of the famine caused by the Nazi regime."

Courtoise, Stephane. "Introduction: The Crimes of Communism," in *The Black Book Of Communism: Crimes, Terror, Repression.* Cambridge, MA: Harvard University Press, 1999, p. 9.

Explanations for the Genocidal Famine

"But it is also beyond doubt that after all, the peasant question is the basis, the quintessence, of the national question. That explains the fact that the peasantry constitutes the main army of the national movement, that there is no powerful national movement without the peasant army, nor can there be. That is what is meant when it is said that in essence, the national question is a peasant question."

Stalin, J. V. "Concerning The National Question in Yugoslavia." Speech delivered in the Yugoslav Commission of the E.C.C.I., March 30, 1925, in *J. V. Stalin Works.* Moscow: Foreign Languages Publishing House, 1954, Vol. 7, 71-72. (Accessed March 11, 2011.)

http://www.marx2mao.com/Stalin/CNQY25.html

"What nonsense. What a foolish rationalization of murder and perversion of Leninist policy. ... I'm sure when that time comes, historians will be able to find sufficient material to make an objective assessment. In addition to our own experience here in the Soviet Union, they will be able to draw on examples of collectivization in the German Democratic Republic, Czechoslovakia, Bulgaria, Romania... There were nowhere near as many victims as in our country... but the worst troubles with collectivization in other countries were a far cry from what happened in the Soviet Union under Stalin.

Collectivization in Romania was a gradual process, carried out in stages. While it elicited local disturbances and resistance, there were no major or widespread riots."

Khrushchev, N. S. "Khrushchev Remembers" in *The Last Testament.* Boston, MA: Little, Brown and Company, 1974, p. 109. (Khrushchev was a former leader of the USSR.)

"The Terror-Famine of 1932-33 was a dual-purpose by-product of collectivization, designed to suppress Ukrainian nationalism and the most important concentration of prosperous peasants at one throw."

Davies, Norman. *Europe: A History*, Oxford University Press, Oxford, 1996, p. 207.

"Ukrainians, being profoundly religious, individualistic, believers in private property, and attached to their plots of land, were obviously unsuitable material for building communism, and this fact was noted by high-ranking Soviet officials. As a nation we were subject to destruction. The remnants of the Ukrainian people were to become material for forming a 'new historical society — the Soviet people,' with the Russian population, language and culture at its core."

Ovsiienko, Vasyl. "Antyradianska knyzhka" (The Anti-Soviet Book) in *Svitlo liudei. Memuary ta publikatsiya*. Knyha II. Kharkiv: Prava liudyny, 2007, pp. 157-158.

"This is why, on the basis of the changed situation, we consider that local, Ukrainian nationalism is the principal danger in Ukraine at the present time."

Kosior, S. V. "The Results and Immediate Tasks of the National Policy in the Ukraine." Article in *Soviet Ukraine Today*. Moscow: Cooperative Publishing Society of Foreign Workers in the USSR, 1934, p. 95.

"Moscow employed famine as a political weapon against the Ukrainians for a second time in the years 1932-33, with this difference, that this time the famine was in its entirety artificially induced and organized. It was the result of a well worked-out plan which was to take in the entire Ukrainian SSR and the Kuban districts which had a Ukrainian population."

Statement of Fedir M. Pihido, engineer and economist. "Famine as an Instrument of Soviet Political Warfare" in *Investigation of Communist Take-Over and Occupation of the Non-Russian Nations of the USSR: Eighth Interim Report of Hearings before the Select Committee on Communist Aggression*. Washington: Gov't. Printing Office, 1954, p. 35.

"Research into the surviving documents that have been released since the collapse of the Soviet Union clearly has shown that the Soviet government used the Famine, which certainly hit the Soviet Union as a whole, and was particularly severe in other areas of peasant resistance, like the Volga and the Don, as a tool to break the Ukrainian peasantry's opposition to collectivization in particular, and also to eliminate the leadership of the Ukrainian Communist Party, which it believed to be too nationalistic and too sympathetic to the plight of the peasantry."

Graziosi, Andrea. *The Ukrainian Weekly*, Sunday, July 25, 2010, p. 4.

"Nowhere did restrictions, purges, repressions and in general all forms of bureaucratic hooliganism assume such murderous sweep as they did in the Ukraine in the struggle against the powerful, deeply-rooted longings of the Ukrainian masses for greater freedom and independence."

Trotsky, Leon. "Problem of the Ukraine" in *Fourth International*. New York, no. 10 (100), (November 1949): pp. 317-319.

http://www.marxists.org/archive/trotsky/1939/04/ukraine.html

"Under the direct leadership and directions of the Central Committee of the Communist Party and personally of comrade Stalin, we smashed the Ukrainian nationalist counterrevolution."

Postyshev, Pavel. *V borotbi za leninsko-stalinsku natsionalnu polityku partii.* Kyiv, Partvydav, 1935, p. 65.

"I remain convinced that, for Stalin to have complete centralized power in his hands, he found it necessary to physically destroy the second-largest Soviet republic, meaning the annihilation of the Ukrainian peasantry, Ukrainian intelligentsia, Ukrainian language, and history as understood by the people; to do away with Ukraine and things Ukrainian as such. The calculation was very simple, very primitive: no people, therefore, no separate country, and thus no problem. Such a policy is GENOCIDE in the classic sense of the word."

Mace, James, "I was Chosen by Your Dead… Legacy of the Famine: Ukraine as a Postgenocidal Society" in *Day and Eternity of James Mace*, compiled by Maryna Zamiatina and Nadiya Tysiachna. Kyiv: Ukrainian Press Group, 2005, p. 58.

"Famine was quite deliberately employed as an instrument of national policy, as the last means of breaking the resistance of the peasantry to the new system where they are divorced from personal ownership of the land and obligated to work on the conditions which the state may dictate to them and deliver up whatever the state may demand from them."

Chamberlin, William Henry. *Russia's Iron Age.* London: Duckworth,1935, pp. 88-89. (Correspondent for *The Christian Science Monitor* in the Soviet Union, 1922–1934.)

"This famine may fairly be called political because it was not the result of any overwhelming natural catastrophe or of such a complete exhaustion of the country's resources in foreign and civil war as preceded and helped to cause the famine 1921-22."

Chamberlin, William Henry. *The Ukraine: A Submerged Nation* New York: The Macmillan Company, 1944, p. 59.

Witnesses to Famine in Ukraine

"I saw the ravages of the famine of 1932-33 in the Ukraine: hordes of families in rags begging at the railway stations, the women lifting up to the compartment window their starving brats which — with drumstick limbs, big cadaverous heads, puffed bellies — looked like embryos out of alcohol bottles…"

Crossman, Richard, ed. *The God That Failed.* New York: Bantam Books, 1965, p.53. (quotation by Arthur Koestler, former communist)

"... On one side, millions of starving peasants, their bodies often swollen from lack of food; on the other, soldiers, members of the GPU carrying out the instructions of the dictatorship of the proletariat. They had gone over the country like a swarm of locusts and taken away everything edible; they

had shot or exiled thousands of peasants, sometimes whole villages; they had reduced some of the most fertile land in the world to a melancholy desert.”

Muggeridge, Malcolm. “War on the Peasants,” *Fortnightly Review*, May 1, 1933.

“On a battlefield men die quickly, they fight back, they are sustained by fellowship and a sense of duty. Here I saw people dying in solitude by slow degrees, dying hideously, without the excuse of sacrifice for a cause. They had been trapped and left to starve, each in his home, by a political decision made in a far-off capital around conference and banquet tables. [...]

The most terrifying sights were the little children with skeleton limbs dangling from balloon-like abdomens. Starvation had wiped every trace of youth from their faces, turning them into tortured gargoyles; only in their eyes still lingered the reminder of childhood. Everywhere we found men and women lying prone, their faces and bellies bloated, their eyes utterly expressionless.

Anger lashed my mind as I drove back to the village. Butter being sent abroad in the midst of the famine! In London, Berlin, Paris I could see with my mind's eye people eating butter stamped with a Soviet trademark. “They must be rich to be able to send out butter,” I could hear them saying. “Here, friends, is the proof of socialism in action.” Driving through the fields, I did not hear the lovely Ukrainian songs so dear to my heart. These people had forgotten how to sing. I could hear only the groans of the dying, and the lip-smacking of fat foreigners enjoying our butter...”

Kravchenko, Victor. *I Chose Freedom: The Personal And Political Life of a Soviet Official.* New York: Charles Scribner's Sons, 1946, pp. 118, 122.

“And the peasant children! Have you ever seen the newspaper photographs of the children in the German camps? They were just like that: their heads like heavy balls on thin little necks, like storks, and one could see each bone of their arms and legs protruding from beneath the skin, how bones joined, and the entire skeleton was stretched over with skin that was like yellow gauze. And the children's faces were aged, tormented, just as if they were seventy years old. And by the spring they no longer had faces

at all. Instead, they had birdlike heads with beaks, or frog heads — thin, wide lips — and some of them resembled fish, mouths open. Not human faces.”

Grossman, Vasily. *Forever Flowing.* New York: Harper & Row, 1972, p. 157.

Consequences of the Famine in Ukraine

Churchill had his first wartime meeting with Stalin in Moscow in August 1942. After formal negotiations during the day, they were having an informal dinner in Stalin's quarters on the last evening before Churchill's departure.

“I [Churchill] asked, 'have the stresses of this war been as bad to you personally as carrying through the policy of the Collective Farms?' This subject immediately roused the Marshal [Stalin]. 'Oh, no,' he said, 'the Collective Farm policy was a terrible struggle.' 'I thought you would have found it bad,' said I, 'because you were not dealing with a few score thousands of aristocrats or big landowners, but with millions of small men.'

'Ten millions,' he said, holding up his hands. 'It was fearful. Four years it lasted. It was absolutely necessary for Russia.”

Churchill, Winston, S. “The Hinge of Fate,” in *The Second World War, Vol. 4.* Boston: Houghton Mifflin Company, 1950, p. 498.

“Hundreds of thousands of lives were lost — maybe even millions. I can't give an exact figure because no one was keeping count. All we knew was that people were dying in enormous numbers.”

Khrushchev, N. S. “Khrushchev Remembers,” in *The Last Testament.* Boston: Little, Brown and Company, 1974, pp. 108-109.

“Imagine the Titanic sinking every day for thirteen years! Such were the losses from the 1933 Famine Genocide in Soviet Ukraine.”

Melanie Bobrowski, interviewed on CITY TV, Toronto, Oct. 4, 1998.

Yet it is well to remember, as Robert Conquest's powerful book obliges us to do, that the forced collectivization of agriculture decreed by the Soviet master and his party likely cost the lives of more people than perished in all countries as a result of the First World War.

Marrus, Michael. "A Page of Infamy and Soviet History." Book review of *Harvest of Sorrow: Soviet Collectivization and the Terror-Famine* by Robert Conquest. *The Globe and Mail*, Toronto, Canada. December 20, 1986.

It was the forced resettlement of a whole people, an ethnic catastrophe. But yet so cleverly were the channels of the GPU – Gulag organized that the cities would have noticed nothing had they not been stricken by a strange three - year famine — a famine that came about without drought and without war.

Solzhenitsyn, Aleksandr I. *The Gulag Archipelago, 1918-1956: An Experiment in Literary Investigation I-II.* New York: Harper & Row, 1974, pp. 54-55.

Cover-up and Denial

The Stalinist totalitarian regime tried hard to ensure that everyone kept silent about the Holodomor, even people who had survived it, as well as their children and grandchildren; so that no one knew about this genocide abroad, and if they found out about it, they would keep silent.

Kramarenko, Oleksandr. "Why isn't the world recognizing the Holodomor as an act of genocide?" *The Day Weekly Digest*, no. 33, Tuesday, October 24, 2006 (Kyiv, Ukraine).

For quite six years the English admirers of Hitler contrived not to learn of the existence of Dachau and Buchenwald. And those who are loudest in denouncing the German concentration camps were often quite unaware, or only very dimly aware, that there are also concentration camps in Russia. Huge events like the Ukraine famine of 1933, involving the deaths of millions of people, have actually escaped the attention of the majority of English Russophiles.

Orwell, George. "Notes on Nationalism," in *England your England, and Other Essays.* London: Seeker & Warburg, 1953, pp. 52-53.

"Duranty was a chain-smoking, scotch drinking vulgar sort of man who made no apologies for his admiration of Stalin. He was held in awe by other journalists, especially young female journalists. He did not fail to use the awe to his advantage, or rather their disadvantage. As Fascism rose in Europe, and Japanese jingoism emerged in the East, Duranty wrote glowing accounts of Stalin's Five-Year Plan. Almost single-handedly did Duranty aid and abet one of the world's most prolific mass murderers, knowing all the while what was going on, but refraining from saying precisely what he knew to be true. He had swallowed the ends-justifies-the-means argument hook, line and sinker. Duranty loved to repeat, when Stalin's atrocities were brought to light, 'you can't make an omelet without breaking a few eggs.' Those 'eggs' were the heads of men, women and children, and those 'few' were merely tens of millions."

Herring, Mark Y. "Useful Idiot," review of *Stalin's Apologist: Walter Duranty, the New York Times' Man in Moscow* by S.J. Taylor. *Contra Mundum*, no. 15 (1995).

http://www.contra-mundum.org/cm/reviews/mh_idiot.pdf

"These philological sophistries, to which we were all driven, served Moscow's purpose of smearing the facts out of recognition and beclouding a situation which, had we reported simply and clearly, might have worked up enough public opinion abroad to force remedial measures. And every correspondent, each in his own measure, was guilty of collaborating in this monstrous hoax on the world."

Lyons, Eugene. *Assignment in Utopia.* New York: Harcourt, Brace and Company, 1937, p. 573. (Moscow correspondent for the United Press.)

Canada on the Holodomor

"We in Canada are bonded to this dark chapter in human history by more than a million Canadians of Ukrainian descent, many of whom lost loved ones in the Holodomor. And so, all Canadians join us in commemoration of this 75th anniversary of the terrible famine of 1932-33. Because what was done to the Ukrainian people was a mortal offence against the values we hold dearest: freedom, democracy, human rights and the rule of law."

Prime Minister Stephen Harper. From a speech at the National Holodomor Commemoration Ceremony. Ottawa, November 28, 2007.

"We have a duty to protect the memory of these people, and to remember other unspeakable acts Ukrainian people have suffered over the years — so we have also ensured students across Ontario also learn about the Holodomor at school by making it part of the curriculum. Remembering these moments is particularly important when we see what is happening in Ukraine now."

Kathleen Wynne, Premier of Ontario. Speech at Holodomor Education Reception at Queen's Park (Ontario Legislature). May 26, 2015.

teacher tip

See assignments on using quotations in part III:
- Using Quotations, p. 204
- Graffiti Walk, p. 208

"Harvest time for a Ukrainian farming family," Kyiv Oblast, 1929.

U.S. Commission on the Ukraine Famine

The US Commission on the Ukraine Famine was established December 13, 1985. Its aim was "to conduct a study of the 1932-1933 Ukrainian Famine in order to expand the world's knowledge of the famine and provide the American public with a better understanding of the Soviet system by revealing the Soviet role." Its findings were delivered to the US Congress on April 22, 1988. Based on the testimony and staff research, the Commission made the following findings:

- There is no doubt that large numbers of inhabitants of the Ukrainian SSR and the North Caucasus Territory starved to death in a man-made famine in 1932-1933, caused by the seizure of the 1932 crop by Soviet authorities.
- The victims of the Ukrainian Famine numbered in the millions.
- Official Soviet allegations of "kulak sabotage," upon which all "difficulties" were blamed during the Famine, are false.
- The Famine was not, as is often alleged, related to drought.
- In 1931-1932, the official Soviet response to a drought-induced grain shortage outside Ukraine was to send aid to the areas affected and to make a series of concessions to the peasantry.
- In mid-1932, following complaints by officials in the Ukrainian SSR that excessive grain procurements had led to localized outbreaks of famine, Moscow reversed course and took an increasingly hard line toward the peasantry.
- The inability of Soviet authorities in Ukraine to meet the grain procurement quota forced them to introduce increasingly severe measures to extract the maximum quantity of grain from the peasants.
- In the fall of 1932 Stalin used the resulting "procurements crisis" in Ukraine as an excuse to tighten his control in Ukraine and to intensify grain seizures further.
- The Ukrainian Famine of 1932-1933 was caused by the maximum extraction of agricultural produce from the rural population.
- Officials in charge of grain seizures also lived in fear of punishment.
- Stalin knew that people were starving to death in Ukraine by late 1932.
- In January 1933, Stalin used the "laxity" of the Ukrainian authorities in seizing grain to strengthen further his control over the Communist Party of Ukraine and mandated actions, which worsened the situation and maximized the loss of life.

- Postyshev had a dual mandate from Moscow: to intensify the grain seizures [and therefore the Famine] in Ukraine and to eliminate such modest national self-assertion as Ukrainians had hitherto been allowed by the USSR.

- While famine also took place during the 1932-1933 agricultural year in the Volga Basin and the North Caucasus Territory as a whole, the invasiveness of Stalin's interventions of both the fall of 1932 and January 1933 in Ukraine are paralleled only in the ethnically Ukrainian Kuban region of the North Caucasus.

- Attempts were made to prevent the starving from travelling to areas where food was more available.

- Joseph Stalin and those around him committed genocide against Ukrainians in 1932-1933.

- The American government had ample and timely information about the Famine but failed to take any steps, which might have ameliorated the situation. Instead, the Administration extended diplomatic recognition to the Soviet government in November 1933, immediately after the Famine.

- During the Famine certain members of the American press corps cooperated with the Soviet government to deny the existence of the Ukrainian Famine.

- Recently, scholarship in both the West and, to a lesser extent, the Soviet Union has made substantial progress in dealing with the Famine. Although official Soviet historians and spokesmen have never given a fully accurate or adequate account, significant progress has been made in recent months.

"No one wanted to die," Mykola Chervotkins.

SOURCE

"U.S. Commission on the Ukraine Famine," report to Congress. Adopted by the Commission, April 19, 1988. Submitted to Congress April 22, 1988. Washington: United States Government Printing Office, 1988. p. 524.

Eyewitness Accounts

Eyewitness accounts are one of the sources of information used by historians to arrive at the truth about a historical event. Using a number of eyewitness reports, students can see how the event affected the lives of ordinary people in a society at a specific time and in a specific place.

US Commission on the Ukraine Famine

The following eyewitness accounts were collected in the course of the work of the US Commission on the Ukraine Famine in the years 1985-88.

CASE STUDY #1. FAMINE TESTIMONY OF SVIATOSLAV KARAVANSKY

Sviatoslav Karavansky

From my childhood years I remember that from 1929, the beginning of industrialization and collectivization, our family and all of the people of Odesa suffered a great shortage of food. Buttermilk, milk, sugar and even bread disappeared from the stores. In the period 1929-30 the whole city turned to the rationing system. The entire population lived on rations. The portions that were handed out continued to decrease, and in the winter of 1933 I, as a dependent, received 200 grams (seven ounces) of black bread per day. My mother, brother and sister received the same ration. Bread was, and still is, the main source of nourishment for the Soviet population. For comparison, let's consider the daily ration of the Soviet soldier. The soldiers of the Red Army received at that time one kilogram (36 ounces) of bread per day. The entire city of Odesa lived on rations which were insufficient for healthy people, but which kept it from starving. The rural population was not subject to rationing, and it perished. People in the villages could not receive any help from their relatives in towns because the city population was hungry, too.

Destroyed church bells, 1930s.

It should be mentioned that the closing of churches preceded the Great Famine. So, the organizer of the famine took into consideration the major role played by the Church in dealing with national disasters like the famine. It is known that during the famine of 1921 in Ukraine churches aided the starving people. During 1932-33, the churches did not function, and the clergy were sent to labour camps, which, in reality, were death camps.

"Playtime in the Village," 1928.

Our family lived in downtown Odesa, and I attended school there. I never saw starving people downtown, but many of the latter were seen on the outskirts of the city. Odesa was a port where foreign sailors and businessmen could always be found, so the authorities took measures not to allow hungry peasants to reach the downtown area. But everyone in Odesa knew that there was a horrible shortage of food in the villages. People swelled from hunger and died. In the school, which I attended from September

1932 to May 1933, the teacher told us that the *kulaks* [or *kurkuls*] were responsible for all the temporary difficulties of the Soviet socialist economy.

My father was employed in the Odesa shipyard, and I heard from adults that a lot of foreign ships in the docks were waiting their turn to be loaded with grain from Odesa grain elevators. My parents wondered how it was possible that such great quantities of food were being exported while the village population was starving. To ask questions about this was dangerous. If a child asked about these things in school, the teachers assumed that he had been taught by his parents, who were thus placed in danger. So, my parents were very careful about telling me not to ask any questions in school, and not to reveal anywhere what was discussed in the family.

"Torgsin," 1933.

The entire population was terrorized by the arrests and trials, which culminated in 1932-33. In those years so-called *torgsins* were opened in Odesa. In *torgsins* anyone could buy for gold and foreign currency all the food that otherwise was distributed through the rationing system. Many people who had small golden crosses or wedding rings brought them to *torgsins.* Once my mother went to *torgsin* as well. She brought back a loaf of black bread, turning the day into a holiday for the entire family. There were rumors in Odesa that people were being arrested for selling human sausage in the market place. There was a saying that the sausages "had been shot." Such accounts were not published in the newspapers, which only praised the wisdom of the party and the great leader, Stalin.

In 1934 my father, as a shipyard employee, got a free ticket for an Odesa-Batumi cruise on the Black Sea. Traveling to Batumi on the liner, he observed that a large number of Ukrainian peasants had migrated to Georgia where there was no food shortage and no famine.

The famine in Ukraine was over, but those who survived fled from Ukraine. I know that in the local schools in the village of Rossosha near Proskurov (now Khmelnytsky) there was no first year class for the 1940-41 school year because the birth rate in 1933 had been zero. In 1953-54 the Soviet Navy also experienced shortages of healthy servicemen because of the zero birth rate in 1933 in Ukraine. The requirements for the service in the navy were reduced because otherwise it was impossible to recruit the necessary number of sailors. I received this information from a navy officer who had served a 10-year term in Mordovia. In 1970 my wife and I met a woman in the village of Tarussa (Kaluga region) who spoke with a strong Ukrainian accent. She told us that she was born near Kyiv. In 1933 she had fled from her native village because of the famine and had found shelter in Tarussa where she later married and settled down, thereby escaping death while her entire family died of starvation.

SOURCE

United States. Commission on the Ukraine Famine. *Investigation of the Ukrainian Famine, 1932-1933: First Interim Report of Meetings And Hearings of And Before the Commission On the Ukraine Famine, Held In 1986.* Washington, D.C.: U.S. Govt. Print. Off. , 1987.

CASE STUDY #2: FAMINE TESTIMONY OF TATIANA PAWLICHKA

In 1932, I was 10 years old, and I remember well what happened in my native village in the Kyiv region. In the spring of that year, we had virtually no seed. The Communists had taken all the grain, and although they saw that we were weak and hungry, they came and searched for more grain. My mother had stashed away some corn that had already sprouted, but they found that, too, and took it. What we did manage to sow, the starving people pulled up out of the ground and ate.

Village home, "Khata." Kyiv Oblast, 1932.

In the villages and on the collective farms (our village had two collectives), a lot of land lay fallow, because people had nothing to sow, and there wasn't enough manpower to do the sowing. Most people couldn't walk, and those few who could had no strength. When, at harvest time, there weren't enough local people to harvest the grain, others were sent in to help on the collectives. These people spoke Russian, and they were given provisions.

After the harvest, the villagers tried to go out in the field to look for gleanings, and the Communists would arrest them and shoot at them, and send them to Siberia. My aunt, Tatiana Rudenko, was taken away. They said she had stolen the property of the collective farm.

That summer, the vegetables couldn't even ripen — people pulled them out of the ground — still green — and ate them. People ate leaves, nettles, milkweed, sedges. By autumn, no one had any chickens or cattle. Here and there, someone had a few potatoes or beets. People coming in from other villages told the very same story. They would travel all over trying to get food. They would fall by the roadside, and none of us could do anything to help. When the ground froze, they were just left lying there dead, in the snow; or, if they died in the house, they were dragged out to the cattle-shed, and they would lie there frozen until spring. There was no one to dig graves.

Cookbook, 1933.

All the train stations were overflowing with starving, dying people. Everyone wanted to go to Russia [the Russian SFSR] because it was said that there was no famine there. Very few [of those who left] returned. They all perished on the way. They weren't allowed into Russia and were turned back at the border. Those who somehow managed to get into Russia could save themselves.

"Children digging for frozen potatoes," Donetsk Oblast, 1933.

In February of 1933, there were so few children left that the schools were closed. By this time, there wasn't a cat, dog or sparrow in the village. In that month, my cousin Mykhailo Rudenko died; a month later my aunt Nastia Klymenko and her son, my cousin Ivan, died, as well as my classmate, Dokia Klymenko.

There was cannibalism in our village. On my farmstead, an 18-year-old boy, Danylo Hukhlib, died, and his mother and younger sisters and brothers cut him up and ate him. The Communists came and took them away, and we never saw them again. People said they took them a little ways off and shot them right away — the little ones and the older ones together.

At that time, I remember, I had heavy, swollen legs. My sister, Tamara, had a large, swollen stomach, and her neck was long and thin like a bird's neck. People didn't look like people — they were more like starving ghosts.

The ground thawed, and they began to take the dead to the ravine in ox carts. The air was filled with the ubiquitous odor of decomposing bodies. The wind carried this odor far and wide. It was thus over all of Ukraine.

teacher tip

For student activities, see assignment for Eyewitness Reports in Part III, pp. 197-198.

"The Road of Sorrow," by Nina Marchenko. From the Collection "Holodomor: Through the Eyes of Ukrainian Artists." Founder and trustee Morgan Williams.

SOURCE

United States. Commission on the Ukraine Famine. *Investigation of the Ukrainian Famine, 1932-1933: First Interim Report of Meetings And Hearings of And Before the Commission On the Ukraine Famine, Held In 1986.* Washington, D.C.: U.S. Govt. Print. Off. , 1987.

Primary Documents

The recent publication and translation of Soviet and Ukrainian archival materials on the Holodomor have made the study of primary documents possible. The following documents are reprinted from the collection *Holodomor of 1932-33 in Ukraine: Documents and Materials*, Ruslan Pyrih, ed., Kyiv: Kyiv Mohyla Academy Publishing House, 2008.

Primary documents are an excellent resource for students to develop critical thinking skills by having them analyze and synthesize information. Teachers are urged to have students practice the Historian's Craft, by having them analyze primary documents as if they were the only information available on the topic. This could be done by analyzing individual documents as a class, or by using a 'jigsaw' exercise to extract basic information from all the documents in a concise and quick manner, using a prepared chart for recording the information. See pages 186-188 for student activities. For instructions on how to analyze a document, please turn to Part III, pages 180-185.

Document #1. Resolution "On safekeeping property of state enterprises, collective farms and cooperatives and strengthening public (socialist) property" (August 7, 1932 excerpt)[15,16]

Section II Excerpts

1. Make all property belonging to collective farms and cooperatives (harvests in the fields, public reserves, livestock, cooperative stock and stores, etc.) equivalent to state property and fully strengthen the protection of this property against theft.
2. Use judicial repressions of the highest degree as measures of social protection against theft of *kolhosp* and collective property: execution by shooting and confiscation of all property, variable under mitigating circumstances to ten years imprisonment with confiscation of all property.

1933 political poster showing that wheat is now socialist property.

15 Communist newspaper, August 9, 1932, "Collectivization of agriculture: the most important resolutions of the Communist Party and Soviet government, 1927-1935," Moscow, 1957, pp. 423-424. Ruslan Pyrih, pp. 46-47.

16 This law made collective farm property equal to state property and provided extremely severe punitive measures for taking as much as few stalks of wheat. This resolution became known as "The Law of Five Ears of Wheat." Stalin would later invoke the law in a January All-Union Politburo resolution.

3. Amnesty cannot be granted to criminals sentenced in cases of collective farm and cooperative property theft.

Section III Excerpts

1. Conduct decisive battle with all anti-public, *kulak*-capitalist elements that use violence and threats, or promote the use of violence and threats, against collective farmers, forcing them to leave or purposefully destroy collective farms.
2. Use measures of judicial repressions for protecting collective farms and collective farmers from violence and threats on the part of kulak and other anti-public elements: imprisonment for five to ten years in a concentration camp.
3. Amnesty cannot be granted to criminals sentenced in these cases.

M. Kalinin, Head, USSR Central Executive Committee
V. Molotov (Skryabin) , Head, Council of Peoples' Commissars
A. Yenukidze , Secretary, USSR Central Executive Committee

"Confiscation of hidden grain," Donetsk Oblast, 1932.

Document #2: Letter from Stalin to Kaganovich on changing Ukrainian SSR leadership (August 11, 1932 excerpt)[17]

The main issue is now Ukraine. Matters in Ukraine are currently extremely bad. Bad from the standpoint of the Party line. They say that in two oblasts of Ukraine (Kyiv and Dnipropetrovsk, I believe), nearly 50 raion Party committees have spoken out against the grain procurement plan as unrealistic. They say the matter is no better in other raion committees. What does this look like? This is not a Party, but a parliament, a caricature of a parliament. Instead of directing the raions [regions], Kosior is always waffling between CC AUCP directives and the demands of raion committees, and he's waffled himself to the end. Lenin was right when he said that a person who lacks the courage to go against the flow at the right moment cannot be a real Bolshevik leader. Bad from the standpoint of the Soviet line. Chubar is no leader. Bad from the standpoint of the GPU. [Stanislaw] Redens is incapable of leading the battle with counterrevolution in such a large and unique republic as Ukraine.

If we do not correct the situation in Ukraine immediately, we will lose Ukraine.

Also keep in mind that within the Ukrainian Communist Party (500,000 members, ha, ha) there is no lack (yes, no lack!) of rotten elements, active and latent *petlurites* and direct agents of Pilsudski. As soon as things get worse, these elements won't hesitate to open a front within (and outside) the Party, against the Party. Worst of all, the Ukrainian leadership does not see these dangers.

Things should not continue this way any longer. It is necessary:

a) to remove Kosior from Ukraine and replace him with you [Kaganovich]; you will retain the post of secretary of the CC AUCP(b);
b) after this, transfer Balitsky to Ukraine as chairman of the Ukrainian GPU (or PP [authorized representative] to Ukraine, as it seems the GPU chairman position in Ukraine does not exist) and he will remain deputy chairman of the [All-Union] OGPU; make Redens a deputy to Balitsky in Ukraine;[18]
c) in a few months replace Chubar with another comrade, say, Hrynko or anybody else, and appoint Chubar to be Molotov's deputy in Moscow (Kosior can be made one of the secretaries of the CC AUCP(b));[19]
d) Set yourself the goal of turning Ukraine into a fortress of the USSR, a real model republic, within the shortest possible time. Don't spare money for this purpose.

---

17 Pyrih, ed., *Holodomor of 1932-33*, pp. 47-49.

18 Vsevold Balitsky (1892-1937) was dispatched to the Ukrainian SSR by CC AUCP(b) Politburo resolution "On a Special OGPU Commissioner for Ukraine" from November 24, 1932. Balitsky was the deputy head of the OGPU joint state political administration, SNK USSR (1931-1934). He headed the GPU political police in Ukraine (1933-1937) and was a member of the Central Oversight Commission of the All-Union Party. Stanislaw Redens (1892-1938) was a member of the Central Committee of the All-Union party (1927-1934) and the head of the Ukrainian SSR republican GPU (1931-1933). He was replaced by Balitsky as head of the Ukrainian GPU in February 1933.

19 Hryhori Hrynko (1890-1938) was the SNK USSR Peoples' Commissar for Finance (1930-1937).

Without these and similar measures (economic and political strengthening of Ukraine starting with the raions along the border, etc.), I repeat once again: we will lose Ukraine. What do you think on this matter?

This requires attention as soon as possible, immediately after [your] arrival in Moscow.

Regards!

J. Stalin
11.VIII.32
P. S. I have spoken to Menzhinsky about Balitsky and Redens. He agrees and fully supports the changes.[20]

RGASPI, fond 81, list 3, file 99, sheets 146-151[21]

"Millions of Ukrainian Peasants," linocut by Oleksandr Nikolayets, 1988.

20 Vyacheslav Menzhinsky (1874-1934) was the head of the SNK USSR OGPU (1926-1934). Ruslan Pyrih, ed, pp. 47-49.
21 Stalin and Kaganovich. *Correspondence. 1931-1936* (Moscow, 2001) Stalin i Kaganovich. Perepiska. 1931-1936, pp. 273-274.

Document #3: Resolution of CC AUCP(b) and USSR SNK on grain procurements in Ukraine, the Northern Caucasus and the Western Oblast, December 14, 1932 [22]

On hearing reports from Comrades Rumiantsev, Secretary of the Western Oblast Party committee; Kosior, Secretary of the CC CP(b)U; Stroganov, Secretary of the Dnipropetrovsk oblast Party committee; and Sheboldaev, Secretary of the North Caucasus regional Party committee, the CC AUCP(b) and the SNK USSR resolve the following:

1. The CC CP(b)U and the Ukrainian SSR RNK, on the personal responsibility of Comrades Kosior and Chubar, shall fully complete the grain and sunflower seed procurement plan by the end of January 1933.

2. The North Caucasus regional Party and executive committees, on the personal responsibility of Comrades Sheboldaev and Larin, shall fully complete the procurement plan for grain by January 10 to 15, 1933, and for sunflower seeds by the end of January 1933.

3. The Western Oblast Party and executive committees, on the personal responsibility of Comrades Rumiantsev and Shelekhes, shall fully complete the procurement plan for grain by January 1, 1933, and for flax by February 1, 1933.

4. In view of extremely poor efforts and the absence of revolutionary vigilance in a number of local Party organizations in Ukraine and the North Caucasus, a significant number of raions has been infiltrated by counterrevolutionary elements: kulaks, former officers, petliurites, supporters of the Kuban Rada, and so on. They have managed to find their way into collective farms as directors and other influential administration members, accountants, storekeepers, threshing floor foremen, and so on. They have succeeded in infiltrating village councils, land management bodies and cooperative societies, and are now trying to direct the work of these organizations against the interests of the proletarian state and Party policy, as well as trying to organize a counterrevolutionary movement and sabotage of the harvest and sowing campaigns. The CC AUCP(b) and SNK USSR order the CC CP(b)U, North Caucasus regional Party and executive committees and the RNK of Ukraine to resolutely root out these counterrevolutionary elements by means of arrest and long-term imprisonment in concentration camps, without stopping short of capital punishment for the most malicious elements.

5. The CC and RNK instruct party and government organizations of the Soviet Union that the worst enemies of the Party, working class, and collective farm peasantry are the saboteurs of grain procurement who have Party membership cards in their pockets. To please kulaks and other anti-Soviet elements, they organize state fraud and double-deals, and fail to complete tasks established by the Party and government. The CC and RNK order appropriate structures to apply austere repressions against these traitors

22 Commanders of the Great Famine: V. Molotov and L. Kaganovich, trips to Ukraine and the Northern Caucasus. 1932-1933 (Kyiv, 2001, p. 399). Komandyry velykoho holodu: poyizdky V. Molotova i L. Kaganovicha v Ukrainu i na Pivnichnyi Kavkaz. 1932-1933. pp. 210-212. Ruslan Pyrih, ed, *Holodomor of 1932-33.*

and enemies of Soviet rule and collective farms, who still carry Party membership cards in their pockets: five to ten year terms of imprisonment in concentration camps and, under certain circumstances, execution by shooting.

6. The CC and RNK point out that instead of the correct Bolshevik implementation of nationality policy, *ukrainization* was carried out mechanically in a number of raions of Ukraine, failing to take into consideration the peculiarities of every raion and without the meticulous selection of Bolshevik cadres. This made it easier for bourgeois-nationalist elements, petliurites and others to create their legal facades and counterrevolutionary cells and organizations.

7. The CC and RNK especially point out to the Party and executive committees of the North Caucasus region that the irresponsible, anti-Bolshevik *ukrainization* which affected nearly half of the raions in the North Caucasus do not correspond to the cultural interests of the population. It was carried out with a complete lack of supervision on the part of territorial agencies over the *ukrainization* of schools and the press, and provided the enemies of Soviet rule with legal facades for organizing resistance to the endeavors of Soviet authorities by kulaks, [czarist] officers, re-emigrating kozaks, members of the Kuban Rada, etc. In order to crush the resistance to grain procurement by kulak elements and their "Party" and non-party flunkeys, the CC and SNK USSR resolve the following:

   a) To relocate the entire population of the most counterrevolutionary Poltava *stanytsia* (in Northern Caucasus) to the northern oblasts of the USSR in the shortest time possible, with the exception of those collective and individual farmers who are truly loyal to Soviet rule and who have not been implicated in grain procurement sabotage. Populate this village with conscientious collective farmers who are Red Army soldiers and are currently working in territories that suffer from shortages and poor quality of land. Transfer all lands, winter crops, buildings, inventory and livestock from the farmers being expelled to these settlers.

      Responsibility for implementing this resolution (paragraph "a") shall rest with Comrades Yagoda, Gamarnik (with Comrade Bulygin as his substitute), Sheboldaev, and Yevdokimov.

   b) Prosecute and sentence traitors of the Party who were arrested in Ukraine for organizing the sabotage of grain procurement to five-ten year terms in concentration camps: former raion secretaries, chairmen of executive committees, directors of land management bodies and chairmen of raion associations of collective farms, specifically: Golovin, Pryhoda, Palamarchuk, Ordelian and Lutsenko in Orikhiv raion; Khoroshko, Us' and Fishman in Balakliya raion; Yaremenko in Nosiv raion; Liashenko in Kobeliaky raion; Lensky, Kosiachenko, Dvornik, Zyka and Dolgov in Velykyi Tokmak raion.

   c) Exile all former communists who were expelled from the Party for sabotaging the sowing and grain procurement campaigns to the northern oblasts as kulaks.

d) Propose that the CC CP(b)U and RNK of Ukraine pay serious attention to the proper implementation of *ukrainization*, to eliminate its mechanical implementation, to expel *petliurites* and other bourgeois-nationalist elements from Party and government organizations, to meticulously select and train Ukrainian Bolshevik cadres and to ensure Party management of and supervision over *ukrainization* on a regular basis.

e) Immediately change the language used in offices of Soviet entities and cooperative societies, as well as all newspapers and magazines in the ukrainized raions of the Northern Caucasus, from Ukrainian to Russian, explaining that Russian is more understandable to Kuban residents. Also, prepare to change the language of instruction at schools to Russian by autumn. The CC and RNK order the regional Party and executive committees to immediately investigate the staff workers of schools in ukrainized raions.

f) In cancellation of a previous resolution, allow delivery of goods to Ukrainian villages and grant Comrades Kosior and Chubar the right to suspend delivery of goods to particularly retrograde raions, until they fulfill the grain procurement plan.

V. Molotov (Skryabin), Chairman of the SNK USSR
J. Stalin , Secretary of the CC AUCP(b)

RGASPI, fond 17, list 3, file 911, sheets 42-44;
TsDAHO Ukrayiny, fond 1, list 20, file 5243, sheets 234-238;
Pyrih R.

"Seizure of kulak grain," Donetsk Oblast, 1932.

Document #4: Report from Balitsky to the OGPU on the mass exodus of villagers from Ukraine, January 22, 1933 [23,24]

"Hunger drives farmers to migrate," Kharkiv Oblast, 1933.

The mass exodus of peasants from villages primarily in Kharkiv, Odesa, Kyiv and from parts of Chernihiv oblasts that began in late December, 1932, can be broken down as follows:

- Kharkiv oblast: Incidents of flight have been registered in 19 raions and 39 villages. A total of 20,129 people have fled. Among them: 7,423 collective farmers, 12,698 private farmers and eight Party activists.

- Odesa oblast: Incidents of flight have been registered in 19 raions, 177 villages and 228 collective farms. A total of 3,447 individuals and 2,642 families have fled. Among them: 1,683 individual collective farmers, 1,259 collective farmer families, 1,320 individual private farmers, 1,007 private farmer families, 438 individual kulaks, 377 kulak families and six Party activists.

- Kyiv oblast: Incidents of flight have been registered in 27 raions and 437 villages. A total of 6,576 people have fled. Among them: 1,287 collective farmers, 3,936 private farmers, 1,244 kulaks and 109 Party activists.

- Chernihiv oblast: Incidents of flight have been registered in nine raions [regions] and 68 villages. A total of 1,541 individuals and 146 families have fled. Among them: 146 individual collective farmers, three collective farmer families, 1,246 private farmers, 124 private farmer families, 141 individual kulaks, 19 kulak families, and five Party activists.

All told, incidents of flight in these oblasts have been registered in 74 raions, 721 villages, and 228 collective farms. A total of 31,693 individuals and 2,789 families have left. Among them: 10,539 individual collective farmers and 1,262 collective farm families, 19,203 individual private farmers and 1,131 private farm families, 1,823 individual kulaks and 396 kulak families and 126 Party activists. In most cases, the incidents of flight can be attributed to the search for work. The fact that malicious non-deliverers of grain prevail

23 On January 23, 1933, the Deputy Head of the All-Union OGPU Georgi Prokofiev submitted this report from Vsevolod Balitsky to Stalin. A handwritten note on the cover letter reads: "To Molotov, Kaganovich, Postyshev, Stalin."

24 Top Secret: From Lubianka to Stalin on the state of the country in 4 volumes (Moscow, 2001, Volume 4) "Sovershenno sekretno." Lubianka - Stalinu o polozhenii v strane: v 4 t. pp. 393-394. Ruslan Pyrih, ed, pp. 83-85.

among those fleeing is evidence that this exodus is from the countryside. Some of those fleeing from their villages take their families along, boarding up their houses and hiding their grain reserves with neighbors and relatives. Some of those fleeing from the villages have buried their grain in the ground. In some villages, those fleeing are primarily the heads of families. Most of those fleeing their villages are headed to Donbas and large industrial centers. The exodus of collective farmers is occurring on a much lower scale than the flight of private farmers. There are also incidents of village council and collective farm chairmen, including "communists," leaving their villages without permission. "Communists" are fleeing from their villages because they are afraid of facing repressions for the sabotage of grain procurement and failure to perform the tasks set by the Party.

Inspections of the Lozova and Sumy railway junctions in Kharkiv oblast, where flight from villages is particularly large in scale, showed high ticket sales for long-distance trains in January this year: 16,500 tickets were sold at Lozova station and 15,000 at Sumy station in January. The growth of ticket sales has also been observed at the Pomoshchna station, Odesa oblast: in November, 879 tickets for long-distance trains were sold, 3,614 in December and 1,617 in the first half of January. No rapid spikes of long-distance train ticket sales have been observed at other railway junctions. In early January, in order to stop the flight from villages in a resolute manner, Ukraine's GPU began arresting the organizers and instigators of the exodus and stepped up intelligence and information-gathering efforts in places where mass exodus had occurred. More than 500 malicious instigators of exodus have been arrested.

Ukraine's GPU has been reporting to the CC CP(b)U and OGPU's SPO [secret political division] on the mass exodus since December 25, 1932. I am issuing additional orders as per your instructions.

V. Balitsky
APRF, fond 3, list 30, file 189, sheets 7-10[25]

"Cemetery, mounds of graves," Kharkiv Oblast, 1933.

25 Pyrih, pp. 83-85.

Document #5: Report from Yagoda to Stalin and Molotov on measures for preventing mass exodus of villagers from the Ukrainian SSR, Northern Caucasus and Belarusian SSR, February 2, 1933 [26]

In order to intercept people fleeing en masse from Ukraine, the Northern Caucasus and Belarus, the OGPU's transport divisions have organized cordons and search groups on the following roadways: N. Caucasus, Ukraine, South-Eastern, Western, Ryazan, Ural, Zlatoustovsk, Oktiabrsk, Moscow-Kazan, Moscow-Belarus-Baltic.

As a result of measures taken from January 22 to 30, 24,961 persons were detained fleeing their places of permanent residence, including 18,379 Ukrainians and 6,225 persons from the Northern Caucasus, and 357 persons from other regions.

The number of people returned to their places of residence is 16,046; 1,016 were arrested; the remaining 7,879 are being investigated

The breakdown of arrests on different roadways is as follows: 2,519 people were detained on the Northern-Caucasian: 2,192 were turned back, 98 were arrested, and 299 are being investigated. On the southern roads 12,842 people were detained, 6,763 sent back, 826 arrested, and 6,250 are being investigated. On the Southeastern, 3,555 people were detained, 2,266 sent back, 32 arrested, and 1,260 are being investigated. On the Western route, 2,274 were detained, 2,270 sent back, and 4 were arrested. On Ryazan-Uralsk, 134 people were detained, 7 were sent back, 127 are being checked. On Sam.-Zlat., 45 persons were detained, 22 were sent back and 23 are being checked. On Oktiabrsk, 427 were detained, 412 sent back, and 15 arrested. On Moscow-Kazan, 191 people were detained, 123 were turned back, and 8 were arrested. On Moscow-Kursk 1710 people were detained, 1,672 were sent back, and 18 arrested. On MBB, 264 people were detained, 249 were turned back and 15 were arrested.

Deputy Chairman, OGPU, *Yagoda*

APRF, fond 3, list 30, file 189, sheets 26-27.[27]

26 *Top Secret: From Lubianka to Stalin,* on the state of the country in 4 volumes (Moscow, 2001, Volume 4) "Sovershenno sekretno." *Lubianka - Stalinu o polozhenii v strane.* V 4 t. p. 398-399.

27 Pyrih. pp. 89-91.

Document #6: Summary of reports from MTS Political Sections in Kyiv oblast on famine, death and the anti-Soviet moods among collective farmers (June 14, 1933 excerpt)[28,29]

- [...] This past spring the oblast encountered serious problems with food supplies. The food relief received from the CC AUCP(b) – a total volume of 19,401 tons – played a crucial role in alleviating the enormous food supply problems faced by Kyiv oblast collective farms during the crucial period of preparing and executing the sowing campaign (March and April). Nevertheless, the situation with collective farm food reserves grew significantly worse in many of the oblast's raions, especially in May and June. In some raions the number of those swollen and dead from famine is growing to dangerous proportions and are having a definite impact on the execution of agricultural and political campaigns... The heads of POs [local Machine Tractor Station political departments] have written the Political Section [of the oblast MTS] about mass starvation and the dying out of entire villages. For instance, the head of the Petrovsky MTS PO, Kamensky raion, writes:

  "...In the last month-and-a-half, incidents of death have been massive in scale. In Rozumievka, 37 people died in the month of May. The situation is especially difficult in the Shliakh Kolhospnyka collective farm of this village. In the Bolshevik Collective Farm in Osota, 120 people died in May. Incidents of mass death have become more frequent than before in the villages of Holykovo, Boltyshka and others. In total 3,336 persons have died in the collective farms of 27 villages of this MTS. Very many children are dying. While in March and April we managed to prevent child deaths thanks to oblast and local aid, in May and the first ten days of June, the rate of mortality was unbelievable: 209 persons in 27 villages."

- The PO of Piatihorsk MTS, Tetiyev raion, reports:

  "...Mortality is reaching catastrophic proportions. In the small village of Nenadykha alone, 113 people died in 20 days during the month of May. Medical clinics have been closed. Many people, especially children, are swollen from famine. They cannot work. There have been many cases of female workers falling in the fields and dying either at home or in the fields. In nurseries, nearly 80 to 70 percent of children are gaunt and swollen. Many schoolchildren are so swollen that they have a hard time walking to school. Urgent relief is required, especially for the children..."

  "...Lately the mortality rate has increased significantly. Up to 2,000 people died in 10 days of June. This is significantly more than during the whole month of May. Incidents of death at work have become more frequent than before..."

  (June 14, 1933 letter from the head of Tetiev MTS PO)

---

28 The report was sent to Lazar Kaganovich, Agriculture Department, CC AUCP(b); Stanislaw Kosior, General Secretary of the CC CP(b)U Politburo and the chairmen of the Political Departments of the USSR and Ukrainian SSR Peoples' Commissariats of Agriculture.

29 Pyrih, pp. 111-114.

"...The number of villages requiring relief has grown: 15 of 17 villages are afflicted; 1,000 people died in the raion during the month of April; 459 people died in the first five days of May. There have been incidents of death during work in the fields. Feeding stations are being closed due to lack of produce. Urgent food aid is needed."

(letter from the head of Tarashcha MTS PO)

"...The rate of mortality has increased in collective farms. Not only slackers, but also good collective farmers are dying. In Sloboda, 120 people died in 10 days. The situation is the same in other villages. People are dying right in the fields while working. Child mortality rates have increased as well, which is particularly dangerous. There is no food aid in the raion. Workforce shortages have been reported in some villages and collective farms. Urgent food aid is needed."

(report from the head of the Tetiev MTS PO)

"...In three villages, Zelena Dubrava, Maidanivka and Hnyzets, acute famine and mortality caused by exhaustion have not been eliminated. In fact their frequency is growing. For instance, in Maidanivka village, 19 people died in March and another 28 in April; 61 people, including 24 able-bodied collective farmers, died in 26 days of May. In these villages there have been incidents of death in the field while working and on the way home from work."

(report from the head of the Olshanka MTS PO, Petrovsky raion).

Similar incidents have been reported by the MTS stations in other raions. According to statistics from 15 MTS political departments, more than 6,000 people have died from exhaustion. [. . .]

Deputy head, Political section, Kyiv oblast MTS,
M. Yehorov

TsDAHO Ukrayiny, fond 1, list 20, file 6276, sheets 55-60.

"Starving children rummaging for food in the rubble," Kharkiv, 1933.

Document #7: Report of the All-Union Resettlement Committee on resettling collective farmers to Ukraine (with table), December 29, 1933[30]

Express; Secret.
To Head of Gulag OGPU Comrade *Berman*

The All-Union Resettlement Committee of the SNK USSR is sending operational report No. 38 on resettlement to Ukraine as of December 28 this year. In addition, the AURC of the SNK reports that the proposed resettlement plan was performed by 104.76%.[31] In total 21,856 collective farms, 117,149 persons, 14,879 horses, 21,898 cows and 38,705 heads of other livestock (the latter includes only swine and sheep) have been relocated. The report is attached.

Deputy Chairman, All-Union Resettlement Committee,
USSR SNK *Rud'*

[ATTACHMENT] Secret

SUMMARY DATA ON ECHELONS OF RESETTLERS SENT TO UKRAINE AS OF DECEMBER 28, 1933:

Source Oblast	Destination Oblast	Number					%
		households	horses	cows	other livestock	Echelons	Plan completion
Gorky	Odesa	2,120	1,348	2,062	2,050	35	106
Ivanov	Donetsk	3,527	1,619	3,498	1,980	44	104
BSSR	Odesa	4,630	3,864	5,295	10,924	61	103
C. Chornoz.	Kharkiv	4,800	2,329	3,472	5,644	80	106.6
Western	Dnipropetrovsk	6,67	5,719	7,571	18,097	109	102.7

1. On 28 December 1933, 329 echelons were dispatched, 21,856 households, 117,149 family members, 14,879 horses, 21,898 cows and 38,705 heads of small livestock.
2. The plan for transporting collective farmers into Ukraine is complete and fulfilled by 104.7%.

Deputy chairman, All Union Resettlement Committee,
USSR SNK *Rud'*

RGAE, fond 5675, list 1, file 33, sheet 56.

30 *Collectivization and famine in Ukraine. 1929-1933.* Kyiv, 1992, p. 734 (*Kolektyvizatsia i holod na Ukraini 1929-1933)* p. 642. Ruslan Pyrih, ed, pp. 121-122.

31 As stated in the document. Further calculations show 104.076%.

Press Articles

Examining articles in the press, students gather information, look for various points of view and gain insight into historical events. By analyzing newspaper articles, students are able to gain an understanding of how people think about a given situation or event at a given time. Gathering important facts about the situation as stated by the press, students can look for evidence of bias in these renditions. The use of multimedia is yet another source of information on an event.

Teachers can access articles from the same time period (1933) in Canada or current media articles on the same topic and compare the attitudes to events.

ARTICLE #1: WORLD FORGETS, CANADA REMEMBERS

Toronto Sun | June 1, 2008 | Eric Margolis

Canada's planned recognition of the 1932-1933 genocide, or Holdomor, in Ukraine is very significant, even if long overdue. It was also apropos for this week's visit of Ukraine's President Viktor Yushchenko, who remains that troubled nation's best hope for democracy and continued independence.

Ottawa's decision was motivated as much by ethnic politics as historic justice, but Prime Minister Stephen Harper's government deserves kudos for doing the right thing.

For eight decades, the greatest mass murder in modern history has been shamefully covered up or ignored. I was shocked to receive letters from young Ukrainian-Canadians saying they had known nothing about the Holdomor until reading about it in my columns. Hopefully, more now will know.

From 1932-33, Josef Stalin and henchmen, Lazar Kaganovich and V.M. Molotov, conducted a merciless campaign to crush resistance by Ukrainian farmers to communism and collectivization. They isolated Ukraine, then cut off all food supplies and seeds. Six to nine million Ukrainians died from the ensuing man-made famine and mass executions of "anti-State elements. Cannibalism became common.

Large numbers of Ukrainians were also murdered during the Great Terror of 1936-38 in which an estimated two million Soviet citizens were shot and the same number died in Stalin's concentration camps.

In the late 1940s and early 1950s, the Soviet penal system reached its zenith: 5.4 million people were prisoners in the gulag or in frigid Siberian exile.

To The Gulag

Some 300,000 more Ukrainians were sent to the gulag under the supervision of Commissar Nikita Khrushchev, and 21,259 were killed in Soviet "pacification" campaigns.

During the same period, Moscow unleashed terror on the tiny Baltic states. From March to May 1949, 95,000 Lithuanians, 27,000 of them children, were sent to concentration camps. In total, 120,000 Lithuanians, 50,000 Latvians and 30,000 Estonians went to the gulag where the death rate was 51% per annum.

While the western world rightly commemorates genocide inflicted on Armenians, Europe's Jews, Cambodians, Rwandans and Bosnians, it shamefully shut its eyes to the Ukrainian Holdomor because it was conducted by a key

"Stalin and the Bones of Ukraine," gouache by Yevhen Luniov, 1989.

wartime ally whom President F.D. Roosevelt hailed as "Uncle Joe."

Nor has the West ever acknowledged genocide against other peoples of the Soviet Union. In the Caucasus, Stalin sent most of the Chechen and Ingush peoples to the gulag, where 500,000 died. Yet when the children of the survivors fought for independence from Russia, the West branded them "Islamic terrorists."

Up to three million Muslims of the Soviet Union died at Stalin's hands, including 1.5 million Kazakhs and Crimean Tatars. No holocaust memorials exist for them.

Nearly 100,000 Moldovans were murdered in a purge conducted by then Commissar Leonid Brezhnev, who would later lead the Soviet Union and be feted by Western leaders.

Add to this butcher's bill Volga Germans, Greeks, Cossacks, Armenians and Poles.

If we keep demanding that Germany and Japan atone for their wartime crimes, is it not time for our governments to finally recognize and atone their alliances with the biggest mass murderer in history, Stalin? His crimes exceeded those of Adolf Hitler by a factor of at least four times. Particularly so in the United States, where the Second World War has become something of a state religion and is invoked endlessly to justify foreign military adventures. Soviet dissident Vladimir Bukovsky demanded a Nuremburg trial for all the Soviet crimes, but unfortunately this will never happen. Most of the criminals are dead.

Canada's recognition of this historic crime is important for two reasons. First, Canada is one of the world's most respected nations. Its acknowledgement of the Holodomor will be heard around the globe. Second, nostalgia for Stalin is on the rise in today's Russia. His memory and politics are being rehabilitated. Russians must be reminded of his crimes and reign of terror.

In *Les abuses de la memoire*, the Bulgarian-born French philosopher Tzvetan Todorov wrote, "Life cannot withstand death, but memory is gaining in its struggle against nothingness."

Refer to Part III for an assignment that can be used with this article, pp. 193-194.

ARTICLE #2: A TALE OF TRUTH AND TWO JOURNALISTS

Report Magazine | March 27, 2000 | Ian Hunter[33]

It is hard to credit that a decade has slipped away since the death of Malcolm Muggeridge on November 14, 1990. The most compellingly readable of journalists, hardly a day goes by that I do not recall one of Muggeridge's insights or marvel afresh at his prophetic vision.

Muggeridge's journalistic integrity was shaped by one searing experience; in 1932 he went to Moscow as correspondent for the Manchester Guardian. Joseph Stalin's twin manias — collectivization of agriculture and dekulakization of peasants — were then at their bloodthirsty zenith, but few Westerners could have guessed it from the sycophantic foreign reporting. The Dean of the Moscow press corps was Walter Duranty of the New York Times. Joseph Alsop would later say of him: "Lying was Duranty's stock in trade."

For two decades Duranty was the most influential foreign correspondent in Russia. His dispatches were regarded as authoritative; indeed Duranty helped to shape U.S. foreign policy. His biographer, Susan Taylor (*Stalin's Apologist*, Oxford University Press, 1990) has demonstrated that Duranty's reporting was a critical factor in President Roosevelt's decision in 1933 to grant official recognition to the Soviet Union.

Duranty, an unattractive, oversexed little man, with a wooden leg, falsified facts, spread lies and half truths, invented occurrences that never happened, and turned a blind eye to the man-made famine that starved to death more than 14 million people (according to an International Commission of Jurists which examined this tragedy in 1988-90). When snippets of the truth began to leak out, Duranty coined the phrase: "You can't make an omelet without breaking eggs." This phrase, or a variant thereof, has since proved useful to a rich variety of ideologues who contend that a worthy end justifies base means. Yet when the Pulitzer committee conferred its prize on Duranty (in 1932, at the height of the famine) they cited his "scholarship, profundity, impartiality, sound judgment, and exceptional clarity."

One story that circulated among Moscow correspondents trying to explain Duranty was that he was a necrophiliac; in exchange for favourable reporting, the Soviet authorities may have allowed him unsupervised night access to the city morgues. Whether true or not (and Duranty's biographer, Susan Taylor, leaves this question open), certain it is that the regime had some sort of hold on Duranty; they showered benefits on him, — a fancy apartment, an automobile, and fresh caviar daily.

Enter Malcolm Muggeridge. In the spring of 1933 Muggeridge did an audacious thing; without permission he set off on a train journey through what had formerly been the breadbasket of the Soviet Union, the Ukraine and North Caucasus. What Muggeridge witnessed, he never forgot. In a series of articles smuggled out in the diplomatic pouch, he described a man-made famine that had become a holocaust: peasants, millions of them, dying like famished cattle, sometimes within sight of full granaries, guarded by the army and police. "At a railway station early one morning, I saw a line of people with their hands tied behind them, being herded into cattle trucks at gunpoint — all so silent and mysterious and horrible in the half light, like some macabre ballet." At a German co-operative farm, an oasis of prosperity in the collectivized wilderness he saw peasants kneeling down in the snow, begging for a crust of bread.

33 Ian Hunter is Professor Emeritus in the Faculty of Law at the University of Western Ontario and was the first biographer of Malcolm Muggeridge.

In his Diary, Muggeridge wrote: "Whatever else I may do or think in the future, I must never pretend that I haven't seen this. Ideas will come and go; but this is more than an idea. It is peasants kneeling down in the snow and asking for bread. Something that I have seen and understood."

But few believed him. His dispatches were cut. He was sacked by the Guardian and forced to leave Russia. Muggeridge was vilified, slandered and abused, not least in the pages of the Manchester Guardian, where sympathy to what was called "the great Soviet experiment" was de rigour. Walter Duranty's voice led the chorus of denunciation and denial, although privately Duranty told a British foreign office acquaintance that at least 10 million people had been starved to death - adding, characteristically, "but they're only Russians."

Beatrice Webb (Muggeridge's aunt by marriage) admitted that "In the Soviet Union, people disappear," but she still denounced Muggeridge's famine reports as "base lies." The Very Reverend Hewlett Johnson, Dean of Canterbury, applauded Stalin's "steady purpose and kindly generosity." George Bernard Shaw made a whirlwind tour and pronounced himself fully satisfied that there was ample food for all in the worker's paradise.

If vindication was a long time coming, it cannot have been sweeter than when Duranty's biographer, Susan Taylor, wrote in 1990: "But for Muggeridge's eyewitness accounts of the famine in the spring of 1933 and his stubborn chronicle of the event, the effects of the crime upon those who suffered might well have remained as hidden from scrutiny as its perpetrators intended. Little thanks he has received for it over the years, although there is a growing number who realize what a singular act of honesty and courage his reportage constituted."

Alas, when these words came to be written, Muggeridge had died. Still, they are worth remembering.

1. Refer to Part III, for activities, pp. 195-196.
2. A more recent news article connecting the Holodomor with present-day Ukraine is located in the Appendix on pp. 299-300.

M. Muggeridge
Manchester Guardian

W. Duranty
New York Times

Literature

Historical fiction on a specific topic provides students with an excellent opportunity to become acquainted with a difficult and emotional event through the eyes of an individual in a story. It gives the event a personal touch and provides a context for understanding historical events.

1. The Rings

Marsha Forchuk Skrypuch

"The Rings" by Canadian author Marsha Forchuk Skrypuch, is one of the stories compiled in *Kobzar's Children: A Century of Untold Ukrainian Stories*, edited by M. F. Skrypuch, Fitzhenry and Whiteside, 2006, an anthology of short historical fiction, memoirs and poems, written about the Ukrainian immigrant experience.

Other short stories on the Holodomor may be found in the compendium *A Hunger Most Cruel*, edited and translated by Roma Franko. One story, "Without Doctors and Priests, without Graves and Crosses," by Olena Zvychayna, is reprinted in Part IV in the Appendix, pp. 290-298.

This story of "The Rings" is set during the 1932-33 Famine-Genocide, which was orchestrated by Stalin in order to starve out Ukrainian farmers — labelled *kulaks* — who refused to give up their land. In the midst of the Famine-Genocide, Stalin invited foreign journalists to tour the countryside so they could see for themselves that there was no famine. Many journalists were sympathetic to the communist cause, and they stayed on the official tour and took things at face value. Others saw the truth but reported lies in order to stay in favor with Stalin. Famous Famine deniers include Walter Duranty of the *New York Times* and playwright George Bernard Shaw. There were a few honest journalists, like Malcolm Muggeridge and Gareth Jones, who heroically reported the truth and were scorned for it.

Entire story "The Rings" found in Part IV Appendix pp. 279-289.

There are rare accounts of people who escaped from Soviet-occupied Ukraine and offered eyewitness testimony about the Famine. "The Rings" is based on a number of firsthand accounts. The following is an excerpt from "The Rings":

> Danylo's sharpest memory was of hunger.
>
> When his father had refused to sign the papers handing over their tiny farm to the state, his family earned the label, *pidkurkul* — or poor farmer who sympathizes with the kulaks.
>
> His father knew that the Communists would send in the Red Army to confiscate their grain, so he had mixed some wheat with the chaff and hid it in the loft. He had also put the best wheat for

sowing, up in the rafters. Danylo's mother had hidden a sack of grain in the chimney.

The soldiers who came were a rough and brutal lot. They were not from the village, and they spoke Russian, not Ukrainian. They brought with them a stabber — a device made of a sharp pronged stick with a bag on the end — to collect evidence of grain.

As one of the soldiers carried an armful of his father's hidden grain to the waiting cart, Danylo rushed forward and grabbed back some stalks of wheat. "Why are you doing this?" he cried.

The man said something in Russian that sounded like a curse. Another Red Army soldier opened the *pich* (oven) and confiscated the fresh loaves of bread baking there. They loaded all the food into the cart and took it away.

A few pieces of stale bread on the rubbish pile had somehow been missed. Danylo's family — his father, his mother, and three younger brothers — survived on these crusts and water for a couple of days. His baby sister Larissa was still at his mother's breast — one less mouth to feed.

Danylo watched as those around him appeared to shrink. His mother remarked one day, as she washed her face, that she could feel every bone in her skull. Later, when Danylo carried the soapy basin of water outside to empty it, he found her wedding ring, which had slipped off. She had not noticed. His mother had not been able to get the silver band past her knuckle for years. Danylo dried it on his shirt, and brought it back in to her. From then on, she wore it on a strip of leather around her neck.

When the crusts of bread were gone, one day passed with no food at all, just water. Danylo's feet and stomach began to swell with the first signs of starvation. His father caught and skinned a stray cat, which sustained them a few more days. But Danylo's four-year-old brother, Anatoly, swelled up and died. Danylo caught a hedgehog, and the remaining family survived on that for a while.

As winter set in, the rats, cats, dogs, and birds in the village disappeared. Danylo learned, like everyone else, that one must eat at least one morsel, each and every day, to keep oneself from swelling. If the swelling set in, his feet and belly would get so huge that he wouldn't be able to move. At that point, he would sit and wait to die. When his mother began to starve, Danylo couldn't bear to look at her body, ballooning out grotesquely, as if it were about to burst. Her swelling caused what little milk she had been able to produce to stop - and so Larissa died. His mother died the next day. Then ten-year-old Vasyl, and then seven-year-old Ivan.

Danylo and his father said prayers for the dead. His father reverently removed the cord that held her wedding ring from around his wife's neck. Before putting it around his own neck, he slipped off his own wedding ring and strung it on the cord.

In their small home, Danylo and his father sat with their dead loved ones for hours — perhaps days. What was time, anyway? It wasn't until the corpses began to stink that they dragged their family beyond the threshold. The village authorities had dug a huge pit in the graveyard. Each morning they sent a cart around to all the houses, collecting the bodies. They dumped the bodies into a pit, until it was full. And then they dug a new one.

teacher tip

The poem "Through the Eyes of a Child" *was written by Halia Dmytryshyn. It is a narrative of events leading to, during and after the Holodomor. The inspiration for this poem is a series of drawings done by schoolchildren. Students can be encouraged to create their own artwork for the poem. Suggestions for an art workshop are provided in Part III, p. 135 and Part IV, p. 269, has instructions for teaching art.*

2. Through the Eyes of a Child

Halia Sawycky-Dmytryshyn

In the 1920s, 1930s, the people of Ukraine,
Lived north of the Black Sea, on beautiful terrain,
in villages, cities, towns and farms
Trees and flowers grew all around.

"Mother Ukraine," by Lidia Siniavskaia, St. Josaphat Catholic School, 2000.

The Ukrainians were hardworking and strong,
Proud of their heritage and bountiful land,
And dearly yearned someday to see their beloved country, Ukraine,
Independent and free!

The people were content, to live their lives as God had meant,
To tend their families, homes, animals and farms,
To pray to God and go to church
To celebrate traditional feasts
To laugh and dance and sing their songs.

And blessed with land rich in minerals and good soil,
Ukrainians lived life filled with hard work and fruitful-toil.

Their fields were vast and ripe with wheat,
The land was rich, black soil ran deep.

They grew all manner of food to eat.
Cabbages, fruit, berries and beets.
Sunflowers, turnips, grain and seeds.

And everyone in Europe knew
That in Ukraine's Bread Basket grew:
The richest grain and golden wheat,
That weaved and danced upon the wind,
And pushed its stalks toward the sun.

"Yellow sunflowers reaching for the sky," by Vera Kowalsky, St. Demetrius Catholic School, 2000.

Baskets were filled and stored away,
Food would be needed each wintry day.
At Harvest's end, the people prayed to
Thank God for all that He gave.
They also prayed in the dark of night,

That no one come to take away,
That which belonged to them, each day.

But in their hearts, Ukrainians knew,
The enemy, not far away was coming closer
everyday.

With guns in hand - the enemy came,
In trucks, on horses too,
In wagons, trains and on foot
By threat of force they swarmed the land.

And took away all food and grain,
Til' only stalks, husks, and empty fields
remained.

The people knew not where to turn,
As hunger took its terrible toll.
Day by day the sadness grew,
The sorrow, fear and despair
They felt was beyond all words to tell.

Mothers held their children's heads and
Pressed them close upon their hearts
To hush their cries - they had not milk or food to give
And many died upon their beds.

People searched and hunted for food
Through meadows, woods and fields,
They took whatever they could find to eat,
leaves, seeds, grass, even tiny birds.
But as time went by,
No matter what they did, However hard they
looked and searched,
All their precious food was gone.

Still, people prayed upon their knees,
And asked for help in their great need.
Candles lit in the dark of the night,
They begged for help in their desperate
plight.

But no help came from near or far,
And it soon became very clear,
Roaming the land like ravaging wolves,
The horror of Famine was here.

"Harvest - bountiful land, hardworking people," by Natalie Trusz, Josyf Cardinal Slipyj Catholic School, 2000.

"Fear Before Terror," by Jaroslaw Fenton, St. Sofia Catholic School, 2000.

Over the land, all you saw,
Were bloated bodies, lying there,
Starving children and people dying,
Death's "Grim Reaper" hovered everywhere.

The land which once was golden and bright,
Turned into darkness overnight.
Ravaged by crops torn out of the ground,
Tears, mingled with blood to stain it brown.

All across Eastern Ukraine,
Crosses and graves covered the terrain.
Death didn't care if you were big or small,
Bodies lay dead where they fell,
Few were left to mourn them all.

"Death At Our Door," by Vasil Hnatkivskyy, St. Josaphat Catholic School, 2000.

After the ruthless communists came,
Millions of people died in Ukraine.

Borders were sealed as though with a shroud,
Help for Ukraine would not be allowed.

No nation would answer her plea,
The world would not know or see,
The Hunger and Genocide brought to be,
By the Communist forces in 1933.

NO ONE ANSWERED UKRAINE'S CALL,

NO ONE HEARD AND

NO ONE SAW

MILLIONS OF UKRAINIANS FALL!

teacher tip

Refer to the lesson "Through the Eyes of a Child" in Part III, p. 135.

The Appendix provides suggestions on how to use art through the lens of the Holodomor, p. 269.

Holodomor: The Aftermath

When examining the aftermath of the Holodomor in Ukraine it is helpful to consider a number of essential questions:

- What are the long-term effects of the Holodomor on the people of Ukraine?
- What effect did the Holodomor have on the demographics of Ukraine?
- What effect did the Holodomor have on Ukrainian language, culture, traditions and, especially, identity?
- What effect did the horrendous loss of life have on the survivors? On their offspring? How did they cope?
- Did collective farms ever prove themselves to be an effective organization for agricultural production? Why or why not?
- Should the perpetrators and the Soviet government be faulted for their actions in implementing the Holodomor?

These and many other questions about Ukraine as a post-genocidal society remain to be researched.

Here are a number of quotations outlining the consequences of the Holodomor:

ON THE MANNER OF IMPLEMENTING FORCED COLLECTIVIZATION

> ***"My friend overheard by chance her parents' conversation. Father [sent to collectivize the farmers] explained that he called Molotov in Moscow and told him that people had nothing to eat and asked for permission to open the granary and feed the people. Molotov answered: 'I forbid. Half will croak, the other half will go into the kolkhoz.' This is how collectivization was realized."***
>
> Russian writer A.A. Andreeva, in an interview in the newspaper *My i mir,* N. 4, 2001.

ALL THOUGHT OF INDEPENDENCE KILLED

> ***"The famine was brought about in Ukraine in order to reduce the number of Ukrainians, resettle in their place people from other parts of the USSR, and in this way kill all thought of independence."***
>
> Statement by Prokopenko, a Party member government plenipotentiary, reported by the OGPU, May 12, 1934.

RUSSIAN COLONIZATION IN UKRAINE

"The current disaster will bring about a preponderantly Russian colonization of Ukraine. It will transform its ethnographic character. In a future time, perhaps very soon, one will no longer be able to speak of a Ukraine, or a Ukrainian people, and thus even of a Ukrainian problem, because Ukraine will become a de facto Russian region."

Report of Italian consul from Kharkiv, May 31, 1933.

TRAUMA

"The late historian James Mace called Ukraine a "post-genocidal society." He became a famine expert, first collecting material for Robert Conquest's **Harvest of Sorrow** ***and later made Ukraine his adopted homeland. He believed that what Ukrainians call Holodomor maimed Ukraine to such an extent that it created a discontinuity in the normal development of the Ukrainian people to this day.***

The orchestrated famine wiped out millions of nationally conscious Ukrainians. The Soviet regime prevented families and individuals from processing both personal and national grief, as for more than 70 years, Ukraine could not address the trauma openly. The problems of today are rooted in the past atrocities and destruction of the spiritual, intellectual and cultural life of successive generations of Ukrainians since the 1930s.

Will acknowledgement by the world community of the Ukrainian genocide ease the effects of the trauma? The Holodomor is not only an event in Ukraine's past — it is an event in its present and its future."

American journalist Irena Chalupa, Dec. 9, 2008.

Dealing with the Aftermath

The psychological effects of extreme violence on people have been studied for only a brief period, and even less time has passed since possible positive interventions for victims of mass violence have been worked on by researchers. The *Harvard Trauma Questionnaire*, the first of its kind, is only several decades old.

Some of the effects of genocide that have been identified are: trauma disorders, disruption of identity and way of understanding the world and disruption of interpersonal relationships. The world appears more threatening to survivors, who feel very vulnerable. Even those who were perpetrators are traumatized. They may shut down their empathetic and compassionate nature, distance themselves from their own behavior, continue to blame the victims for their misfortunes and hold on to the ideology that motivated and justified the violence.

Barbara Coloroso suggests in her book *Extraordinary Evil: A Brief History of Genocide*, that there are a number of steps to be taken for victims to begin to heal:

- Take care of the dead. Find the bodies and give them a proper funeral.
- Support surviving orphans.
- Create public remembrance rituals.
- Adequately treat all sorts of physical, mental, and emotional trauma.
- Bring the guilty to justice and to account, even if it is only for historical justice and acknowledgement of their crimes.
- Provide reparations or compensation for survivors.
- Heal the community through economic, social, cultural and educational programs.
- Address issues of forgiveness for and reconciliation with perpetrators, henchmen and observers. This may be difficult, and should not be forced, as healing by acknowledging the genocide may have to precede them.

Ukraine after the Holodomor

For close to half a century after the Holodomor, both the perpetrators and the survivors were forced into silence inside the Soviet Union. None of the steps towards healing (as outlined above by Barbara Coloroso) were permitted to restore the broken and traumatized society in Ukraine. Only in 1987 did General Secretary of the Communist Party of Ukraine V. Shcherbytsky, use the term "famine" to describe the horrors of 1933. Prior to the late 1980s, anyone caught talking about the Famine was subject to repressions for "anti-Soviet behaviour" by the Soviet government. Survivors were afraid to tell their children of the horrors they had lived through for fear of discovery by Soviet authorities.

What effect did this enforced secrecy, cover-up and denial have on the people of Ukraine — social, physiological, psychological and economic?

What effect did it have on the children who witnessed the Famine, were denied a normal childhood, and were traumatized by what they had seen?

For most of its 70-year existence, the Soviet Union either ignored or gave a narrow ideological interpretation to historically controversial issues, especially those dealing with the abuse of human rights. Since independence in 1991, Ukraine has had a relatively brief period of time to explore and interpret its difficult past and relearn its buried historical memory. Only recently, with the opening of former Soviet Ukrainian and Russian archives to researchers and analysts, has it been possible for this forbidden past to be dealt with.

The Holodomor was the most prominent omission in Ukraine's history under Soviet rule. The topic of the genocidal famine was subject to a constant and relentless Soviet "disinformation" campaign, both inside and outside the borders of the USSR. This barrage of half-truths, deflections and denials was aided by the indifference of Western governments and journalists during the 1930s. Thus the combination of a Soviet-enforced silence on the generations of people in Ukraine and international ignorance about the Holodomor left a huge blank spot in Ukrainian historical consciousness for generations. More importantly, not only were the survivors unable to express and deal with their trauma, the Holodomor has left Ukrainian society with a wound that cannot heal without reconciliation and acknowledgement, both inside Ukraine today and by the world community.

...a constant and relentless Soviet "disinformation" campaign

The Holodomor left a huge blank space in Ukrainian historical consciousness for generations.

In order to enforce the policies that brought about the horrors of the Holodomor, the perpetrators, be they local secret police agents or leading members of the Politburo, had to renounce a portion of their humanity. This is significant because these same people and their successors continued to rule the USSR until its collapse. Will authorities today pursue justice for the criminal actions of the people responsible?

Should the perpetrators be condemned for what they did?

Studies done in post-genocidal Rwanda show that an individual's identity, way of understanding the world, spirituality, emotional state and interpersonal relationships are all negatively affected by the experience of widespread violence and death. The Rwandan studies found that the techniques of clinical psychology were best suited for the healing of trauma and the promotion of reconciliation and forgiveness between perpetrator and victim. The admission of wrongdoing and the process of reconciliation and forgiveness are critical factors in the healing of trauma, regardless of a trauma's origin. If trauma was left untreated, it was found that victims were much more sensitive and aggressive towards perceived threats. In such cases victims could resort to "defensive violence," believing such a course of action to be in their best interest. These traumas are trans-generational, which means that the trauma has been transferred, passed on, from those victims who had suffered first hand to their descendants and to the generations to follow. The process of this transference of trauma is described as a complex post-traumatic stress disorder mechanism. Without treatment this past trauma can go untreated for generations.

Little research has been done on the significant consequences of the Holodomor, be they psychological or social or to family structures and identity. To be identified as a patriotic Ukrainian was deemed to be enough to be arrested, imprisoned or sent to the Gulag and accused of "Ukrainian nationalism." Thus, survivors had to decide how they would present themselves in Soviet society. This has influenced the ethnic composition of Ukraine after the 1930s. Some Ukrainians sought the path of least resistance and used the Russian language and adopted the Soviet culture of the rulers of the Soviet Union to feel safe. In some cases, Russians and Belarusians were brought in to farm the empty villages in Ukraine. The policy of Russification, which replaced Ukrainization in the 1930s, had a severe cultural and social impact on Ukrainian society, that continues to be felt to this day in independent Ukraine.

To be identified as a patriotic Ukrainian was deemed to be enough to be arrested, imprisoned or sent to the Gulag and accused of "Ukrainian nationalism."

Truth and reconciliation methods help to overcome the lasting effects of trauma dealt by genocide. The continual denial of the genocide by Russia has furthered the traumatic effects that keep victims and their descendants from being able to come to terms with the trauma that they have experienced personally and as a community. In order to begin to heal the wounds of this genocide, acknowledgment is needed on the world stage, which would begin the process of reconciliation and healing for Ukrainians worldwide.

Today we find many Ukrainians who have grown up under this policy of Russification, who speak Russian, but are loyal to Ukraine and support Ukrainian sovereignty.

This process of healing, reconciliation and forgiveness has been stunted in Ukraine and coming to terms with the Ukrainian genocide is greatly complicated by historical, diplomatic, societal and cultural issues. Andrea Graziosi, an Italian historian of Ukrainian, Russian and Soviet history, notes that the study and analysis of the Holodomor will challenge and force a change in the collective memory of twentieth-century European history.

...analysis of the Holodomor will challenge and force a change in the collective memory of twentieth-century European history.

Graziosi is confident that for moral and intellectual reasons, the awareness and study of the Holodomor will continue to grow and build on work already done during the previous decades. Bearing this in mind, the following section "Breaking the Silence" summarizes steps taken to date to raise awareness of the Holodomor. It also addresses the problems that have arisen as a result of these initiatives in today's post-genocidal Ukraine.

Breaking the Silence

There were hundreds of thousands of refugees from Soviet Ukraine after WWII, many brought to Germany to work as slave labourers *(Ostarbeiter)*. Some of them had survived both the Famine and Nazi brutality and had reached the West. In their new countries, they lived in constant fear of being sent back to the Soviet Union or feared reprisals against their relatives by Soviet authorities. As a result, many remained silent about the trauma of the Holodomor as long as the Soviet Union was still in existence.

In 1985 a Commission on the Ukraine Famine was established to report to the US Congress on the Famine of 1932-33. Its findings were delivered in 1988 and confirmed that millions in Ukraine and the Northern Caucasus (especially in the Kuban) had died in a human-made famine created by the rulers of the Soviet Union.

In 1986 Robert Conquest, a noted scholar of the Soviet Union, published his book *The Harvest of Sorrow: Soviet Collectivization and the Terror-Famine*. The award-winning documentary film *Harvest of Despair* was produced by the Ukrainian Famine Research Committee in Toronto (now the Ukrainian Canadian Research and Documentation Centre, **www.ucrdc.org**), which houses an extensive archive of witness and survivor testimonies. They presented a different version of events in the 1930s in the USSR. These cracks in the "iceberg of silence" in the West began to extend to Ukraine, which was undergoing a period of *glasnost* (openness) in the late 1980s.

Today, there are still important officials in Russia and worldwide who deny that the Holodomor in Ukraine was a genocide, stating that starvation occurred across the Soviet Union, and ignoring the fact that Ukraine was specifically targeted with exceedingly harsh treatment. Historians and researchers are analyzing the private correspondence of Stalin, Molotov and Kaganovich, the perpetrators, and primary documents of the USSR. This analysis suggests that Moscow had specific plans for Ukraine and feared losing Ukraine because of its efforts to gain independence. The resistance and uprisings demonstrated by farmers against collectivization and Soviet authority attest to that fact.

Holodomor monument in Edmonton, 1983.

The first monument in Canada to the victims of the Holodomor was created by Ludmilla Temertey and erected in Edmonton, Alberta in 1983. Annual commemorations of the Holodomor, with the few remaining survivors in attendance, are held and dedicated to those deliberately starved to death in Ukraine. Special commemorations are held worldwide on the fourth Saturday in November.

Across Canada, students commemorate Holodomor Memorial Day on the fourth Friday in November in their schools. The initiative came into effect in November 2008 with the TDSB (Toronto District School Board), then was followed by other school boards such as the TCDSB (Toronto Catholic District School Board), the DPCDSB (Dufferin-Peel Catholic District School Board), the HWDSB (Hamilton Wentworth District School Board), the RCSD (Regina Catholic School District) and the ECSD (Edmonton Catholic School District).

On that day, a special announcement is read over the PA followed with a moment of silence. Also, prayers and exhibits, films and special lessons or ceremonies remember and commemorate the millions of victims of the Holodomor, of whom at least 31% were children under the age of ten.

Recognizing the Holodomor as Genocide

The Government of Ukraine officially recognized the Holodomor as genocide in 2006. In 2008 the Government of Canada recognized the Holodomor as genocide. The Holodomor became the fifth genocide to be officially recognized in Canada. This was followed by five of the Provincial Legislatures: Saskatchewan, Manitoba, Alberta, Ontario and Quebec, which designated the fourth Saturday in November as Holodomor Memorial Day. These provinces have also made efforts to include the Holodomor as a topic incorporated into certain courses in their school curricula.

Many countries have also recognized the Holodomor as a genocide. In effect, these recognitions pronounce: "you are human, you are part of us, you were wronged, you see that we care, our hearts are heavy" (p. 222, *The Forgiving Self* by Robert Karen). These steps are helpful to victims and their descendants as they travel on the difficult healing road to forgiveness and reconciliation.

STATEMENT BY THE *VEKHOVNA RADA* (PARLIAMENT OF UKRAINE), NOV. 28, 2006.
Excerpt sourced from the Ukrainian Canadian Congress archives

№ № 376–V | 28.11.2006
The Verkhovna Rada (Parliament) of Ukraine:

- Honouring the memory of millions of compatriots, who became victims of the 1932-33 Holodomor in Ukraine and of its aftermaths;
- Respecting all individuals, who survived this horrific tragedy in the history of the Ukrainian people;
- Realizing its moral duty before the past and future generations of Ukrainians as well as recognizing the necessity of restoring the historic justice and strengthening of intolerance of the society to any manifestations of violence;
- Noting that for many decades the tragedy of the 1932-33 Holodomor in Ukraine was officially denied by the authorities of the Union of Soviet Socialist Republics;
- Condemning the criminal acts of the totalitarian regime of the Union of Soviet Socialist Republics, that were aimed at the organization of the Holodomor, which resulted in the annihilation of millions of people, destruction of the social foundation of the Ukrainian people and of its centuries-old traditions, spiritual culture and ethnic distinctive character...
- Recognizing, in accordance with the Convention on the Prevention and Punishment of the Crime of Genocide of 9 December 1948, the 1932-1933 Holodomor in Ukraine as a purposeful act of mass annihilation of people, has adopted this Law.

Article 1. The 1932-1933 Holodomor in Ukraine is an act of genocide of the Ukrainian people.

President of Ukraine
Viktor Yushchenko
28 November 2006

Viktor Yushchenko
(President, 2005 - 2010)

Parliament of Canada

CONSOLIDATION CODIFICATION [Abridged Version]

Ukrainian Famine and
Genocide ("Holodomor")
Memorial Day Act

S.C. 2008, c. 19
Assented to 2008- 05- 29 to December 10, 2012

Published by the Minister of Justice at the following address:
http://laws-lois.justice.gc.ca

TABLE OF PROVISIONS

S.C. 2008, c. 19

An Act to establish a Ukrainian Famine and Genocide ("Holodomor") Memorial Day and to recognize the Ukrainian Famine of 1932-33 as an act of genocide

[Assented to 29th May 2008]

Preamble WHEREAS the Ukrainian Famine and Genocide of 1932-33 known as the Holodomor was deliberately planned and executed by the Soviet regime under Joseph Stalin to systematically destroy the Ukrainian people's aspirations for a free and independent Ukraine, and subsequently caused the death of millions of Ukrainians in 1932 and 1933;

WHEREAS that forced collectivization by the Soviet regime under Joseph Stalin also caused the death of millions of other ethnic minorities within the former Soviet Union;

WHEREAS 2007-08 marks the 75th anniversary of the Ukrainian Famine and Genocide of 1932-33;

WHEREAS on November 26, 1998, the President of Ukraine issued a Presidential Decree establishing that the fourth Saturday in November be recognized as a National Day of Remembrance for the victims of this mass atrocity;

WHEREAS on June 19, 2003, the Senate of Canada unanimously adopted a motion calling on the Government of Canada to recognize the Ukrainian Famine of 1932-33 as an act of genocide;

WHEREAS on November 28, 2006, Ukraine's Parliament voted to recognize the Ukrainian Famine of 1932-33 as an act of genocide against the Ukrainian people;

WHEREAS the parliaments of Argentina, Austria, Estonia, Georgia, Hungary, Lithuania, Poland and the United States of America and the senates of Australia and Canada have recognized the forced Ukrainian Famine of 1932-33 as a genocide against the Ukrainian people;

WHEREAS the fourth Saturday in November has been recognized by Ukrainian communities throughout the world as a day to remember the victims of the Ukrainian Famine and Genocide of 1932-33 and to promote the fundamental freedoms of a democratic society;

WHEREAS it is recognized that information about the Ukrainian Famine and Genocide of 1932-33 was suppressed, distorted or destroyed by Soviet authorities;

WHEREAS it is only now that truthful and accurate information is emerging from the former Soviet Union about the Ukrainian Famine and Genocide of 1932-33;

WHEREAS many survivors of the Ukrainian Famine and Genocide of 1932-33 have immigrated to Canada and have made a positive contribution to Canadian society;

WHEREAS Canada, as a party to the Convention on the Prevention and Punishment of the Crime of Genocide of December 9, 1948, condemns all genocides;

AND WHEREAS Canadians cherish democracy, defend human rights, and value the diversity and multicultural nature of Canadian society;

NOW, THEREFORE, Her Majesty, by and with the advice and consent of the Senate and House of Commons of Canada, enacts as follows:

SHORT TITLE
Short title 1.
This Act may be cited as the Ukrainian Famine and Genocide ("Holodomor") Memorial Day Act.

Ukrainian Famine and Genocide ("Holodomor") Memorial Day

Not a legal holiday

2.
Throughout Canada, in each and every year, the fourth Saturday in November shall be known as "Ukrainian Famine and Genocide ("Holodomor") Memorial Day".
3.
For greater certainty, Ukrainian Famine and Genocide ("Holodomor") Memorial Day is not a legal holiday or a non-juridical day.

Legislative Assembly of Manitoba

BILL 217
THE UKRAINIAN FAMINE AND GENOCIDE MEMORIAL DAY ACT

Royal Assent given June 12, 2008

WHEREAS 2007-08 marks the 75th anniversary of the Ukrainian Famine and Genocide of 1932-33, which is being recognized by the international community;

AND WHEREAS it is recognized that Soviet authorities denied, concealed or destroyed information about the Ukrainian Famine and Genocide of 1932-33, and it is only now that accurate information about this horrific event is emerging;

AND WHEREAS some survivors of the Ukrainian Famine and Genocide of 1932-33 and their descendants have made their home in Manitoba and have contributed richly to Manitoban society;

AND WHEREAS Manitobans cherish democratic freedoms, defend human rights and are passionately committed to the principles of diversity and multiculturalism;

THEREFORE HER MAJESTY, by and with the advice and consent of the Legislative Assembly of Manitoba, enacts as follows:

Ukrainian Famine and Genocide Memorial Day

1. In each year, the fourth Saturday in November is to be known throughout Manitoba as "Ukrainian Famine and Genocide Memorial Day."

2. This Act may be referred to as chapter U8 of the Continuing Consolidation of the Statutes of Manitoba.

3. This Act comes into force on the day it receives royal* assent.

*Explanatory Note

This Bill proclaims the fourth Saturday of November in each year as "Ukrainian Famine and Genocide Memorial Day."

Legislative Assembly of Alberta

UKRAINIAN FAMINE AND GENOCIDE (HOLODOMOR) MEMORIAL DAY ACT

2008 Bill 37, First Session, 27th Legislature, 57 Elizabeth II

Preamble

WHEREAS millions of Ukrainians perished as a result of the Ukrainian Famine and Genocide (Holodomor) of 1932-33;

WHEREAS the term "Holodomor" is a Ukrainian word that means "extermination by means of starvation" and is used to describe the Ukrainian Famine and Genocide (Holodomor) of 1932-33;

WHEREAS it is recognized that the Soviet authorities denied, concealed or destroyed information about the Ukrainian Famine and Genocide (Holodomor) of 1932-33 and that accurate information about this tragic event is only now being made available;

WHEREAS the Organization for Security and Co-operation in Europe (OSCE), the largest regional security organization in the world, passed a resolution that welcomes the recognition of the Holodomor in the United Nations, by the United Nations Educational, Scientific and Cultural Organization (UNESCO) and by the national parliaments of a number of the OSCE participating States;

WHEREAS the OSCE strongly encourages all parliaments to adopt acts regarding recognition of the Holodomor;

WHEREAS some of the survivors of the Ukrainian Famine and Genocide (Holodomor) of 1932-33 and their descendants reside in Alberta and have contributed greatly to Alberta's cultural, economic, political and educational life;

WHEREAS the people of Alberta value democratic freedoms, human rights and the rule of law, honour the values of compassion and honesty, and cherish the multicultural vibrancy of the Province;

WHEREAS the 4th Saturday in November has been recognized by the Parliament of Canada and by other Legislatures in Canada as a day to commemorate the Ukrainian Famine and Genocide (Holodomor) of 1932-33;

WHEREAS 2008 marks the 75th Anniversary of the Ukrainian Famine and Genocide (Holodomor) of 1932-33; and

WHEREAS it is important and fitting to observe Ukrainian Famine and Genocide (Holodomor) Memorial Day for the purposes of recognizing the Ukrainian Famine and Genocide (Holodomor) of 1932-33 and of reflecting on the horrific legacy of this event;

THEREFORE HER MAJESTY, by and with the advice and consent of the Legislative Assembly of Alberta, enacts as follows: Ukrainian Famine and Genocide (Holodomor) Memorial Day. The 4th Saturday in November in each year is proclaimed as "Ukrainian Famine and Genocide (Holodomor) Memorial Day."

Legislative Assembly of Ontario

Bill 147, 2009

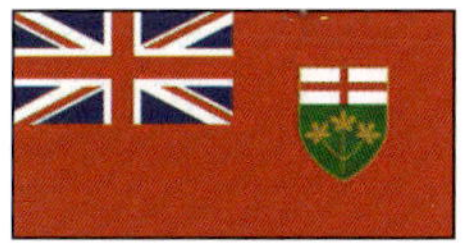

EXPLANATORY NOTE (Not part of the law): The purpose of the Bill is to make the fourth Saturday in November in each year Holodomor Memorial Day.

An Act to proclaim Holodomor Memorial Day

Preamble

The Holodomor is the name given to the genocide by famine that occurred in Ukraine from 1932 to 1933. As many as 10 million Ukrainians perished as victims of a man-made famine under Joseph Stalin's regime, with 25,000 dying each day at the peak of the famine.

The Government of Ukraine, the United States House of Representatives, the United States Senate, the Parliament of Canada, the Senate of Canada, the Governments of Alberta, Manitoba and Saskatchewan, UNESCO, the United Nations and over 40 other jurisdictions around the world have officially condemned the Holodomor or recognized it as genocide. Ukraine has established the fourth Saturday in November in each year as the annual day to commemorate the victims of the Holodomor.

On May 29, 2008, the Ukrainian Famine and Genocide ("Holodomor") Memorial Day Act (Canada) was enacted to recognize the famine as an act of genocide and to establish throughout Canada the Ukrainian Famine and Genocide ("Holodomor") Memorial Day on the fourth Saturday in November in each year.

To memorialize those who perished, it is appropriate to extend to Ontario the annual commemoration of the victims of the Ukrainian genocide by famine. A memorial day provides an opportunity to reflect on and to educate the public about the enduring lessons of the Holodomor and other crimes against humanity.

Therefore, Her Majesty, by and with the advice and consent of the Legislative Assembly of the Province of Ontario, enacts as follows:

Holodomor Memorial Day

1. Throughout Ontario, the fourth Saturday in November in each year is proclaimed Holodomor Memorial Day to memorialize those who perished as victims of genocide by famine that occurred in Ukraine from 1932 to 1933.

Commencement

2. This Act comes into force on the day it receives Royal Assent.

Short title

3. The short title of this Act is the Holodomor Memorial Day Act, 2009.

Legislative Assembly of Saskatchewan

The Ukrainian Famine and Genocide (Holodomor)
Memorial Day Act
being
Chapter U-0.1 of The Statutes of Saskatchewan, 2008
(effective May 14, 2008).
UKRAINIAN FAMINE AND GENOCIDE
(HOLODOMOR) MEMORIAL DAY

UKRAINIAN FAMINE AND GENOCIDE (HOLODOMOR) MEMORIAL DAY
CHAPTER U-0.1
An Act to recognize the Ukrainian Famine and Genocide (Holodomor)
Preamble

WHEREAS the Ukrainian Famine and Genocide (Holodomor) of 1932-33 has been recognized by the United Nations and by the international community;

AND WHEREAS it is recognized that the Soviet authorities denied, concealed or destroyed information about the Ukrainian Famine and Genocide (Holodomor) of 1932-33 and that accurate information about this horrible event is only now being made available;

AND WHEREAS some of the survivors of the Ukrainian Famine and Genocide (Holodomor) of 1932-33 and their descendants reside in Saskatchewan and have contributed greatly to Saskatchewan's cultural, economic, political and educational life;

AND WHEREAS the people of Saskatchewan prize democratic freedoms, human rights and the Rule of Law, appreciate the values of compassion and honesty and cherish the multicultural vibrancy of the province;

AND WHEREAS the fourth Saturday in November has been recognized by other Legislatures in Canada as a day to remember the Ukrainian Famine and Genocide (Holodomor) of 1932-33;

THEREFORE HER MAJESTY, by and with the advice and consent of the Legislative Assembly of Saskatchewan, enacts as follows:

Short title

1. This Act may be cited as The Ukrainian Famine and Genocide (Holodomor) Memorial Day Act.

Ukrainian Famine and Genocide (Holodomor) Memorial Day

2. The fourth Saturday in November in each year is declared to be "Ukrainian Famine and Genocide (Holodomor) Memorial Day" for the purposes of recognizing the

Ukrainian Famine and Genocide (Holodomor) of 1932-33 and of reflecting on the lessons to be learned from that event.
2008, c.U-0.1, s.2.

Coming into force

3. This Act comes into force on assent.
2008, c.U-0.1, s.3.

4.
c. U-0.1

UKRAINIAN FAMINE AND GENOCIDE
(HOLODOMOR) MEMORIAL DAY
REGINA, SASKATCHEWAN

Holodomor Memorial Day at St. Mary's Ukrainian Catholic Church in Mississauga, Ontario, 2012. (Community leaders and politicians)

Québec National Assembly

Bill 390

(2010, chapter 14)

An Act to proclaim Ukrainian Famine and Genocide (Holodomor) Memorial Day

Introduced 25 November 2009
Passed in principle 2 June 2010
Passed 4 June 2010
Assented to 4 June 2010

AS the Holodomor is the name given to the great famine and genocide that occurred in Ukraine in 1932 and 1933;

AS millions of Ukrainians perished as victims of a famine deliberately induced by the Soviet regime under Joseph Stalin;

AS the forced collectivization of agriculture imposed by the Soviet regime under Joseph Stalin resulted in the death of millions among the other peoples of the former Soviet Union;

AS the President of Ukraine issued a Presidential Decree on 26 November 1998 establishing the fourth Saturday in November as a National Day of Remembrance for the victims of this mass atrocity;

AS, in recent years, a number of countries have in various ways acknowledged the Holodomor in Ukraine as historical fact;

AS there is a Ukrainian community in Québec;

AS Quebecers are committed to defending democratic values and human rights and as they reject intolerance;

THE PARLIAMENT OF QUÉBEC ENACTS AS FOLLOWS:

- The fourth Saturday in November in each year is proclaimed Ukrainian Famine and Genocide (Holodomor) Memorial Day.

- For greater certainty, Ukrainian Famine and Genocide (Holodomor) Memorial Day is not a legal holiday or a non-juridical day.

- This Act comes into force on 4 June 2010.

Assemblée Nationale
Projet de loi no 390

Loi proclamant le Jour commémoratif de la famine et du génocide ukrainiens (l'Holodomor)

Présenté par
Madame Louise Beaudoin
Députée de Rosemont

CONSIDÉRANT que l'Holodomor désigne la famine et le génocide qui ont sévi en Ukraine en 1932 et 1933 ;

CONSIDÉRANT que des millions d'Ukrainiens ont alors péri, victimes de la famine provoquée délibérément par le régime soviétique de Joseph Staline en vue d'anéantir les aspirations du peuple ukrainien à la liberté et à l'indépendance de l'Ukraine ;

CONSIDÉRANT que le 26 novembre 1998, le président de l'Ukraine a pris un décret présidentiel désignant le quatrième samedi de novembre comme Jour national du souvenir en mémoire des victimes de cette atrocité collective ;

CONSIDÉRANT que, sur le plan international, plusieurs pays ont, de diverses façons, reconnu au cours des dernières années l'existence de l'Holodomor en Ukraine ;

CONSIDÉRANT la présence au Québec d'une communauté ukrainienne ;

CONSIDÉRANT que nos concitoyens d'origine ukrainienne tiennent profondément à perpétuer la mémoire des victimes de la famine et du génocide ukrainiens de 1932 et 1933 ;

CONSIDÉRANT la volonté des Québécois de défendre les valeurs démocratiques et les droits de la personne ainsi que leur refus de l'intolérance et de l'exclusion ethnique ;

LE PARLEMENT DU QUÉBEC DÉCRÈTE CE QUI SUIT :

1. Le quatrième samedi de novembre de chaque année est proclamé Jour commémoratif de la famine et du génocide ukrainiens (l'Holodomor).

2. La présente loi entre en vigueur le *(indiquer ici la date de la sanction de la présente loi).*

Notable People and the Holodomor

Balytsky, Vsevolod — Headed the GPU in the Ukrainian SSR in the 1930s. He was a key player, together with Pavel Postyshev, in the executions of the Ukrainian intelligentsia and the replacement of leading party figures in villages. He was executed in 1937 during the Great Terror.

Chamberlin, William Henry — An American historian and journalist who was the Moscow correspondent for the *Christian Science Monitor* from 1922-1934. He reported about the Famine in Ukraine and wrote the book *Russia's Iron Age*, in 1934.

Conquest, Robert — Respected British historian of the Soviet Union whose works include *The Great Terror*, *Harvest of Sorrow: Soviet Collectivization and the Terror Famine* (the first scholarly monograph on the Holodomor), and *Reflections on a Ravaged Century*.

Duranty, Walter — A journalist who served as the Moscow Bureau Chief for *The New York Times*. Cooperating with Soviet authorities, he reported that there was no famine or starvation in the Ukrainian SSR. He was awarded the Pulitzer Prize for his 1931 accounts on the Soviet Union. Duranty wrote "You can't make an omelet without breaking eggs" in reference to the consequences of collectivization.

Herriot, Edouard — A two-time premier of France, he visited the USSR in the summer of 1933. While in Ukraine he was given a tour of a "Potemkin village," a showcase collective farm and other similar model sites in Ukraine. He later declared there was no famine in Ukraine and that any news of famine was due to anti-Soviet lies. This strongly influenced European public opinion.

Innitzer, Cardinal Theodor — The Archbishop of Vienna who attempted to organize relief for the starving farmers during the Holodomor. His archives include rare photographs of the Holodomor.

Jones, Gareth — A Welsh investigative journalist who reported about media censorship in the Soviet Union, the arrests of peasant-farmers, and mass starvation in Soviet Ukraine after travelling there in 1933. Walter Duranty wrote reports contradicting Jones' coverage, stating that there was no starvation in Ukraine. Jones died under mysterious circumstances in 1935 in Manchuria.

Kaganovich, Lazar — A leading Communists in the 1930s and one of Stalin's closest colleagues and henchmen. Along with Viacheslav Molotov, Kaganovich was responsible for implementing **collectivization** and monitoring grain confiscation in the Northern Caucasus region (**Kuban**)

and in Ukraine, when farmers could not meet impossible grain quotas. He saw all shortages as sabotage that needed to be dealt with by force. A leading Bolshevik in Ukraine and the Soviet Union, he developed a fearsome reputation for his murderous actions during the Holodomor. He died in 1991.

Khataievich, Mendel — Second Secretary of the Communist Party of Ukraine, 1932-33. He monitored the confiscation of crops in Ukraine.

Kosior, Stanislav — First Secretary of the Communist Party of Ukraine from 1928-38. Responsible for collectivization in Ukraine and the Holodomor. He was executed during the Great Terror.

Lemkin, Raphael — An eminent lawyer of Polish-Jewish descent who coined the term "genocide" and helped draft the UN Convention on the Prevention and Punishment of the Crime of Genocide. Lemkin was familiar with the Holodomor and argued that it was a classic case of genocide (1953).

Lenin, Vladimir — A Russian Communist revolutionary and leader of the Bolshevik Party who played a key role in transforming the Russian Empire into the Soviet Union. He was the first leader of the USSR (1922-1924).

Mace, James — American historian and leading Holodomor researcher, who worked with Robert Conquest. He served as Staff Director for the US Congressional Commission on the Ukraine Famine. Mace was a leading figure in encouraging Holodomor research in Ukraine.

Molotov, Viacheslav — A leading Communist in the USSR and trusted ally of Stalin. He personally oversaw the confiscation of crops in Ukraine. He negotiated the Molotov-Ribbentrop Non-Aggression Pact with Nazi Germany which led to the invasion of Poland and the start of WWII.

Morozov, Pavlik — Supposedly, a Soviet boy who was glorified in Soviet propaganda for reporting his father to the authorities for hiding grain during **collectivization**. He became a role model for defending loyalty to the state, rather than his own family.

Muggeridge, Malcolm — English journalist and author who published articles about the Holodomor in the *Manchester Guardian* in the 1930s. He was libeled by Duranty and later prohibited from travelling to the USSR.

Postyshev, Pavel — Stalin's deputy in Ukraine from January 1933, responsible for the realization of **grain procurement quotas**. In 1933 he unleashed a campaign against the Ukrainian intelligentsia, Party members and cultural workers. He was executed during the Great Terror.

Shaw, George Bernard — British writer and Soviet sympathizer who denied the existence of a famine in Ukraine after being guided on a staged **Potemkin village** tour.

Skrypnyk, Mykola — Head of the Ukrainian People's Commissariat of Education and Ukrainian Bolshevik leader who supported and furthered Ukrainization efforts in the 1920s. He believed Ukraine would thrive in a federation rather than in a centralized state. Attacked by Pavel Postyshev as a protector of nationalists, he is thought to have committed suicide in 1933 once Ukrainization policies were reversed, and he witnessed the massive destruction of his nation.

Stalin, Joseph — General Secretary of the Soviet Communist Party and *de facto* dictator of the USSR from 1928-1953. Responsible for the Holodomor and the Great Terror of the 1930s. Leader of the Soviet Union during the Second World War (1939 - 1945). He was the chief architect of the genocide in Ukraine.

Trotsky, Leon — Leading Bolshevik during the Russian Revolution and the early years of the Soviet Union. Organized the **Red Army** and was a rival to Stalin for leadership of the Soviet Union after Lenin's death in 1924. Trotsky was exiled and ultimately murdered by Stalin's agents in 1940.

Webb, Beatrice and Sidney — Influential British socialists and economists who visited the Soviet Union in 1932-1933. As prominent scholars (co-founders of the London School of Economics), they went on to praise Stalin's grain procurement plan in Ukraine in 1933. They reiterated the falsifications of the Soviet leadership with respect to the famine and supported the Soviet leadership's use of any means to carry out industrialization.

Have students research one or more "Notable People" and write a more comprehensive biography of the person(s).

Glossary

teacher tip **This glossary can be used with "Read More" found in Part II, pp. 34-41.**

Aa

Accomplice — An individual or group that knowingly helps another commit a wrongful act.

Bb

Bidniak — (pl. *bidniaky*) A Soviet term devised to describe the poorest farmers in Ukraine during the 1920s and 1930s, it translates as "the poor." *Read more: #15*

Blacklist — In 1932, Ukrainian villages that failed to deliver the amount of grain demanded by the state were placed on blacklists as punishment. These villages were then surrounded by armed militia, which confiscated almost all foodstuffs and stopped the movement of goods and food into the area, resulting in the starvation of the residents. Over one-third of all Ukrainian villages experienced this form of punishment, which led to starvation. *Read more: #24*

Bolsheviks — Members of the more radical wing of the Social Democratic Workers' Party who advocated for the immediate seizure of power by the **proletariat** (workers). They organized the Russian Revolution of November 1917 under the leadership of **Lenin**. This term was later replaced by the term Communist Party of the Soviet Union (CPSU). *Read more: #4*

Breadbasket of Europe — Ukraine is known for its black, fertile soil, *chornozem*, which has enabled its people to grow and export vast amounts of grain for centuries, earning the country the nickname the "Breadbasket of Europe."

***Buksyr* brigades** — Special requisition units of Soviet Party members and activists who searched homes and villages for hidden food, confiscating and destroying food and property.

Bystander — An individual or group that sees or hears about an event or crime but does not intervene to stop it.

Cc

Collectivization — A policy adopted by the Soviet government to reorganize agriculture by doing away with private ownership of land and setting up collective farms controlled by the state. All farmers were forced to give up their land, animals and equipment to the state without compensation and to become employees of the collective farm. Forced collectivization of about five million farms in Ukraine was part of the first Five-Year Plan (1928-1933). 📖 *Read more: #18*

Commissar — Title of an official in charge of a Soviet government department, comparable to a minister.

Commissariat — Government department in the Soviet Union.

Communism — A political ideology that advocates the creation of a classless society in which private property is abolished. A concept first developed by Karl Marx.

Dd

Dekulakization — A Soviet policy to eliminate the most productive and independent farmers, who were labelled as *kulaks* (in Russian) and *kurkuls* (in Ukrainian). *Kulaks* were singled out for destruction by the Soviet Government.

Ff

Famine — An extreme shortage of food, usually caused by crop failure or overpopulation, resulting in hunger, starvation and death. The Holodomor is called a man-made famine as it was not a result of crop failure or overpopulation but the result of government policies.

Five-Year Plan — A wide-ranging blueprint for developing and regulating the state's economy prepared in the Soviet Union every five years. The policy of collectivization of agriculture and large-scale, rapid **industrialization** were the centerpieces of the First Five-Year Plan (1928-1933).

Gg

Genocide — The term is used here as was defined by the 1948 Convention on the Prevention and Punishment of the Crime of Genocide (Article 2), which states that genocide is "any of the following acts committed with intent to destroy, in whole or in part, a national, ethnical, racial or religious group," including:

a) killing members of the group;

b) causing serious bodily or mental harm to members of the group;

c) deliberately inflicting on the group conditions of life calculated to bring about its physical destruction in whole or in part;

d) imposing measures intended to prevent births within the group;

e) forcibly transferring children of the group to another group.

Gleaning — The act of gathering grain left over in fields from the harvest that would otherwise be left to rot. Gleaning was outlawed in the Soviet Union by the "Law of Five Stalks of Grain" (1932) and made punishable by death or imprisonment in the Gulag. *Read more: #21 & #28*

GPU — The intelligence service/secret police of the Soviet Union and the predecessor of the NKVD and the KGB. Each Soviet republic had its own GPU, subordinated to the central all-Union OGPU. *Read more: #14*

Grain procurement quota — The amount of grain set by officials that each collective farm was required to provide to the state on a regular basis. Farmers were forced to hand over their grain, and only after state quotas were filled could farmers keep grain to feed themselves. In many cases the procurements were so high that farmers were forced to hand over their seed grain. *Read more: #21*

Gulag — A system of concentration camps and exile settlements, usually in the northern parts of the Soviet Union, in which prisoners and resisters of the system were imprisoned and often worked to death. *Read more: #17*

Hh

Henchman — A loyal and trusted individual who supports and aids a person of power and carries out their dishonest, immoral or criminal activities.

Holodomor — A term used to describe the Genocidal Famine in Ukraine in 1932-33. It comes from the Ukrainian words *holod* (hunger) and *moryty* (to inflict death) – in other words, "death inflicted by starvation."

Ii

Indigenization — A policy by which each republic was encouraged to develop its native language and culture (e.g., Ukrainization), adopted in the 1920s by the Bolsheviks/Communists in an attempt to gain the support and cooperation of the various national republics that composed the Soviet Union. *See Korenizatsiia.* *Read more: #13*

Industrialization — The process of developing industries on a large scale to transform an agricultural society into an industrial one; includes the development of manufacturing, technological innovation, assembly lines, one of the two major goals of the first Five-Year Plan.

Intelligentsia — The best-educated people of a society who are considered to be its cultural, artistic, spiritual and political leaders.

Internal passport — A document introduced in the Soviet Union in 1932 that was given to city workers but not to farmers in Ukraine. It served as an identity card, and was

required to buy a railway ticket for travel. The internal passport system prohibited Ukrainian farmers from fleeing or leaving their villages in search of food.
📖 *Read more: #25*

Kk

Karbovanets — (pl. *karbovantsi*) Unit of currency in Soviet Ukraine equivalent to the Russian ruble.

KGB — The national state security agency and secret police for the Soviet Union from 1954-1991; preceded by the OGPU and the NKVD.

Kharkiv — The capital city of the Ukrainian SSR from 1922-1934, located in the eastern part of Ukraine.

Khutir — (pl. *khutory*) A single, private, self-contained homestead in Ukraine prior to collectivization.

Kolhosp (Ukr.)/***kolkhoz*** (Rus.) — A Soviet collective farm run by the state where all farmers were employees of the collective farm.

Komsomol — The Communist Youth League, which was the youth wing of the Soviet Communist Party. Komsomol members were used to search homes and villages, to confiscate and destroy food and other valuables, and also to pose as regular Ukrainians during the staged Potemkin village-style visits of prominent persons to the Ukrainian SSR in the 1930s. 📖 *Read more: #18*

Korenizatsiia — A policy introduced in 1923 that called for a concerted effort to recruit non-Russians to the Party and the state apparatus. Soviet officials were instructed to use local languages and to support culture and social development of the nationalities of the USSR. The Ukrainian version of this policy was called Ukrainization. *See also Indigenization.* 📖 *Read more: #13*

Kuban — A geographic area situated in the North Caucasus region of the RSFSR, adjacent to southeastern Ukraine. Prior to the Holodomor, it had a large ethnic Ukrainian population. During the 1920s, the Ukrainian SSR supported Ukrainian language education and cultural life in the Kuban. The area was subject to the same "special" decrees as Ukraine and the death toll there during the Holodomor was very high.
📖 *Read more: #27*

Kurkul (Ukr.) — (pl. *kulaki* in Russian, *kurkuly* in Ukrainian) A Soviet term used to describe a successful farmer who supposedly used his riches to manipulate village life and politics. A negative term, it was used at the beginning of collectivization to label any farmer who owned a productive farm and could afford to hire help. Later, any farmer who resisted collectivization or refused to join the collective farm could be labelled a *kulak*. Deemed by the state to be leaders of villages and resisters to the Soviet policy of collectivization, whole families were arrested, deported or executed. At least half a million men, women, and children in Ukraine were labelled as kulaks. 📖 *Read more: #15*

Ll

Law of Five Stalks of Grain — This law, enacted on August 7, 1932, declared all collective farm items to be state property. It forbade gleaning and punished anyone caught picking leftover grains from the fields of the collective farms. Punishment could be death or imprisonment in a Gulag concentration camp. 📖 *Read more: #28*

Little Russian — A term used until the early 20th century to describe the inhabitants of Ukraine in the Russian Empire, denying them a separate national identity.

Nn

New Economic Policy (NEP) — Instituted by Vladimir Lenin, it allowed independent farmers a measure of freedom in selling their grain on the open market. Small businesses were also allowed to operate. In effect from 1921-1927, it was introduced to stabilize the economy after the Civil War. 📖 *Read more: #12*

NKVD — The name of the secret police agency in the USSR during 1934-1954, preceded by the Cheka and OGPU. 📖 *Read more: #14*

Oo

Oblast — An administrative division or province that was introduced in Ukraine in 1932. At that time there were seven oblasts.

OGPU — The secret police of the USSR that investigated and combated what were deemed "anti-Soviet activities" in the Soviet Union in 1923-1934. 📖 *Read more: #14*

Onlooker — *See Bystander.*

Pp

Perpetrator — Someone who organizes or carries out an illegal, harmful or immoral action, such as genocide.

Petliurite/Petliurites — A person who was deemed to support independence for Ukraine. This label was derived from the name of Symon Petliura, a leader who fought for Ukrainian independence from 1918 to 1926. Petliurites were deemed enemies of the state by Soviet authorities. 📖 *Read more: #7*

Politburo — At Party congresses, Communist Party members would elect a Central Committee that would choose a Politburo (Political Bureau), which in practice ran the Soviet Union. The *de-facto* head of the Soviet government was the General Secretary of the Communist Party. Although elections were held for the Supreme Soviet, a legislative body, in reality the country was run by the Politburo, a small group of top Party officials. (Similar to a Cabinet) 📖 *Read more: #23*

Pood or ***Pud*** — A measure of grain, equal to 16.38 kg. or 36.11 lbs.

Potemkin village — A façade or staged village created to disguise or divert attention from the real conditions of life. During the Holodomor, Soviets took "useful idiots," foreign journalists, and political leaders on tours of Ukrainian towns and villages that had been cleaned up and/or fabricated to show no signs of starvation and suffering. Members of the Komsomol or actors posed as typical Ukrainians during these tours.

Proletariat — Term for the working or wage-earning class, often used in Marxist and Communist theory.

Propyska (Ukr.) — (*propiska* in Russian) A permit showing proof of residence in the Soviet Union, used to control the movement of people. Without a *propyska*, one could not work or live in a given city or town or travel.

Rr

Raion — (pl. *raiony*) An administrative region or district (county) within an oblast.

Red Army — The army of the Soviet Union; it was used to brutally put down revolts during the Holodomor.

Rescuer — An individual or group that saves another from a dangerous or distressful situation, like genocide.

Resister — An individual or group that actively opposes an action, such as the policies of a government.

Russification — A policy of assimilation undertaken by the Soviet government in which non-Russians were to adopt a Russian national, linguistic and cultural identity. This was done to de-nationalize Soviet minorities and make them into "Soviets" and to solidify control over 120+ diverse national groups, the largest being Ukrainians.

Ss

Seksot — (pl. *seksoty*) An informant of the secret police or government agency. Pavlik Morozov, a young boy who supposedly reported on his parents hiding grain in the 1930s, was held up as a model *seksot*.

Seredniak — (pl. *seredniaky*) A Soviet term devised to describe the middle-income farmers in Ukraine.

Siberia — A remote and underdeveloped region in the northeastern Soviet Union where resisters and other persons considered "enemies of the people" were deported as punishment.

Soviet — An adjective describing something of or relating to the Soviet Union; an elected government council in the Soviet Union.

Steel prod — A tool used by the specialist *buksyr* brigades to prod the earth in search of hidden food during the Holodomor.

Tt

Torgsin stores — Special stores created by the Soviet government in the 1930s where starving people could trade valuables such as wedding bands and crosses for small amounts of food. The gold collected at these stores provided a major revenue source for the Soviet economy.

Treaty of Brest-Litovsk (March 1918) — The treaty that ended the First World War on the Eastern Front; signed by the Germans, Bolshevik Russia, and Ukraine in which the Bolsheviks recognized Ukraine as an independent country and acknowledged its territorial integrity. *Read more: #5*

Totalitarian — A centralized system of government that is dictatorial in nature and demands and implements complete subordination in all aspects of life to the state (e.g. USSR).

Twenty-five-thousanders (25,000ers) — Dedicated Communist activists recruited by the Party to leave their homes and jobs in the city and move to rural areas to improve collective farm performance, organization, and discipline. They met resistance from Ukrainian farmers both for their lack of knowledge of agriculture and as a foreign presence, since many of them were Russian-speakers from the cities of Ukraine and Russia. *Read more: #18*

Uu

Ukrainian Autocephalous Orthodox Church (UAOC) — The Ukrainian Autocephalous (independent) Orthodox Church was established in 1921. It was a Ukrainian national church, independent of the Russian church. The leadership of the Church was purged and the UAOC was liquidated by the Soviet regime in 1930. *Read more: #3*

Ukrainization — A policy of developing, promoting, and increasing the use of Ukrainian language and culture in various facets of public life. In the 1920s Ukrainization was part of the early Soviet policy of indigenization but eventually was looked upon as a threat to Soviet rule by Stalin and discontinued. 📖 *(Read more: #13)*

Upstander — An individual or group that takes positive action on behalf of others, particularly when it may be easier to do nothing.

Useful idiot — An individual who is manipulated into supporting or naively supports and furthers a cause about which he or she has insufficient knowledge; in the 1930s a term used to describe a Western socialist sympathizer who supported the Soviet Union without knowing or understanding the true nature of Soviet actions, policies, and their implications.

Ukrainian SSR — The Ukrainian Soviet Socialist Republic was one of the national republics (provinces) that belonged to the USSR between 1922 and 1991. Also known as Soviet Ukraine. 📖 *(Read more: #23)*

USSR — The Union of Soviet Socialist Republics was a federation of Soviet states ruled by the Communist Party from Moscow, 1922-1991. Also known as the Soviet Union.

Vv

Victim — An individual or group that is the target of cruel or unjust treatment.

Ww

White Sea Canal/*Bilomor Kanal/Belomor Kanal* — An infamous Soviet modernization project, built using labour from the Gulag in the 1930s. Political prisoners endured extremely harsh working conditions. Thousands of intellectuals and workers perished during the construction of the White Sea Canal. Used as a means of eliminating enemies of the Soviet state. 📖 *(Read more: #17)*

PART III

Learning Activities

IN THIS SECTION

Lesson Plans

Class Projects

Assignments

Student Worksheets

Rubrics

"The Last Road," by Nina Marchenko. Oil on canvas, panel from triptych, 1998-2000. From the collection "Holodomor: Through the Eyes of Ukrainian Artists." Founder & trustee Morgan Williams.

This section consists of suggestions and lesson ideas for the teaching of the Holodomor in grades 6-12. Included are media studies, analyses of newspaper articles, memoirs of survivors, and document analyses. Lesson plans and assignments are usually followed by rubrics for assessment.

As critical and historical thinking are crucial to any study of history and social studies, teachers are provided with a variety of assignments for gleaning information and encouraging research, analysis, and synthesis of information.

OPPOSING VIEWPOINTS

> ***"I remain convinced that for Stalin to have complete consolidated power in his hands, he found it necessary to physically destroy the second largest Soviet republic, meaning the annihilation of the Ukrainian peasantry, Ukrainian intelligentsia, Ukrainian language and history as understood by the people: to do away with Ukraine and all things Ukrainian as such. The calculation was very simple, very primitive: no people, therefore no separate country, and thus no problem. Such a policy is Genocide in the classic sense of the word."***
>
> James Mace, Holodomor scholar, USA
> "I was chosen by your dead." *Day and Eternity of James Mace.* Kyiv: Ukrainian Press Group, 2005, p. 58.

> ***"Enemies of communists say that! They are the enemies of communism. People who are politically unaware, who are politically blind... I twice travelled to the Ukraine... of course I saw nothing of the kind there. Those allegations are absurd. Absurd!"***
>
> Viacheslav Molotov, Foreign Minister of the Soviet Union, 1986.

teacher tip

The above quotations on opposing viewpoints may be used for a learning activity.

Lesson: Activities for Introducing the Topic

Halia Sawycky-Dmytryshyn and Valentina Kuryliw

*It is essential that in introducing a **topic**, students are encouraged to search for an explanation of why such an event occurred and that they are engaged in the further study and exploration of various resources to arrive at their own conclusions. Students need to be emotionally involved, the topic needs to touch their humanity – they need to express their feelings and question what happened and why. Only then does the teaching begin.*

The introduction can be done with the entire class, asking for feedback from students using brainstorming techniques. Suggestions for materials to use in brainstorming:

- Picture of the event (e.g., before and after photos)
- Monument
- Brief story
- Quotation
- Related activities in this section of the resource:
    - "Bread and Butter" activity
    - Eyewitness account
    - Newspaper article

The introduction may also be done in student groups using the suggestions below:

- Analyzing a picture, students can deduce what has transpired and then investigate the event concerned. This is part of the craft of an historian. As "young detectives" students will try to understand what happened from the limited information provided in class, and therefore, be encouraged to continue studying the topic.

- Discussing a quotation from an eyewitness account of the Holodmor, such as a child who remembers a rhyme or a saying of the time.

    a. *"The hammer and sickle – mean death and starvation."*

    b. *"Wake up Taras, and look around you.
Not a cow or pig in sight, nor a morsel to eat,
Only Stalin's portrait on the wall."*
N. Mychajlowska, 11 years old in 1933

- Choosing a quotation on the consequences of the Famine, e.g., A. Graziosi, p. 68.

- Viewing a portion of a film, e.g., *Genocide Revealed - Education Version* (26 minutes) with a focus question to bring about discussion.

- Viewing the first 11 minutes of *Soviet Story*, which deals with social engineering and Marxist ideology.

- Listening to DVD accounts of survivors who were children in the 1930s in Ukraine. *(Use Worksheet #2, pp. 199-200 and/or Worksheet #4, pp. 233-234) – What did they all say? What happened? Why did it occur?*

- Examining written eyewitness accounts, ending with a discussion.

- Reading excerpts from historical fiction: e.g., *The Rings (pp. 98-99), Maria, Stones Under the Scythe.*

- Reading a short story: *e.g. The Rings (pp. 279-289), Without Priests, Without Graves and Crosses (pp. 290-298).*

- Reading a newspaper article about a Holodomor Memorial Day commemoration, for example. What was known? How did the world perceive the Genocidal Famine? *(pp. 94-95).*

- Listening to a song, reading a poem, *e.g., Through the Eyes of a Child (pp. 100-102).*

teacher tip

Short stories may be found in the Appendix, pp. 279-298 or on www.education.holodomor.ca/teaching-materials/the-rings/

Soup kitchen, Odesa during the Holodomor.

Lesson: Art Workshop - "Through the Eyes of a Child"

Halia Sawycky-Dmytryshyn

This one-day workshop explores the subject of the Genocidal Famine in Ukraine. The project provides a learning opportunity for students to reflect on and express their knowledge and thoughts about the Famine by painting images of these events.

teacher tip

For teachers unfamiliar with art projects, refer to the Appendix, pp. 269-278, for an overview of art theory, art education principles, and the basics of art production.

Grade Level:
Grade 5 to 10

Curriculum Fit / Specific Expectations / Learning Outcomes:
Select expectations you wish to cover from either English language arts, social studies, history, genocide, social justice, politics, law or religious studies and provide an assessment to share with the students at the outset.

Materials Required:

- Paint, brushes, paper, paint mixing palettes, water, newspapers/paper towels (for more information about these materials, refer to Appendix p. 277.)
- Poem "Through the Eyes of a Child" by Halia Sawycky-Dmytryshyn, see Part II, pp. 100-102.
- Choose visual aids listed in "Visual Motivational Strategies," on pp. 271-273 in the Appendix.

GOAL

To allow students the opportunity to paint meaningful paintings with a view to Art Elements and Principles, based on the subject of the Genocidal Famine of 1932-1933 in Ukraine.

OBJECTIVES

To present an overview of the events leading up to and including the Genocidal Famine in Ukraine in 1932-1933 through:

Motivational Strategies (see "Motivation," pp. 270-277 in Appendix)

- Engage students emotionally in the events.
- Help students identify with the people and events.
- Allow students to express their ideas and feelings in a meaningful way when they go on to paint.

Art Expression (see Art Elements, Art Principles, and Art Materials, pp. 273-277)

- Present students with some basic concepts of art elements and principles.
- Help students begin their composition by a brief discussion of contour lines, sketching or drawing an outline using chalk on construction paper.
- Give students the opportunity to use good quality watercolour cake paints and a variety of artists' brushes and all the art supplies needed to paint in a comfortable ambient atmosphere with enough time to plan, paint and complete a painting.

Planning the Art Workshop Project

An art workshop of one day shares many of the same characteristics as an on-going art program, but due to time constraints, it needs to be condensed, intense and focused on the goals and objectives of the project.

Preparation for the workshop is very important. The teacher should not only plan and prepare for the topic assuming most students know very little, but should also prepare additional information for students with advanced knowledge. The planning must be thorough and flexible enough to accommodate students of different ages, grades, skill and knowledge levels, yet sufficiently structured to engage and challenge the students.

MOTIVATIONAL STRATEGIES

Overview Presentation

Each full-day workshop consists of a verbal and a visual overview presentation (approximately 60 minutes) of the events in Ukraine from the early 1930s to the human-made Genocidal Famine in 1932-1933. The verbal component includes a question-answer approach, narratives, and discussion interspersed with visuals — pictures, charts, quotes, books that challenge, contradict, emphasize and aid the thinking process. See pp. 271-277 in the Appendix for more information about these visual aids.

The Genocidal Famine of Ukraine is a painful subject. It is the story of millions who were starved to death in their own land, by a regime that wanted to bring Ukraine under a communal collective system. The following points should be raised in the discussion:

- The conditions in Ukraine in the 1920s and early 1930s
- The general characteristics of the Ukrainian people of those times
- The socio-political policies and edicts of Stalin and the Soviet Communist government during the 1920s and 1930s
- The Soviet economic plan for Ukraine, which included collectivization and industrialization
- The crushing of Ukrainians' dream for national liberation
- Collectivization – what it meant for the Ukrainian people
- Results of collectivization – displacement of people, mass national starvation
- International response to the Famine in Ukraine

Example of Discussion

As a teacher, I wanted to present the events of 1932-1933 in a manner that not only reviewed and reinforced information students may already possess, but to provide further insight into the Famine-Genocide story. Students would be able to identify and become emotionally involved with the events, and therefore better able to create meaningful art.

To this end, I began each presentation by asking all the children to close their eyes for one moment, and to cast their minds back through time to envision life in Ukraine in the early 1930s. Questions were posed to make children think of their personal connections to the people of those times and thereby, to help them identify with the period and people.

One simple open-ended question was "What do you think the people of Ukraine grew in their fields in the 1930s?" This question is suitable for brainstorming even with younger students or with students without topic-specific background knowledge. Accept all ideas. They will be confirmed or abandoned during the class question and answer session and classifying strategy activities.

Sample questions:

- Where is Ukraine located?
- Who has friends of Ukrainian heritage?
- Who in this class has family living in Ukraine? As hands go up, children respond.
  My grandmother, grandfather, uncle, cousin... lived there.
- What do you think life was like for them in those days before television, before computers, before malls, before cars or telephones?
- What would you have been doing in those times? Going to school? Working in the fields?

These questions invite students to make comparisons to their own lives today. Various pictures are held up as the discussion progresses and questions are brainstormed. All answers are accepted. For example:

- What do you think Ukrainians were like at that time?
  Children's responses: *"happy, religious, loyal, independent, sad, liked to sing, proud, poor, hardworking"*
- How did they live, socialize, celebrate, and earn a living?
  "lived and worked on a farm, celebrated Easter"
- What kind of clothing was common for them to wear?
  "rags, old, itchy"
- What did they eat, grow, sell, and produce?
  "wheat, vegetables, pickles"
- How did they express their creativity and value their culture?
  "dancing, singing, embroidery"

- What did we inherit from them that continues today?
  "love of dancing, music, delicious food"

List of Brainstormed Words

The answers to the questions in the section above may be made into a list and re-read or chanted often during the project. The list below is an example of brainstormed words, which describe and answer the question "What kind of people lived in Ukraine in the 1930s?" This list describes traits that establish positive feelings towards the people of Ukraine. This list may be chanted before each activity on the Holodomor.

- Example of List of Brainstormed Answers

What kind of people lived in Ukraine?

Strong
Strong-minded
Hardworking
Active
Joyful
Family-oriented
Proud
Loyal
Good neighbours
Helpful
Religious
Patriotic
Nationalistic
Sad
Traditional
Stubborn
Kind
Just
Very independent

Student art, Jara Wowk, St. Sofia Catholic School, Mississauga, 2000.

Student art, Andrew Kikhard, St. Demetrius Catholic School, Toronto, 2000.

In my class such questions were posed, probed and heartily discussed in a lively interactive manner by students. Approximately 45 minutes later, a verbal picture of the people of Ukraine emerged. Other questions followed to build a picture of the times and the issues facing them:

- What kind of government did the people have?
- Was it a safe, stable time? If not, what made it uncertain, dangerous?
- What was happening to the social structure?

Discussion continued about what happened in the 1930s when Communists took away individual farms to collectivize the land.

- Why was Ukraine known as the "Breadbasket of Europe?"
- What was collectivization? What did it mean for Ukraine?
- What edicts did Stalin and the Communist regime impose on the people?
- Did people resist the take-over? Did they fight, yield?
- How could they have resisted?
- How did food disappear? Where did it go? Who took it away?
- Why couldn't the hungry get food from neighbours? From neighbouring regions, countries, Canada?
- What did the people do to survive?
- What happened to the churches, priests, teachers and leaders of the country? Did they leave? How were they silenced?

The children responded with many answers: *"wheat quotas increased, people could not survive on what was left, eventually, nothing was left at all."*

- What happened then? Answers included: *"hunger, pain, starvation, death, sorrow, horror."*

The discussion session is very important. Children envision in their minds what it might have been like for some of their ancestors, what they might have seen and experienced. These images may be sad, awful, cruel, but the events occurred and were real. These images fuel their imaginations and inspire their art.

If the art materials are handed out at this point, the results might not reflect what students are capable of producing. Because older students want to paint more realistically, some may hesitate and be reluctant to paint from memory or their imaginations the way younger children do. Sometimes without concrete objects or models to observe, they can only guess at figures/ objects and size/shape/space relationships. Some students may not want to risk putting their ideas down on paper yet, especially with a new teacher present only for the day.

The students may need more tools and art skills at this point. The practical skills are the building blocks of art—lines, shapes and colours. These skills are a means, not an end in themselves in art education, but they enhance children's efforts. In this situation, teachers may want to conduct the exercises presented in "Art Elements and Art Principles" on pp. 273-277 in the Appendix.

Student art, Christina Cholkan, Josyf Cardinal Slipyj Catholic School, Toronto, 2000.

ART EXPRESSION

Read the poem "Through the Eyes of a Child" in class and use it as a springboard to student art activities. The poem is found in Part II, pp. 100-102.

Stage 1

The practical part of the workshop can begin with some simple exercises. The chalkboard serves this purpose well, along with teaching boards and information, with display visuals, lines, shapes, colours, textures, patterns, etc. For an example of discussion at this stage and student activities, see pp. 269-277 in the Appendix.

Children should imagine an image that reflects their understanding of the poem. They should use coloured chalk only, not pencils, for outlining/sketching in the basic shapes of their composition/imagined image. They do not need to include details, just the larger shapes so that the outlined shapes are designed in a manner pleasing to the child.

Stage 2

At this point, art production points are presented. The young artist needs to keep in mind:

- Paper size and the figure/object relationship – size of object in relation to the paper size
- Not to be concerned with "erasing" chalk lines because the opaque watercolour paint

"Yellow sunflowers reaching for the sky," by Vera Kowalsky, St. Demetrius Catholic School, Toronto, 2000.

will cover most "mistakes" and some chalk lines that remain and show usually become part of the painting adding depth and texture.

- To be aware of paint application principles – always start with lighter colours first (not unlike pysanka and batik dying methods). One can darken light colours easily but not lighten dark ones.

"Fear Before Terror," by Jaroslaw Fenton, St. Sofia Catholic School, Mississauga, 2000.

- To practice the brush size principle – large brushes are for large objects and backgrounds, medium brushes are for smaller areas where using the large flat brushes even sideways won't do, and fine brushes are only for small areas and details for intricate designs or for outlining when the painting is completed.
- To offset the concern some students have with realistic endeavours, many small black and white newspaper clippings of people in the news in a variety of poses are provided. The students are able to select pictures, not to be copied, but to aid them in positioning figures, objects, scenes, action and people in motion on their drawing papers.

This is the last step before painting. Desks are arranged in groups of 4 and 6, facing one another. Students share only trays of paints. They each have their own set of brushes, can of water, paint mixing palette and paper towels. All desks are covered with newspaper and water cans are filled. When using hard cake paints, brushes need to be handled properly, so a demonstration of this follows as well as mention of clean-up procedures. For more information about art materials, see pp. 277-278 in the Appendix.

Stage 3

It's painting time! The children will have most of the afternoon for painting. They can fill in the shapes they created in Stage 1 and/or create a new image based on the poem. During this time the teacher's job is just as important as before. Children need further motivation and encouragement as they begin their work. This is the time to speak with individual students, provide suggestions, comments, and encouragement, answer questions and help with problems when needed.

Students may:

- ask for help anytime
- talk, chat and discuss freely and quietly among themselves
- trade paint trays with permission of those children whose colours they wish to use
- ponder and paint a second painting, time permitting.

Students should:

- reflect, savour and enjoy this painting time!

By participating in this project, these students create a wealth of art about a painful period in the history of Ukraine through their own eyes. Not only is this an educational, creative and rewarding project, but the art work will go on to become an inspiration to others.

teacher tip

Consult the poem "Through the Eyes of a Child" by Halia Sawycky-Dmytryshyn as a teaching aid to acquaint students with conditions of life in Ukraine in the 1920s and 1930s (Part II, pp. 100-102) and make comparisons to the student art produced.

"Mother Ukraine," by Lidia Siniavskaia, St. Josaphat Catholic School, Toronto, 2000.

Student art by Yaroslaw Mikolaenko, Josyf Cardinal Slipyj Catholic School, Toronto, 2000.

Lesson: Bread and Butter Activity

Halia Sawycky-Dmytryshyn

This lesson involves reading the book Little Red Hen, *found online. Students are directly involved in the making of butter, which is then taken away before they can eat it to create understanding of what it feels like to have food taken away.*

Grade Level:

Junior Kindergarten to grade 12. The lesson is geared toward elementary students, but may be used with high school students and adults.

Curriculum Fit / Specific Expectations / Learning Outcomes:

Students will learn through a holistic and experiential approach by actively participating in a combination of activities including: **storytelling** and **shared reading** of the *Little Red Hen,* emphasizing **the use of voice** and the sharing of bread and making of butter. Through these activities students will gain understanding of the injustice of having food forcibly taken away from those who produced it. Hunger is a sensitive topic which needs to be approached in a creative and meaningful manner, especially at the elementary school level.

Materials Required:

- The book *Little Red Hen*
  www.enchantedlearning.com/stories/fairytale/littleredhen/story/
  - Most versions of this folk tale include three friends or neighbours. e.g. dog, cat, and pig and Little Red Hen and her chicks.
  - It tells the story of producing bread, starting with planting grain, growing and harvesting, threshing, milling flour, and finally baking flour into bread to feed Little Red Hen's hungry baby chicks.

Jars for making butter.

- Plastic butter knives (one for each student)
- Paper plates or serviettes (one for each student)
- Bowl for buttermilk
- *Bread:* The teacher should purchase several loaves of sliced bread from a local bakery or baked babka, paska, or bread made by Baba (granny).
- *Butter:* It is recommended that you make the butter with your class, as this activity is simple and economical and the effect and results are awe-inspiring and memorable. The following recipe is proposed.

BUTTER RECIPE

Ingredients

- 35% whipping cream (room temperature)
- Small jar (with a tight fitting lid) for each student (visit a discount outlet)

Instructions

1. Fill jar ½ full with whipping cream.
2. Tighten the lid on the jar.
3. Holding both ends of the jar, vigorously shake the jar for several minutes until butter separates from buttermilk and forms into a lump.
4. Pour off the liquid buttermilk into the bowl provided by the teacher.
5. Spread butter on bread.
6. Enjoy!

Set-up Required:

- Fill the jars (one for each student) half-way with 35% whipping cream. **NOTE:** If you think that you are going to repeat this activity, keep the jars and clean them for re-use. However, it really makes this activity more interesting for students when they take jars home and shake up the butter for their family.
- Pre-cut or slice the bread.
- Set aside the paper/plastic plates, serviettes, container/bowl, and butter knives.

The tasks may be completed sequentially in one lesson or you may choose parts of the lesson to complete according to the resources and time available.

☑ **PRE-TASK ACTIVITIES**

- Introduce the Holodomor and the significance of wheat for the Ukrainian people both during the Holodomor and today. The following excerpt may be read to the students:
  - *Wheat is a precious crop throughout the world today and has been for thousands of years. This was especially true of "The Bread Basket of Europe," as Ukraine was known in the early nineteenth and twentieth centuries. Wheat (flour) harvested one autumn had to last a family until the next harvest (usually in August). This wheat provided flour that was used in many ways during the year – especially in baking bread. Planting wheat to milling it into flour is a long and intensive process with many steps. In the 1930s, the Communist government in Moscow imposed quotas on Ukraine's grain, which left families struggling, trying to save tiny amounts of wheat to see them through the cold harsh winter that followed. Because troops were brought in to take away all wheat and later, all food from farmers, millions of men, women and children were starved to death as a result of this man-made Famine.*

☑ **TASK 1**

- Provide each child with a glass jar with the whipping cream inside.
- Have the students shake the butter while completing task two.

☑ **TASK 2**

- Read the *Little Red Hen* to your class, modelling expression and voice.
  NOTE: It is important when reading the story to change the ending so that when the bread is finally baked and smeared with butter, and the hen and her chicks are ready to eat the bread, a fox comes by who did nothing to help produce the bread and takes away the hen's bread.
- Discussion – Make analogies of the events to the Holodomor. They should feel the injustice of the neighbour or a bully coming by and forcefully taking the bread away from the hen and her chicks who worked for it (children can recognize the injustice of having someone taking away the fruit of their labour).
- Re-read or retell the *Little Red Hen.*
  - Invite students to participate in the hen's hard-working journey, while her friends refuse to help her because they only want to play.
  - Get students involved in telling the story by repeating various phrases or omitting words from the text. For example, "Who will help me plant?" "Not I said the cat." "Not I said the dog." "Not I said the pig." Have the students repeat and read the phrases with expression and with appropriate voice.
- When the butter is ready, there will be clumps. Help students open the jar and pour out the buttermilk into a bowl, leaving the butter in the jar.
- Provide each student with a piece of bread, a butter knife, and a paper plate or serviette.
- Have students butter their bread.
- When the students are ready to eat the bread with butter hold up your hand and say "STOP! Do not eat the bread and butter. They belong to me, not you! Even though you baked the bread and turned the butter, it does not belong to you!"
- Then the teacher takes the bread and butter away – while explaining that this is what happened to Ukrainians during the forced Famine.

☑ **POST-TASK ACTIVITIES**

- Give the bread and butter back to the students.
- Discussion - Talk about the feelings of a person who had worked hard, but who had the fruits of their labour taken away without compensation.
  NOTE: Include in the discussion that the Holodomor is an example of extreme bullying or genocide as we understand it, where force is used by a bully to get what they want, regardless of the consequences. With the Holodomor, it was the Communist government in Moscow that used force to take away Ukrainian food. This led to millions of Ukrainian deaths by starvation in the years of 1932 and 1933.

Lesson: Reflecting on Holodomor Documentaries

This lesson focuses on visual media to stimulate reflection on the Holodomor. Worksheets are provided for students to explore their viewing experience. Teachers may select one or more worksheets to meet their expectations.

Suggested Documentary DVDs:

- *Genocide Revealed – Educational Version (26 min.)* - Grades 9-12
- *Harvest of Despair (55 min.)* - Grades 9-12
- *Soviet Story (11 min.)* - Grades 9-12
- *Holodomor, Voices of Survivors (30 min.)* - Grades 6-12

Grade Level:
See above

Curriculum Fit / Specific Expectations / Learning Outcomes:
Select expectations you wish to cover from either English language arts, social studies, history, genocide, religious studies, politics, law, or social justice courses and provide an assessment to share with the students at the outset.

Materials Required:

- Online sources of documentary:
    - *Harvest of Despair:* **http://video.google.ca/videoplay?docid=3897393411603039499#** or **http://www.youtube.com/watch?v=VXkgGdZC6uQ**
- Copies of either Worksheet #1 and #2 for any DVD listed above
- And/or copies of Worksheet #3 for *Harvest of Despair*
- Copies of Worksheet #4 or #5 for *Genocide Revealed*

Set-up Required:

- Screen to view documentary
- DVD player

Harvest of Despair is one of several documentaries that present the story of the Holodomor. It is easily available and a good source of information. It may be used as a pre-task activity providing students with information that they may require to successfully complete their learning task. In this section, we provide three worksheets that teachers may duplicate for their students. Students may work in groups or individually after they have viewed the documentary.

The educational version of *Genocide Revealed* contains two segments, 26 min. and 52 min. It is one of the most recent documentaries on the Holodomor, that draws upon new resources and eyewitness accounts.

For *Soviet Story* and *Holodomor, Voices of Survivors*, refer to p. 258 in Part IV for a description of the DVD.

WORKSHEET #1: GENERIC ANALYSIS OF DVD

Generic Analysis of *Harvest of Despair, Genocide Revealed, Soviet Story,* or *Holodomor, Voices of Survivors.*

- ☑ **Pre-task activity:** viewing of the film.
- ☑ **Task:** completing the film analysis form provided in Worksheet #1.
- ☑ **Post-task reflection:** sharing views with students in a small group.

WORKSHEET #2: DEFINITIONS

Students identify the players in a genocidal action such as the Holodomor.

WORKSHEET #3: HARVEST OF DESPAIR (DVD)

Students use the information in the documentary to answer questions on *Harvest of Despair.*

WORKSHEETS #4 or #5: GENOCIDE REVEALED (DVD)

Worksheet #4 accompanies the 26-minute version of the DVD *Genocide Revealed,* which is appropriate for grades 6-12. Worksheet #5 supports the 52-minute version of the DVD and is suitable for grades 11 and 12.

- ☑ **Pre-task activity:** viewing of the film.
- ☑ **Task:** responding to questions, class discussion.
- ☑ **Post task activity:** individual reflection on the answers and new questions that arose during the class discussion.

Worksheet #1: Generic Analysis of Documentaries

Harvest of Despair, Genocide Revealed, Soviet Story,
OR *Holodomor, Voices of Survivors*

After viewing the documentary answer the following questions.

1. Name of film:

2. Date of production:

3. Producer:

4. The period or epoch presented in the film:

5. The main idea presented in the documentary:

6. Sources of information:

7. The central figures in the film:

photocopy for students to fill out

8. Additional aids used by the film director to put the main idea across:

9. If you were the director, what would you add to the film to emphasize the main idea?

10. Was this a fair presentation of the main idea? Explain, giving three specific reasons/examples for your argument:

11. Make a drawing that expresses one major item in the documentary that impressed you:

photocopy for students to fill out

Worksheet #2: Definitions of Genocide Terms

Harvest of Despair, Genocide Revealed,
***OR Holodomor, Voices of Survivors* (DVDs)**

A. Write a definition for each of the following words before viewing the documentary:

Perpetrator –

____

____

Bystander –

____

____

Henchman –

____

____

Victim –

____

____

Onlooker –

____

____

Rescuer –

____

____

B. After viewing the film, identify the following

The perpetrators in the film were:

____

____

The henchmen were:

The victims or targets were:

The bystanders were:

The onlookers were:

The rescuers were:

C. Make a drawing that expresses one major idea in the film that impressed you:

photocopy for students to fill out

Worksheet #3: Harvest of Despair Documentary

Analysis of *Harvest of Despair*

It is suggested to view the DVD in two segments: 1) The first half gives background information and events leading to the Genocidal Famine; 2) the second half deals with the Famine and the cover-up.

After viewing the film, the class may be divided into groups of 4-5 students each. These groups discuss the questions on the worksheet below and report their findings to the class as a whole. The findings can be recorded on a chart with each subsequent group adding to the notes of the the previous group's information recorded on the chart. Conclusions can be drawn out in a class discussion based on the findings of each group.

a) Discuss the following questions in your group and record your answers for sharing with the whole class:

1. What evidence exists that the Famine was man-made?

2. What events led to the Genocidal Famine?

3. What evidence is there that the Genocidal Famine was directed specifically against the Ukrainian people?

4. How many people died as a result of the Genocidal Famine? What percent of the population?

5. Select one eyewitness in the film. Describe the living conditions of their family. Describe their testimony.

photocopy for students to fill out

6. Describe one scene from the film illustrating the horrors of the Genocide.

7. List the actions taken by Soviet Government officials that led to the Genocidal Famine in Ukraine.

b) After viewing the second part of the film, discuss and answer these questions individually or in groups, as directed by the teacher.

1. Western nations knew about the starvation of millions in Ukraine. Suggest reasons why they were silent about this tragedy in 1932-33.

2. Why was there a media cover-up inside and outside the Soviet Union? Explain.

3. What role did Malcolm Muggeridge and Walter Duranty play in the media coverage of the Ukrainian Famine in 1933?

photocopy for students to fill out

4. Who were the perpetrators?

...the victims?

...the observers/bystanders?

5. Should the perpetrators be exposed and held accountable for crimes against humanity? Why or why not? Suggest what could be done even after they have died.

photocopy for students to fill out

Worksheet #4: Genocide Revealed Documentary

EDUCATIONAL VERSION

(26 min.) - Suggested for Grades 6 to 12

1. What is the main message of the film?

____

____

____

2. a) Who are the main characters in the film?

____

____

____

b) Who were the victims? Who were the perpetrators?

____

____

____

3. Why was grain so important for the Soviet Union?

____

____

____

4. Why did the Ukrainian Genocidal Famine occur?

____

____

____

5. a) What is collectivization?

____

____

photocopy for students to fill out

b) What methods did Stalin use against the Ukrainian farmers to bring about collectivization? Explain.

____

____

____

6. What evidence exists that the Ukrainian Genocidal Famine occurred?

____

____

____

7. a) How does the 1948 UN Convention define genocide?

____

____

____

b) Why is the Holodomor considered to be an act of genocide? Be specific.

____

____

____

8. In your opinion, was it morally justifiable to force farmers to work on the collective farms? Explain.

____

____

9. In your opinion, why do some countries and people (politicians, historians and journalists) continue to deny the Holodomor today?

____

____

10. Suggest one thing that global society can do to prevent genocide in the future:

____

____

Worksheet #5: Genocide Revealed Documentary

EDUCATIONAL VERSION

(52 min) - Suggested for Grades 11 and 12

1. What is the main message of the film?

2. a) Who are the main characters in the film?

   b) Who were the victims? Who were the perpetrators?

3. What categories/groups of people did Stalin destroy in the late 1920s and early 1930s? Why was this done?

4. Why was grain so important for the Soviet Union?

photocopy for students to fill out

5. According to eyewitness accounts, what did some Ukrainians do to survive starvation between 1932 – 1933? Be specific.

6. What evidence exists that the Ukrainian Genocidal Famine occurred?

7. a) How does Raphael Lemkin define genocide in the 1948 UN Convention?

   b) Why is the Holodomor considered to be an act of genocide? Be specific.

8. a) What is collectivization?

   b) What methods did Stalin use against the Ukrainian farmers to bring about collectivization? Explain.

photocopy for students to fill out

9. According to Professor Serbyn, the Soviet state exported "...1.5 million tons of grain out of a total of 3 million tons..." Explain why grain and other food was being exported from Ukraine while Ukrainian farmers starved to death in 1933.

10. In your opinion, was it morally justifiable to force farmers to work on the collective farms? Explain.

11. Why did it take over 50 years for information on the Ukrainian Famine to become widely known?

12. In your opinion, why do some countries and people (politicians, historians and journalists) continue to deny the Holodomor today?

13. The Holodomor was largely ignored and denied outside and inside of Ukraine for some 50 years. How might the news of a possible genocide be dealt with in today's globalized society?

14. What is the historical importance/significance of the Holodomor today?

15. What can global society do to prevent genocide in the future?

photocopy for students to fill out

Lesson: The Holodomor through Short Stories

*Reading **short stories** about historical events is an excellent way to engage students in gathering factual information about a topic. A story provides the context to elicit empathy from a difficult issue.*

Lesson #1: Group Project
"Without Doctors and Priests, without Graves and Crosses" short story by Olena Zvychayna (pp.290-298), responding to a short story using learning activities such as writing a diamante poem, an editorial, a feature story, or a tableaux.

Lesson #2: Daily Life During the Holodomor (Grades 6-12)
A story about the Holodomor, includes activities such as drawing and writing captions, p. 164.

Lesson #3: Elements of Reading a Short Story (Grades 6-10)
A short story about the Holodomor, includes a worksheet and rubric, pp. 165-167.

Lesson #4: Analysis of a Short Story (Grades 9-12)
Analysis of a short story about the Holodomor, includes a worksheet, pp. 168-171.

LESSON #1: GROUP PROJECT

Grade Level:
Grades 9 to 12

Curriculum Fit / Specific Expectations / Learning Outcomes:
Select outcomes you wish to cover from either English language arts or social studies, history, politics, law, social justice, genocide, and religious studies and prepare an assessment to share with students at the outset.

Materials Required:

- Copies for each student of the short story, "Without Doctors and Priests, without Graves and Crosses," from *A Hunger Most Cruel*, by Olena Zvychayna, see Part IV, pp. 290-298, or "The Rings," Part IV, pp. 279-289
- Copies of Group Project Instruction Sheet for each student, pp. 162-163

Set-up Required:
Create student groups.

☑ PRE-TASK ACTIVITIES

- Teachers make copies of the short story, "Without Doctors and Priests, without Graves and Crosses," from *A Hunger Most Cruel*, by Olena Zvychayna, available in Part IV, pp. 290-298. The author takes the audience on an imaginary guided tour of Kharkiv during the Holodomor. An alternate short story is "The Rings" from *Kobzar's Children* by Marsha Skrypuch, also in Part IV, pp. 279-289.

- The teacher decides the learning outcome(s) that will be addressed in the activity and assessment, and communicates this to the students.

- Review the meanings of these words with the students, and ask them to keep these words in mind while reading the text: *intolerance, stereotypes, prejudices, discrimination, scapegoating, democracy and human rights, individual and collective responsibility, bystanders, rescuers, and perpetrators*. Define the words (15 minutes).

- Create groups of four students each. In each group assign roles such as leader, recorder, observer and presenter.

- Have students individually read the text, "Without Doctors and Priests, without Graves and Crosses," by Olena Zvychayna.

- Have the groups of students discuss the tasks in this assignment and choose one to work on (20 minutes). The list of tasks is on the instruction sheet on the following page.

- Students present their task activity to the class.

This lesson could be used as a culminating activity. An alternative short story, "The Rings," is found on pp. 279-289.

Lesson #1: Group Project Instruction Sheet

Oksana Kuryliw

"Without Doctors and Priests, Without Graves and Crosses"
by Olena Zvychayna

NOTE: An alternate short story is "The Rings" from Kobzar's Children *by Marsha Skrypuch. Each group has a choice of doing one of the following (20 minutes):*

a) FEATURE STORY — You are **investigative reporters** and have read the above short story. Write a **feature story**, which will deal with one or more of the concepts: *intolerance, stereotypes, prejudices, discrimination, scapegoating, democracy and human rights, individual and collective responsibility, bystanders, rescuers, and perpetrators.*

NOTE: Feature stories deal with human interest, a personal or historical issue, and/or an exposé.

b) EDITORIAL — You are **writing an editorial** on the situation presented to you in the short story.

Editorial writing puts forward a position, supports it with researched facts, statistics, details and illustrations and then discusses what should be done about the situation. Biases, if any, should be confirmed up front. The concepts *intolerance, stereotypes, prejudices, discrimination, scapegoating, democracy and human rights, individual and collective responsibility, bystanders, rescuers, and perpetrators,* as well as the story should be kept in mind when composing the editorial.

photocopy for students to fill out

c) DIAMANTE POEM — Write a **diamante poem**, using one of the concepts: *intolerance, stereotypes, prejudices, discrimination, scapegoating, democracy and human rights, individual and collective responsibility, bystanders, rescuers, and perpetrators,* keeping the short story in mind.

In a diamante poem:

- Line 1 consists of a one-word **subject (noun)**.
- Line 2 consists of two **adjectives** about the subject.
- Line 3 consists of three **participles** that refer to the subject.
- Line 4 consists of four words: **two that relate** to the **subject** and **two** that relate to the **opposite** of the subject (noun).
- Line 5 consists of three **participles that refer to the noun-opposite** of the subject.
- Line 6 consists of two **adjectives** that describe the noun-opposite of the subject.
- Line 7 consists of one word: a **noun-opposite** of the subject in Line 1.

This **diamante** is an ideal form to use with a **tan gram pattern** because it is meant to take the shape of a diamond ♦. Both a tan gram and diamante have seven parts; both have a geometric aspect. It is a real challenge to arrange the seven pieces into a shape that communicates the verbal message of the seven lines of the diamante.

See **http://www.mixbook.com/photo-books/all/tangram-poems-5451699** for examples.

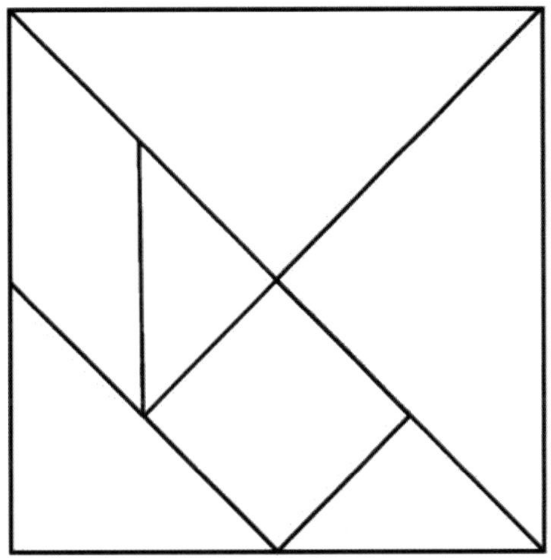

d) TABLEAUX — Create a **series of tableaux** based on the text that represents the concepts: *intolerance, stereotypes, prejudices, discrimination, scapegoating, democracy and human rights, individual and collective responsibility, bystanders, rescuers, and perpetrators.*

NOTE: A tableau is a dramatic activity where you physically construct a significant scene from literature through body placement, facial expressions, and the use of a few props. It is helpful to have an audience identify the "freeze frame," its importance, and the significance of the characters, their actions, and reactions in writing.

photocopy for students to fill out

e) CHORAL READING — Create a **choral reading** making sure *intolerance, stereotypes, prejudices, discrimination, scapegoating, democracy and human rights, individual and collective responsibility, bystanders, rescuers, and perpetrators* are used in the choral reading in a dramatic fashion.

Each group will **show, read** or **demonstrate** their completed work to the class (10 minutes).

☑ **POST TASK ACTIVITY**

REFLECTION — Have the students individually write what activity most helped them to understand the Holodomor. Ask the students to meet in their groups to share their reflections.

☑ **ASSESSMENT**

The teacher decides the assessment according to the learning outcome that was established.

Lesson #2: Daily Life During the Holodomor

This understanding through literature activity focuses on the daily life of people in Ukraine.

Grade Level:
Grades 6 to 12

Curriculum Fit / Specific Expectations / Learning Outcomes:
Please select outcomes you wish to cover from either English language arts, social studies, history, politics, law, social justice, genocide, and religious studies and prepare an assessment to share with the students at the outset.

Materials Required:

- A copy for each student of one story from any of the following publications:
  - *A Hunger Most Cruel: The Human Face of the 1932-1933 Terror-Famine in Soviet Ukraine*, A. Dimarov, Y. Hutsalo, O. Zvychayna. Language Lanterns Publications, 2002. Recommended reading: short stories by Anatoliy Dimarov, Yevhen Hutsalo, Olena Zvychayna. See Part IV, pp. 290-298.
  - "The Rings," in *Kobzar's Children*, Marsha Forchuk Skrypuch. Fitzhenry & Whiteside, 2006. See Part IV, pp. 279-289.

Set-up Required:
Create student groups.

☑ **PRE-TASK ACTIVITY**

Students read a story.

☑ **TASK 1 RESPONDING TO LITERATURE**

Students are asked to depict their impressions of the story by drawing an image that expresses how they felt, and writing a caption to explain their drawing.

☑ **POST-TASK ACTIVITY**

REFLECTION — What impact does this story have on you as a citizen? Students make notes individually, discuss the question in small groups, and then have a reporter from each group share their conclusions with the class. How would you compare the life of a child growing up in Soviet Ukraine in the 1930s to the life of a student in Canada today?

Lesson #3: Elements of Reading a Short Story

Grade Level:
Grade 6 to 10

Curriculum Fit / Specific Expectations / Learning Outcomes:
Select outcomes you wish to cover from either English language arts or social studies, history, politics, law, social justice, genocide, and religious studies and prepare an assessment to share with the students at the outset.

Materials Required:

- Copies of one of the stories from:
  - *A Hunger Most Cruel: The Human Face of the 1932-1933 Terror-Famine in Soviet Ukraine*, A. Dimarov, Y. Hutsalo, O. Zvychayna. Language Lanterns Publications, 2002 (short stories). See Part IV, pp. 290-298.
  - Documentary DVD on the Holodomor – *Genocide Revealed, Harvest of Despair,* or the *Soviet Story*
- Copies of the worksheet are on the next page for each student.

Set-up Required:
Equipment for viewing DVD.

☑ **PRE-TASK ACTIVITY**

- Show *Genocide Revealed* or the first 11 minutes of *Soviet Story* to give students a background about what was happening in Soviet Ukraine.
- Discuss the conditions of life and human rights in Soviet Ukraine. This could be done by brainstorming with the entire class.

☑ **TASK**

- Students read a story and complete a response to the literature assignment using the worksheet on p. 166.

☑ **ASSESSMENT**

- Use your rubric or the Assessment Rubric provided on p. 167.

Worksheet #1: Elements of Reading a Short Story

FOR GRADES 6-10

photocopy for students to fill out

Name of Story:

____

Read the story. Complete the questions below:

1. Select the 5 events that you consider to be most significant and list them in the order in which they occurred.

   a. __________________________________

   b. __________________________________

   c. __________________________________

   d. __________________________________

   e. __________________________________

2. Of these events, which do you think is the:

   c) Saddest? ______________________________

   d) Least believable? __________________________

   e) Happiest? ______________________________

   f) Most believable? __________________________

   g) Strangest? ______________________________

   h) Most terrifying? __________________________

3. Place yourself as the main character in the story and write a letter to your aunt explaining your feelings about your situation (1 page).

4. What are the consequences of these events on the life of the main character in the story? Decide on two possible scenarios.

Assessment Rubric: Elements of a Short Story

Knowledge/ Understanding	LEVEL 4	LEVEL 3	LEVEL 2	LEVEL 1
Uses facts from the short story to develop the letter.	Shows a high degree of effectiveness in using facts from the short story to develop the letter.	Shows considerable effectiveness in using facts from the short story to develop the letter.	Shows some effectiveness in using facts from the short story to develop the letter.	Shows a limited degree of effectiveness in using facts from the short story to develop the letter.
Demonstrates understanding of key ideas, concepts, terminology, and themes.	Demonstrates a high degree of understanding of key information, ideas, concepts, terminology, and themes.	Demonstrates considerable understanding of key information, ideas, concepts, terminology, and themes.	Demonstrates some understanding of key information, ideas, concepts, terminology, and themes.	Demonstrates a limited degree of understanding of key information, ideas, concepts, terminology, and themes.

Thinking	LEVEL 4	LEVEL 3	LEVEL 2	LEVEL 1
Analyzes and synthesizes information.	Analyzes and synthesizes information with a high degree of effectiveness.	Analyzes and synthesizes information with considerable effectiveness.	Analyzes and synthesizes information with some effectiveness.	Analyzes and synthesizes information with a limited degree of effectiveness.

Communication	LEVEL 4	LEVEL 3	LEVEL 2	LEVEL 1
Communicates position and ideas clearly.	Communicates information with a high degree of clarity.	Communicates information with considerable clarity.	Communicates information with some clarity.	Communicates information with a limited degree of clarity.
Uses proper conventions of language, grammar, and punctuation.	Uses proper conventions of language, grammar, and punctuation with a high degree of effectiveness.	Uses proper conventions of language, grammar, and punctuation with considerable effectiveness.	Uses proper conventions of language, grammar, and punctuation with some effectiveness.	Uses proper conventions of language, grammar, and punctuation with a limited degree of effectiveness.

Application	LEVEL 4	LEVEL 3	LEVEL 2	LEVEL 1
Draws appropriate conclusions in the chosen role.	Draws appropriate conclusions in the chosen role with a high degree of effectiveness.	Draws appropriate conclusions in the chosen role with considerable effectiveness.	Draws appropriate conclusions in the chosen role with some effectiveness.	Draws appropriate conclusions in the chosen role with a limited degree of effectiveness.
Uses persuasive images, words, and phrases true to role, audience, and format.	Shows a high degree of effectiveness in choosing persuasive images, words, and phrases that are true to role, audience, and format.	Shows considerable effectiveness in choosing persuasive images, words, and phrases that are true to role, audience, and format.	Shows some effectiveness in choosing persuasive images, words, and phrases that are true to role, audience, and format.	Shows limited effectiveness in choosing persuasive images, words, and phrases that are true to role, audience, and format.

photocopy for students to fill out

Lesson #4: Analysis of a Short Story

Grade Level:
Grades 9 to 12

Curriculum Fit / Specific Expectations / Learning Outcomes:
Please select outcomes you wish to cover from either English language arts or social studies, history, politics, law, social justice, genocide, and religious studies and prepare an assessment to share with the students at the outset.

Materials Required:

- Documentary DVDs: *Genocide Revealed* (Educational version), *Harvest of Despair* or first 11 minutes of *Soviet Story*
- Compilation of short stories from: *A Hunger Most Cruel: The Human Face of the 1932-1933 Terror- Famine in Soviet Ukraine*, A. Dimarov, Y. Hutsalo, O. Zvychayna. Language Lanterns Publications, 2002
- Recommended reading: story by Olena Zvychayna. Part IV, pp. 290-298
- "The Rings," *Kobzar's Children*, Marsha Forchuk Skrypuch, Fitzhenry & Whiteside, 2006. Part IV, pp. 279-289. Also available at **www.holodomor.ca/education**
- Copy of accompanying Worksheet #2 for each student, p. 169

Set-up Required:

- Equipment for viewing DVD
- Create student groups.

☑ **PRE-TASK ACTIVITY**

- Show the first part of any of the above-mentioned DVDs, which depict conditions of life in Soviet Ukraine in 1933.
- Brainstorm for words describing the conditions the conditions of life and human rights in Soviet Ukraine.
- Students read a story and complete the assignment using the worksheet "Analysis of a Short Story."

Worksheet #2: Analysis of a Short Story

GRADES 9-12

Title of story:

____

____

Author:

____

____

Description of the main character:

____

____

____

____

Main Plot:

____

____

____

____

Living Conditions:

____

____

____

____

Victims were:

____

____

____

photocopy for students to fill out

photocopy for students to fill out

Perpetrators were:

____

____

____

____

Henchmen were:

____

____

____

____

Bystanders/Observers were:

____

____

____

____

Rescuers were:

____

____

____

____

Examples of human rights abuses:

1. ______________________________

2. ______________________________

Examples of discrimination:

1. ______________________________

2. ______________________________

Effects on the human condition:

____

____

____

____

Two key items I learned from the story were:

1. ____

2. ____

Students share their answers in small groups.

Typical house (khata) in rural Ukraine, Chernihiv Oblast, 1977.

Project: Historical Fiction Book Review

The ***Historical Fiction Book Review*** *assignment is an excellent motivator for students of all levels to become hooked on history by reading an interesting novel based on historical facts. It is especially well suited as a means for students who are not academically inclined to learn of historical events. This assignment enables students to study key ideas, events, groups and individuals from a different historical period through literature. It encourages empathy for the characters in the narrative, with whom they may identify, to understand their challenges and to reflect on the commonality of human actions in specific circumstances, regardless of time or place. In studying the daily life of a book's characters, students also have the opportunity to learn about the political, social, economic, religious and cultural life of the times, their effect on the human condition and their consequences on the individual and society.*

In this project, students have the opportunity to analyze the historical significance of the Holodomor in the lives of the individuals and groups in the novel, compare and contrast that with their own lives, and examine the influence of historical events and ideas on our contemporary way of life. Through this written assignment students will develop their abilities to analyze, synthesize, think critically and clearly communicate their ideas.

Grade Level:
Grades 7 to 12

Curriculum Fit / Specific Expectations / Learning Outcomes:
Select outcomes you wish to cover from either English language arts, social studies, history, politics, law, social justice, genocide, and religious studies and prepare an assessment to share with the students at the outset.

Materials Required:

- Copies of the instruction sheet, checklist, and rubric for each student
- Select the historical novel(s) to be studied.

Recommended novels:

- *Maria: A Chronicle of a Life*
  Author: Ulas Samchuk
  Translator: Roma Franko
  Publisher: Language Lanterns Publications (2011)
  ISBN-10: 0987775006 Website: **www.ucrdc.org**
- *Stones Under the Scythe*
  Author: Olha Mak
  Translator: Vera Kachmarskyj
  Publisher: iUniverse.com (2011)
  ISBN-10: 1462010385 Website: **www.ucrdc.org**

Set-up Required:

- (Optional) If several suitable novels are available for this assignment, create a display of these books for students to examine.

☑ **PRE-TASK ACTIVITY**

- Discuss with students how novels can be a good source of historical information.
- Introduce the Historical Fiction Book Review assignment to students using the Instruction Sheet on p. 175. Go over expectations and criteria for assessment using the rubric on p. 174.
- You may wish to read a few pages or a chapter from a historical fiction novel and model how to extract historical information.
- Students select a historical fiction novel that deals with the time period covered by the Holodomor.
- **NOTE:** It is advisable to share selected book titles with students, provide them with a suggested book, or visit the library that has ensured that books on the topic are available.

☑ **TASK**

- Students read the novel and complete the checklist on p. 176.

☑ **ASSESSMENT**

- Determine the assessment according to the learning outcomes selected, or use the rubric on p. 174.

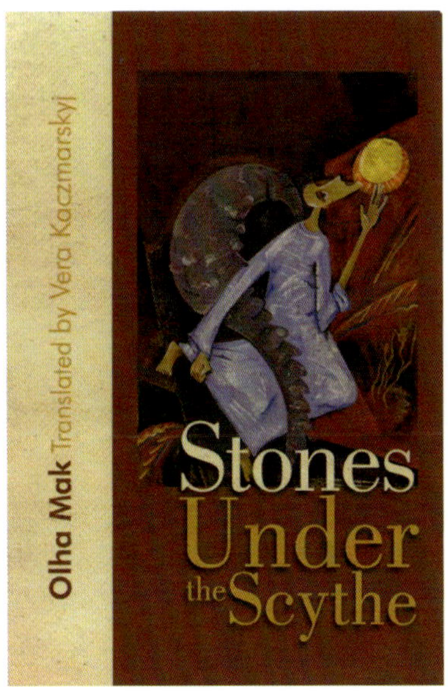

Assessment Rubric: Historical Fiction Book Review

Knowledge/ Understanding	LEVEL 4	LEVEL 3	LEVEL 2	LEVEL 1
Demonstrates knowledge of relevant historical terminology, facts, and ideas.	Demonstrates thorough knowledge of relevant historical terminology, facts, and ideas.	Demonstrates considerable knowledge of relevant historical terminology, facts, and ideas.	Demonstrates some knowledge of relevant historical terminology, facts, and ideas.	Demonstrates limited knowledge of relevant historical terminology, facts, and ideas.
Demonstrates understanding of author's key ideas and themes.	Demonstrates a thorough understanding of author's key ideas and themes.	Demonstrates considerable understanding of author's key, ideas and themes.	Demonstrates some understanding of author's key ideas, concepts and themes.	Demonstrates a limited understanding of author's key ideas and themes.

Thinking	LEVEL 4	LEVEL 3	LEVEL 2	LEVEL 1
Uses historical evidence to draw logical conclusions about key themes, characters, setting, and lifestyle.	Uses historical evidence to draw logical conclusions about key themes, characters, setting, and lifestyle with a high degree of effectiveness.	Uses historical evidence to draw logical conclusions about key themes, characters, setting, and lifestyle with considerable effectiveness.	Uses historical evidence to draw logical conclusions about key themes, characters, setting, and lifestyle with some effectiveness.	Uses historical evidence to draw logical conclusions about key themes, characters, setting, and lifestyle with a limited degree of effectiveness.
Analyzes and evaluates key ideas and information.	Analyzes and evaluates key ideas and information with a high degree of effectiveness.	Analyzes and evaluates key ideas and information with considerable effectiveness.	Analyzes and evaluates key ideas and information with some effectiveness.	Analyzes and evaluates key ideas and information with a limited degree of effectiveness.

Communication	LEVEL 4	LEVEL 3	LEVEL 2	LEVEL 1
Expresses ideas.	Expresses ideas with a high degree of clarity.	Expresses ideas with considerable clarity.	Expresses ideas with some clarity.	Expresses ideas with a limited degree of clarity.
Organizes information.	Organizes information with a high degree of logic.	Organizes information with considerable logic.	Organizes information with some logic.	Organizes information with a limited degree of logic.
Uses proper conventions of language, grammar, and punctuation.	Uses proper conventions of language, grammar, and punctuation with a high degree of effectiveness.	Uses proper conventions of language, grammar, and punctuation with considerable effectiveness.	Uses proper conventions of language, grammar, and punctuation with some effectiveness.	Uses proper conventions of language, grammar, and punctuation with a limited degree of effectiveness.

Application	LEVEL 4	LEVEL 3	LEVEL 2	LEVEL 1
Applies knowledge of relevant concepts and literary skills (e.g., tone, point of view, audience, style) to draw supported conclusions about the book's purpose and effectiveness.	Applies knowledge of relevant concepts and skills with a high degree of effectiveness to draw supported conclusions about the book's purpose and effectiveness.	Applies knowledge of relevant concepts and skills with considerable effectiveness to draw supported conclusions about the book's purpose and effectiveness.	Applies knowledge of relevant concepts and skills with some effectiveness to draw supported conclusions about the book's purpose and effectiveness.	Applies knowledge of relevant concepts and skills with a limited degree of effectiveness to draw supported conclusions about the book's purpose and effectiveness.

photocopy for students to fill out

Instruction Sheet: Historical Fiction Book Review

1,000 words / 100 Marks

Assignment due: ____________________

Format

- title page
- write on every other line
- number pages
- use paragraphs
- write up to 1,000 words

Select a historical novel about the life of an individual or event that reflects the chosen historical period. Read the novel and write a book review that includes all of the components below.

Presentation

Introduction	>	State the title of the novel, author, publisher, date published and number of pages.
	>	Include a short biography on the author (date of birth, place of residence, experiences that influenced their work, other works, etc.).
Main plot	>	State the historical periods covered in the novel, summarize the plot, and describe the main characters (100-200 words).
Main emphasis	>	Select three aspects of life described in the novel (e.g., political, economic, religious, military, cultural, social). How are they presented? What did you learn, for example, about the social conditions in the society? Describe what life was like using three specific events or facts from the story for each of the aspects of life.
Analysis	>	Analyze the style used to tell the story. Was the novel well written? Logically presented? Difficult to read? Why? Did the author present a realistic account of life during those times? Support your reflections with concrete facts. Did the author include maps, pictures or known historical figures? What is the novel's audience, tone and point of view? What are the main themes?
Conclusion	>	Your overall impression of the book. Would you recommend this book? Why or why not?

photocopy for students to fill out

photocopy for students to fill out

Checklist: Historical Fiction Book Review

Please complete the following checklist prior to submitting your book review. Checklist must be submitted along with the assignment.

☐ I have read the assigned book in its entirety.

The introductory paragraphs of my book review include:

☐ the name of the book
☐ the name of the author
☐ the publisher, date and location of publication
☐ the number of pages in the book
☐ the author's relevant biographical information (e.g., date of birth, place of residence, education, experiences that influenced their work, relevant affiliations, other works, etc.)

The body of my book review includes:

☐ a brief summary of the book's plot
☐ a brief description of the main characters
☐ the book's audience, tone, and point of view
☐ the main ideas or themes in the book
☐ a description of three aspects of life (e.g., political, economic, religious, military, cultural, personal) with three examples for each
☐ a critique of the author's style (e.g., Are the order of events in the book logical? Is the story convincing? Is the book confusing to read?)

The concluding paragraphs of my book review include:

☐ My overall impression of the book
☐ My opinion for recommending the book to someone else… why or why not?
☐ Title page for my assignment
☐ Citations for any quotations or ideas I have used in my assignment
☐ My editing notes

☐ I have checked the rubric to make sure my assignment addresses the expectations.

Lesson: Historical Novel Analysis

Maria: A Chronicle of Life

*This **historical novel lesson** encourages students to think critically about history through the identification an analysis of continuity and change. Students read excerpts from a historical novel to extract information about the events, people, and time period portrayed. They explore sections of Ulas Samchuk's* Maria: A Chronicle of a Life, *to compare and contrast life in Ukraine before and during the Holodomor. Students identify similarities and differences through examining various aspects of life, including in political, social, and cultural realms, and record their findings in a Venn diagram.*

Grade Level:
Grades 9 to 12

Curriculum Fit / Specific Expectations / Learning Outcomes:
Select outcomes you wish to cover from either English language arts, social studies, history, politics, law, social justice, genocide, and religious studies, and prepare an assessment to share with the students at the outset.

Materials Required:

- Find a copy of *Maria: A Chronicle of a Life* in the library.
- Choose excerpt from the book. Make copies for the class.
- Copies of the Venn diagram, p. 179, for each student

Set-up Required:
Students will work at their desks.

☑ **PRE-TASK ACTIVITIES**

- Discuss with students how novels can be a good source of historical information.
- Distribute the excerpts and the Venn diagram graphic organizer to students.
- Introduce the Venn diagram to students. Explain how it is used to compare and contrast information.
- Prompt students to consider the following when reading the excerpts:
    - What has changed? What evidence exists to show the changes took place? Why did things change? Who was affected by the changes? Who made the changes?
    - What has stayed the same? What evidence exists to show things have stayed the same or not? Why did things stay the same or why did they change?
    - Were the changes positive or negative? Explain.

☑ **TASK ACTIVITIES**

- Students read the excerpts from the book.
- Students record similarities in the inner portion of the diagram where the circles overlap and the differences in the outer portions of the diagram under the appropriate headings.

☑ **POST-TASK ACTIVITIES**

- Students submit a paragraph about their conclusions based on their analysis of the information extracted from the excerpts.

"Despair in Ukraine," by Anna Romaniak.

Worksheet: Venn Diagram

Similarities and Differences Between Life Before and During the Holodomor

Name: ____________________________ **Date:** ____________________________

Complete the following Venn Diagram to show life in a Ukrainian village before the Holodomor (1920s) in the left circle, and life during the Holodomor (1933) in the right circle. In the middle of the diagram, where the circles overlap, record how life was the same before and during the Holodomor.

photocopy for students to fill out

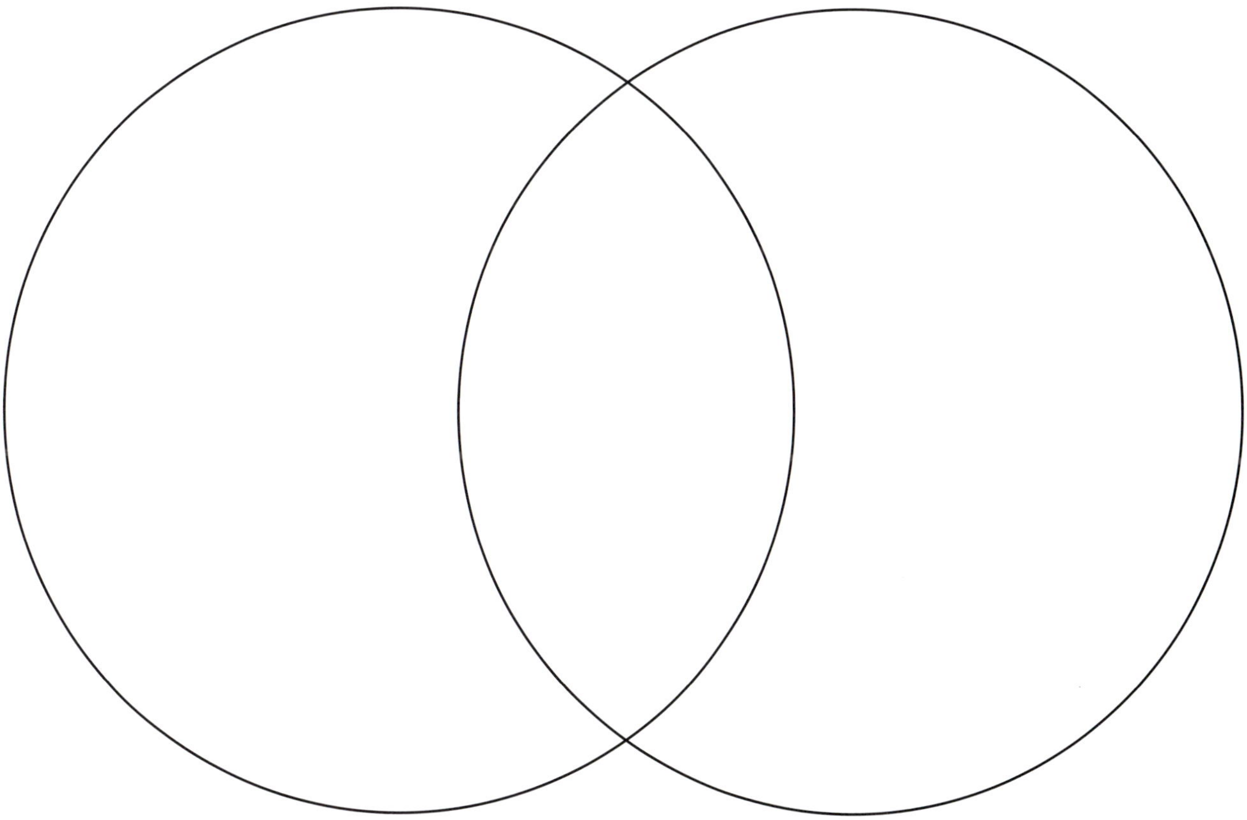

Lesson: Analysis of a Historical Document

*In analyzing a **historical document**, students develop critical thinking skills. There are three suggested stages for analyzing a historical document adapted to various age groups, and each is progressively more difficult and requires greater skills. It is important to approach the analysis of a historical document in this sequence. This analysis gives students an opportunity to practice the historian's craft by examining a primary document as a key resource in understanding a specific event. By examining such a document, the students use the "historical method" to re-construct the narrative of the event. In this manner, students act like detectives in extracting information.*

teacher tip

Each group may receive the same document to work on, or different documents from the same time period.

Worksheet #1: Analysis of a Historical Document (Grades 6-8)

Worksheet #2: Analysis of a Historical Document (Grades 9-10)

Worksheet #3: Analysis of a Historical Document (Grades 11-12)

Grade Level:
Grades 6 to 12

Curriculum Fit / Specific Expectations / Learning Outcomes:
Select outcomes you wish to cover from either English language arts, social studies, history, politics, law, social justice, genocide, and religious studies, and prepare an assessment to share with the students at the outset.

Materials Required:

- Student copies of the historical documents on the Holodomor, Part II, pp. 81-93 and the assignment on the worksheet appropriate for the grade level. Teachers may choose the documents they want their students to examine.
- Suggested documents from Ruslan Pyrih's book, *Holodomor of 1932-33 in Ukraine: Documents and Materials* (Kyiv: Mohyla Academy Publishing House, 2008). Excerpts are found in Part II, pp. 81-93:
    - Resolution: "On safekeeping property of state enterprises, collective farms and cooperatives and strengthening public (socialist) property" (excerpt) August 7, 1932, Part II, pp. 81-82.
    - Letter from Stalin to Kaganovich on changing Ukrainian SSR Leadership (excerpt), August 11, 1932. Stalin and Kaganovich Correspondence 1931-1936 (Moscow, 2001), Part II, pp. 83-84.

- "Resolution of the CC AUCP(b) and USSR SNK on grain procurement in Ukraine, the Northern Caucasus and the Western Oblast," December 14, 1932, part II, pp 85-87.
- Report from "Balitsky to the OGPU on the mass exodus of villagers from Ukraine," January 22, 1933, Part II, pp. 88-89.
- Report from "Yagoda to Stalin and Molotov on measures for preventing mass exodus of villagers from the Ukrainian SSR, Northern Caucasus and Belorussian SSR," February 2, 1933, Part II, p. 90.
- Summary of reports from "MTS Political Sections in Kyiv Oblast on famine, death and the anti-Soviet moods among collective farmers (excerpt)," June 14, 1933, Part II, pp. 91-92.
- Report of the "All-Union Resettlement Committee on resettling collective farmers in Ukraine" (with table), December 29, 1933, Part II, p. 93.

Set-up Required:

- Organize students into groups of 5-6 students in each.
- Prepare chart paper for recording student findings for display in the class. **NOTE**: Teachers may wish to designate the reading and analysis of a historical document as a pre-task activity, followed by viewing a film or reading literature or a historical essay. **For example**: DVDs, excerpts from literature, newspaper articles, etc. See pp. 133-134 for ideas.

☑ **PRE-TASK ACTIVITIES**

1. **It is recommended that the teacher analyze one document with the entire class to model expectations. Only then should students attempt to analyze a document on their own. This type of modeling is crucial whenever a new skill is introduced.**

2. **These documents may be found in Part II, pp. 81-93 and on the website www.education.holodomor.ca/educational-resources-list/pyrih-documents/**

☑ **TASK**

- Have students take on roles within the group (leader, presenter, recorder, researcher, timekeeper, etc.). All students are also researchers.
- Have students analyze the document as outlined for their grade level. The presenter reports the findings to the class, which are recorded on the blackboard or on chart paper.

photocopy for students to fill out

Worksheet #1: Analysis of a Historical Document

FOR GRADES 6-8

Work in groups of 4-6 students each. Divide the group roles among yourselves (leader, recorder, presenter, researcher, timekeeper). Analyze the document using the questions below. The presenter reports the findings to the class, which are recorded on the blackboard or on chart paper.

Each group may receive the same document to work on, or different documents from the same time period.

Stage 1: Analysis of a historical document

a) Who is the author of the document?

b) Is it a single individual or a group of people?

c) What can we learn about the author's position, social class, nationality, and political views from the document?

d) When and where was the document written?

e) Who was the intended reader of the document?

f) What do we learn about the times from this document? (5 items)

g) In your opinion, is the document credible? Why or why not?

h) Is the language of the document easy to understand?

i) Is it addressed to more than one individual? Explain.

j) What main ideas are expressed in the document?

Follow-up assignment for individual students:

Write a one-page essay using the information taken from the group's analysis of the document, explaining what you learned about the Ukrainian Genocide in 1932-33. Use the terms *perpetrator, victim, rescuer, bystander* when relevant.

Worksheet #2: Analysis of a Historical Document

FOR GRADES 9-10

Work in groups of 4-6 students each. Divide the group roles among yourselves — leader, recorder, presenter, researcher, timekeeper. Analyze the document using the questions below. The presenter reports the findings to the class, which are recorded on the blackboard or on chart paper.

Each group may receive the same document to work on, or different documents from the same time period.

Stage 1: Analysis of a historical document

a) Who is the author of the document?

b) Is it a single individual or a group of people?

c) What can we learn about the author's position, social class, nationality, and political views from the document?

d) When and where was the document written?

e) Who was the intended reader of the document?

f) What do we learn about the times from this document? (5 items)

g) In your opinion, is the document credible? Why or why not?

h) Is the language of the document easy to understand?

i) Is it addressed to more than one individual? Explain.

j) What main ideas are expressed in the document?

Stage 2:

1. What is the purpose of this document?
2. Is it a convincing document that logically outlines its position?
3. Does it entertain?
4. Is it emotionally charged? If so, select words from the document that illustrate this.
5. What is the genre of the document? (Formal/official, letter, etc.)
6. Is it grammatically correct, with proper punctuation, etc.?
7. What are your general impressions about the document?

Follow-up assignment for individual students:

Write a one-page essay using the information taken from the group's analysis of the document, explaining what you learned about the Ukrainian Genocide in 1932-33. Use the terms *perpetrator, victim, rescuer, bystander* when relevant.

Worksheet #3: Analysis of a Historical Document

FOR GRADES 11-12

Work in groups of 4-6 students each. Divide the group roles among yourselves—leader, recorder, presenter, researcher, timekeeper. Analyze the document using the questions below. The presenter reports the findings to the class, which are recorded on the blackboard or on a chart paper.

Each group may receive the same document to work on, or different documents from the same time period.

photocopy for students to fill out

Stage 1: Analysis of a historical document

a) Who is the author of the document?

b) Is it a single individual or a group of people?

c) What can we learn about the author's position, social class, nationality, and political views from the document?

d) When and where was the document written?

e) Who was the intended reader of the document?

f) What do we learn about the times from this document? (5 items)

g) In your opinion, is the document credible? Why or why not?

h) Is the language of the document easy to understand?

i) Is it addressed to more than one individual? Explain.

j) What main ideas are expressed in the document?

Stage 2:

1. What is the purpose of this document?
2. Is it a convincing document that logically outlines its position?
3. Does it entertain?
4. Is it emotionally charged? If so, select words from the document that illustrate this.
5. What is the genre of the document? (Formal/official, letter, etc.)
6. Is it grammatically correctly, with proper punctuation, etc.?
7. What are your general impressions about this document?

Stage 3:
A critical analysis of the document. Use your imagination:

a) How important is this document? Be investigative.

b) Is it telling the truth?

c) What evidence is presented to support its claims?

d) What other points of view might there be on the subject under discussion?

e) What can you learn about the society from which it came? (5 things)

f) What were the society's values/beliefs? What was important to that society?

g) What does this document mean to me? What have I learned? Be sure to examine it by looking at concepts like perpetrators, victims, bystanders, rescuers, henchmen.

Follow-up assignment for individual students:

Write a one-page essay using the information taken from the group's analysis of the document, explaining what you learned about the Ukrainian Genocide in 1932-33. Use the terms *perpetrator, victim, rescuer, bystander* when relevant.

Soviet hramota, *Soviet certificate of achievement in schools, UCRDC Toronto.*

Project: Holodomor Jigsaw

Valentina Kuryliw

*The **Holodomor Jigsaw** learning strategy requires higher order critical thinking skills. It is a cooperative learning strategy in which each student works in two groups (home group and expert group) to deal with a complex assignment requiring the efficient analysis of a number of primary materials. In this activity, students are divided into "Expert" groups responsible for reading and thoroughly comprehending a primary source document on the Holodomor. They consult with other students who are responsible for analyzing the same document before presenting the key facts, ideas, and importance of their primary source to their "Home" group members. This strategy allows students to obtain an in-depth understanding of several key primary sources in a short period of time, and is an opportunity to teach each other. It also teaches students about teamwork, accountability, and communicating clearly.*

Grade Level:
Grades 10 to 12

Curriculum Fit / Specific Expectations / Learning Outcomes:
Please select outcomes you wish to cover from either social studies, history, politics, law, social justice, genocide,religious studies, and prepare an assessment to share with the students at the outset.

Materials Required:

- One copy of each primary source document per group of four students from Part II, pp. 81-93 of this learning resource OR from the book, *Holodomor of 1932-33 in Ukraine: Documents and Materials*, compiled by Ruslan Pyrih (Kyiv: Kyiv Mohyla Academy Publishing House, 2008)
- Copies of Jigsaw Chart on which each student will fill out information regarding the documents

Setup required:

- Prepare copies of the primary source documents. Put the same identifying number on each copy of the same document.
- Clearly explain the Jigsaw procedure, step by step.
- Divide students into Home and Expert groups.

For larger classes, six groups are recommended for each "Home" group using a different document.

☑ **TASK**

- The teacher analyzes a single document with the whole class to ensure that students know what is expected, i.e. models expectations.
- Divide class into groups of four to six students. These will be students' "Home" groups (four groups min; six groups max).
- Assign each student in the "Home" group a different primary source document to analyze. For example, each "Home" group will have documents numbered 1, 2, 3, 4, (5, 6 if needed).
- Each student is to receive a Jigsaw Chart to complete.
- Students read and conduct a preliminary analysis of their individual document.
- Create four to six new "Expert" groups comprised of students who analyzed the same document but are in different "Home" groups. For example, all Document #1s are from one "Expert" group, Document #2s are from second "Expert" group, etc.
- "Expert" groups choose one classmate to fulfill each of the following roles:
  - group leader (ensures everyone has the opportunity to participate and that opinions are respected)
  - time keeper (ensures the discussion is on topic and manages the group's discussion time)
  - recorder (records the group's interpretation, analysis, and evidence)
- Students discuss their interpretation and analysis within their "Expert" group and come to a consensus about the most important points.
- Students then return to their "Home" groups to teach their peers about their primary source. Group members make notes on a chart provided by the teacher, based on the information communicated by members of each "Expert" group (example document 1, 2, 3, 4, 5, 6). Thus, all documents will have been analyzed in a short period of time. This is done by students teaching each other about all the documents involved.
- All tasks should be completed within a specified amount of time.

Variations

- Documents or artifacts may consist of photographs, newspaper articles, video clips, audio clips, poetry, artwork, quotations, caricatures, etc.
- A Jigsaw assignment could be created using different types of artifacts. The Jigsaw Document Chart artifacts can be used. See p. 188.

☑ **POST-TASK ACTIVITIES**

- Students may compare two of the primary sources in a written paragraph assignment.
- Data may be used for subsequent activities and assignments (e.g. reflections, essays, presentations, debates, etc.).

photocopy for students to fill out

Holodomor Jigsaw Chart

Name of Document	Author Date created Location	Primary source type (e.g., article, letter, etc.)	Intended audience	What is the artifact about? Be specific.	Why was it created? What is the anticipated consequence? Provide evidence.	Is there evidence of bias? Identify any emotionally charged words.	What is important about this primary source?

Lesson: Reinterpreting History

Historians write about an issue, event or person from a particular point of view. If historians reach similar conclusions, their shared view of history becomes the "standard" interpretation. However, over time new generations of historians re-examine the event, and in light of new evidence, values and biases, may come to a substantially different interpretation.

Grade Level:
Grades 11 to 12

Curriculum Fit / Specific Expectations / Learning Outcomes:
Select outcomes you wish to cover from either English language arts, social studies, history, politics, law, social justice, genocide, or religious studies and prepare an assessment to share with students at the outset.

Materials Required:

- Any of the folllowing documentaries:
  - *Harvest of Despair* (55 min.)
  - *Genocide Revealed* (26 min.)
  - *Soviet Story* (first 11 min.)
  - *Holodomor, Voices of Survivors* (30 min.)
- Copies for each student of one eyewitness account in Part II, pp. 77-80 or the essay "The Holodomor, 1932-1933," by V. Kuryliw, pp. 21-28

Set-up Required:

- Equipment for viewing documentary
- Create student groups.

Recommended as a culminating activity.

☑ PRE-TASK ACTIVITIES

- Students experience different perspectives on the Genocidal Famine by reading an eyewitness account, watching a documentary or reading "The Holodomor: 1932-1933," V. Kuryliw's essay from Part II, pp. 21-28.

☑ TASK ACTIVITY: REINTERPRETING HISTORY

THE HOLODOMOR 1932-1933[34]

- In groups of 4 students create a list of 10 historical issues, events or people that you think have undergone a substantial change in interpretation as a result of the passage of time. Group your examples and explain reasons for the change.
- In your group discuss the following questions: If you wanted the most reliable information on the Ukrainian Famine, would you prefer to hear from a person who was recently involved in the event itself, or would you prefer to hear from a person who was 80 or more years removed from the event? Can you suggest advantages and disadvantages of both sources of information? What strengths and weaknesses would each have? This may be done in chart form.
- Write a one-page essay called *Searching for Truth*. Do we get nearer to the truth the closer we are to the event or the more removed we are from it? Suggest reasons to support your position using the "The Holodomor 1932-1933" essay as your example.
- Read the quotation below. What does it mean? How does it relate to the Holodomor?

> ***"The intrusion of history is not just theoretical. It is also the legacy of being an accomplice or a victim, or just an onlooker. In each case, history entails the uncomfortable presence of earlier unresolved roles."***
>
> Charles S. Maier, historian, Harvard University.

☑ POST-TASK ACTIVITY

REFLECTION – How has my view of history been affected by this activity?

34 Adapted from "Vision and Revision in History." *CBC News in Review*, Teaching Guide, 1995. p. 30.

Lesson: Raphael Lemkin

*Information about **Lemkin**'s contributions to justice are provided in Part II, pp. 57-64.*

Grade Level:
Grades 10 to 12

Curriculum Fit / Specific Expectations / Learning Outcomes:
Select outcomes you wish to cover from either social studies, history, politics, law, social justice, genocide, or religious studies and prepare an assessment to share with students at the outset.

Materials Required:

- Text of the UN Convention on the Prevention and Punishment of the Crime of Genocide available online at **https://treaties.un.org/doc/publication/unts/volume%2078/volume-78-i-1021-english.pdf**
  Click on "Text of the Convention" or excerpts of the Convention from Part II, pg. 59 and pp. 62-64.
- Copies for each student of either "Excerpts from Raphael Lemkin's Soviet Genocide in Ukraine" in Part II, pp. 60-61 or the full text in Part IV, pp. 262-266
- Copies of the question sheet for each student, found on p. 192

Set-up Required:
N/A

☑ **PRE-TASK ACTIVITY**

- The class should discuss the UN Convention on Genocide by reviewing excerpts of the document, p. 59 and pp. 62-64, or visit website listed above.
- Teachers should discuss Raphael Lemkin's contribution to the concept of genocide.

☑ **TASK**

- Students read excerpts from Raphael Lemkin's "Soviet Genocide in the Ukraine" Part II, pp. 60-61, or Part IV, pp. 262-266.
- In groups or individually answer the questions on p. 192.

☑ **POST-TASK ACTIVITY**

- What more do you want to know about the Holodomor of 1932-1933?
- In your opinion, is the Holodomor related to the events unfolding in Ukraine since 2013? Explain.

Worksheet: Raphael Lemkin on the Holodomor

Read the handout with excerpts from Raphael Lemkin's, "Soviet Genocide in the Ukraine." In groups or individually, answer the following questions:

1. What reason does Lemkin give for the Soviet attack on the Ukrainian population in the 1930s?
2. What is meant by "Russification?" What are its implications for Ukrainians?
3. According to Lemkin, how did the Soviets plan to destroy the Ukrainian nation?
4. List the 4 steps by which this destruction was attempted. How was each step carried out?
5. According to Lemkin, why was it necessary to destroy a large number of Ukrainian farmers?
6. How did the Soviets plan and carry out the Genocidal Famine in Ukraine?
7. According to Lemkin, how does the Ukrainian Genocide differ from the Holocaust?
8. What evidence has Lemkin presented that this was indeed an attempt to destroy a culture and a nation?
9. What are your feelings about Lemkin's ideas on the "Soviet Genocide in Ukraine." Explain in one paragraph.
10. What contribution do you think Raphael Lemkin made by devoting so much of his life to trying to make genocide a criminal act? In your opinion should a sovereign state have the right to declare internal enemies and dispose of them?

Bonus: Who do you believe were the perpetrators of the Ukrainian Genocidal Famine? How should they be remembered or portrayed?

photocopy for students to fill out

Lesson: The Holodomor in the Press

This set of activities provides an opportunity for students to learn about the Genocidal Famine while developing the skills to analyze opinion pieces in newspapers. Students will learn to identify the main idea of an article and the reasons for it being written. They will use a specific newspaper article to learn how to analyze and examine different viewpoints in news articles and examine the sources or lack of sources to back up points of views.

> **Worksheet #1:** "World Forgets, Canada Remembers" by Eric Margolis
> **Worksheet #2:** "A Tale of Truth and Two Journalists" by Ian Hunter

Lesson #1: "World Forgets, Canada Remembers"

Eric Margolis, "World Forgets, Canada Remembers," *Toronto Sun*, June 1, 2008

Grade Level:
Grades 10 to 12

Curriculum Fit / Specific Expectations / Learning Outcomes:
Select outcomes you wish to cover from media studies, English language arts, social studies, history, politics, law, social justice, genocide, or religious studies and prepare an assessment to share with students at the outset.

Materials Required:

- Copies of the article for each student see Part II, pp. 94-95
- Copies of Worksheet #1 for analyzing an opinion piece article, p. 194

Set-up Required:
N/A

photocopy for students to fill out

☑ **TASK**

- Read the article by Eric Margolis, "World Forgets, Canada Remembers," *Toronto Sun*, June 1, 2008 and answer the questions suggested for analyzing an opinion piece article using Worksheet #1, p. 194.

teacher tip

An additional newspaper article can be found in the Appendix, pp. 299-300, "Behind Ukraine's protest are memories of Moscow's famine" by Marta Baziuk, *Globe and Mail*, Dec. 11, 2013.

photocopy for students to fill out

Worksheet #1: "World Forgets, Canada Remembers"

By Eric Margolis, *Toronto Sun*, June 1, 2008

Read Eric Margolis' article and answer the following questions:

Stage 1

1. What event led to the writing of the article?
2. What is the main idea of the article?
3. Select several facts/arguments (3 minimum), which support the main idea.
4. Does the author provide enough factual material to support his ideas (quotes witnesses, provides statistics, states his sources of information)? Was he an eyewitness to events, or was the information obtained through a news service?
5. In your opinion, is the reportage true, balanced or biased? Explain.
6. Are different viewpoints presented? Is this article an editorial (i.e. the author's own ideas). Is it informative, is it convincing, is it balanced?
7. What do you think of the article and its point of view? Explain.

NOTE: Stage 1 questions can be used for the analysis of any newspaper article.

Stage 2

a) According to the author, why did the Soviet Union want to destroy the Ukrainian farmers as such?

b) Who were the perpetrators/henchmen of the Holodomor?

c) What other actions besides the use of starvation were used against the Ukrainian population? Which other groups of people within the Soviet Union also suffered from the actions of the Soviet government?

d) State two reasons why Canada recognized the Holodomor. Do you think Canada can do more to acknowledge the Holodomor? Explain.

e) How did Western nations deal with the Holodomor? Did nations commemorate it? Explain.

f) In his article, Margolis states that "If we keep demanding that Germany and Japan atone for their wartime crimes, is it not time for our governments to finally recognize and atone their alliances with the biggest mass murderer in history, Stalin?" Do you agree or disagree with this statement? Explain why. Give one or two suggestions as to what can be done to atone for these tragic events in history.

Lesson #2: "A Tale of Truth and Two Journalists"

Ian Hunter. "A Tale of Truth and Two Journalists," *Report Magazine*, March 27, 2000

Grade Level:
Grades 10 to 12

Curriculum Fit / Specific Expectations / Learning Outcomes:
Select outcomes you wish to cover from media studies, English language arts, social studies, history, politics, law, social justice, genocide, or religious studies and prepare an assessment to share with students at the outset.

Materials Required:

- Copies of the article for each student. See Part II, pp. 96-97
- Copies of the Worksheet #2 for analyzing an article, p. 196

Set-up Required:
N/A

☑ **TASK**

- Read Ian Hunter's article, "A Tale of Truth and Two Journalists," March 27, 2000, in *Report Magazine* and answer the questions on Worksheet #2.

Empty house, Kharkiv Oblast, 1933.

Worksheet #2: "A Tale of Truth and Two Journalists"

By Ian Hunter, *Report Magazine*, March 27, 2000

Read Ian Hunter's article and answer the following questions:

Stage 1

1. What event led to the writing of the article?
2. What is the main idea of the article?
3. Select several facts/arguments (3 minimum), that support the main idea.
4. Does the author provide enough factual material to support his ideas (quotes witnesses, provides statistics, states his sources of information)? Was he an eyewitness to events, or was the information obtained through a news service?
5. Is the reportage, in your opinion, true, balanced or biased? Explain.
6. Are different viewpoints presented? Is this article an editorial (author's own ideas), is it informative, is it convincing, is it balanced?
7. What do you think of the article and its point of view? Explain.

NOTE: Stage 1 questions can be used for the analysis of any newspaper article.

photocopy for students to fill out

Stage 2

a. How did Muggeridge and Duranty present events in Ukraine in 1933? Use the chart below.

b. What explanation is given for discrepancies between the writings of the two journalists? In your opinion, who told the truth? Explain why.

c. Write a short letter to the editor about how you feel about Duranty and his Pulitzer Prize for journalism.

OPPOSING VIEWPOINTS ON HOLODOMOR

Both journalists wrote about the Holodomor, but each presented his own point of view. List each journalist's ideas in the chart below.

Malcolm Muggeridge	Walter Duranty

Lesson: Analyzing Eyewitness Accounts

*The power of **eyewitness accounts** comes from their immediacy. Accounts of historical events can have an emotional impact on students. These accounts help them to understand the past by looking at events through the eyes of the people who lived them. They offer an interesting and rewarding learning experience and perspective.*

Grade Level:
Grades 6 to 12

Curriculum Fit / Specific Expectations / Learning Outcomes:
Select outcomes you wish to cover from either English language arts, social studies, history, politics, law, social justice, genocide, or religious studies and prepare an assessment to share with the students at the outset.

Suggested Pre-Task Activities for background information on the Holodomor:

DVDs:

- *Holodomor—Let Their Memory Be Eternal* by CanadInns (15 min.) that can be ordered through **mcindy@canadinns.com**
- *Soviet Story* (first 11 min.)
- *Genocide Revealed* – Educational Version (26 min.)
- *Holodomor, Voices of Survivors* (30 min.)

Websites:

- **www.holodomorsurvivors.ca**
- **www.sharethestory.ca**

Materials Suggested:

- Student copies of eyewitness accounts Part II, pp. 77-80
- Each of three groups will receive one of the two eyewitness accounts.
- Make copies of Case Studies #1 (pp. 77-78) and #2 (pp. 79-80) of eyewitness accounts.
- Copies of culminating activity, assessment form for interviews, and rubric for writing an article

Set-up Required:

- Equipment for viewing DVD
- Form six groups of students.

Worksheet #1: Working with Transcripts
Worksheet #2: Working with Documentaries
Culminating Activity: Conducting an interview and writing an article. An assessment form and rubric are provided.

Worksheet #1: Working with Transcripts

Eyewitness Accounts

Students will be divided into six groups. Three groups will receive Eyewitness Account #1 (pp.78-79) and three groups will receive Eyewitness Account #2 (pp. 79-80). Students will read the eyewitness account and answer the following questions in their groups:

1. Identify the eyewitness (age, gender and location) and the historical event in his/her life.

2. How did this event affect his/her life? Give 3 to 5 specific examples.

3. What did you learn about the event from this account? (Why and where did it happen? Who were the perpetrators and victims?)

photocopy for students to fill out

Worksheet #2: Working with Documentaries

Eyewitness Accounts

View the DVD "Holodomor—Let Their Memory Be Eternal" by Canad Inns, a 26-minute production that includes the accounts of 12 Holodomor survivors, or view DVD "Holodomor, Voices of Survivors," available at **www.ucrdc.org.ca**

Answer the following questions:

a) Gather 10 facts about the Holodomor from the accounts of the survivors.

1. ______________________________

2. ______________________________

3. ______________________________

4. ______________________________

5. ______________________________

6. ______________________________

7. ______________________________

8. ______________________________

9. ______________________________

10. ______________________________

b) According to the survivors, who were the:

perpetrators? ______________________________

henchmen? ______________________________

victims? ______________________________

c) What evidence was given that the Famine was deliberate?

____

____

photocopy for students to fill out

d) How did some people survive?

e) Select an incident described by a survivor that was especially distressing:

f) Select an incident described by a survivor that was especially memorable or uplifting:

g) Describe the survivors:

Culminating Activity: Interview and Press Article

Stage 1: Interview

Prepare a newspaper article on the basis of an interview you conduct with an eyewitness of a historical event of the twentieth century, such as the Holodomor. Choose one individual to interview and one event in the life of that person.

Interview Strategy and Preparation:

- In groups of four, prepare 10 general questions to start your interview and hand in the prepared questions.
- Choose only one person to interview.
- Conduct an interview with an eyewitness of a historical event by recording the answers on paper or video.
- Find out what daily life was like at that time: religious, military, economic (work, prices) political, social issues of the day.
- Select one significant historical event in his/her life.
- How did this event affect his/her life?
- What did you learn that was new about the Holodomor from this interview?
- Analyze and organize the gathered information.

NOTE: Use the Assessment Form for Interview on p. 202.

Stage 2: Newspaper Article

Format:

- *Introduction*: Identify a) the person interviewed; b) the event; c) location and date of the event. Make sure your introduction engages the reader.
- *Body*: After completing Stage 1 above, present concrete information that you gathered. Give specific examples about the political, economic, military, religious and social issues in the country at the time of the event.
- *Conclusion*: Include your personal observations of what you learned preparing this project.

Preparation:

- Create a title for your article.
- Write your fascinating article, using **only** the information you gathered from the interview.
- Attach your rough notes to the back of your assignment.

NOTE: Use the Assessment Rubric for News Article on p. 203.

photocopy for students to fill out

Assessment Form: Interview and Press Article

Note: If you prefer, this form may be used for both Stage 1 and Stage 2 of the activity.

Name: ______________________________ Date: ______________

CRITERIA	MARK	RECEIVED MARK	COMMENTS
Preparation: Title for article; 10 questions; title page; rough work included.	10		
Organization: *Introduction:* catches interest and provides essential information; *Body:* sequential organization of ideas, events, paragraphs related to the main theme; *Conclusion:* summary and comments of author.	25		
Content: Sufficient information provided; facts are related to theme and tied to historical event; there is a balance between personal and historical information outlining the daily life of the eyewitness.	25		
Language: Vocabulary, proper grammar, style, punctuation.	25		
Appearance: Originality, neatness, illustrations, picture, maps, creativity	15		
TOTAL MARK	100		

Knowledge/ Understanding	Level _______
Critical Thinking/ Research	Level _______
Communications	Level _______
Application	Level _______

photocopy for students to fill out

Assessment Rubric: Press Article

Knowledge/ Understanding	LEVEL 4	LEVEL 3	LEVEL 2	LEVEL 1
Uses anecdotal evidence from interview to support conclusions drawn in article.	Uses anecdotal evidence from interview to support conclusions drawn in the article with a high degree of effectiveness.	Uses anecdotal evidence from interview to support conclusions drawn in the article with considerable effectiveness.	Uses anecdotal evidence from interview to support conclusions drawn in the article with some effectiveness.	Uses anecdotal evidence from interview to support conclusions drawn in the article with a limited degree of effectiveness.
Demonstrates understanding of key historical concepts, information, terminology, and themes.	Demonstrates a high degree of understanding of key historical concepts, information, terminology, and themes.	Demonstrates considerable understanding of key historical concepts, information, terminology, and themes.	Demonstrates some understanding of key historical concepts, information, terminology, and themes.	Demonstrates a limited degree of understanding of key historical concepts, information, terminology, and themes.

Thinking	LEVEL 4	LEVEL 3	LEVEL 2	LEVEL 1
Develops thorough, exhaustive interview questions.	Develops thorough, exhaustive interview questions with a high degree of effectiveness.	Develops thorough, exhaustive interview questions with considerable effectiveness.	Develops thorough, exhaustive interview questions with some effectiveness.	Develops thorough, exhaustive interview questions with a limited degree of effectiveness.

Communication	LEVEL 4	LEVEL 3	LEVEL 2	LEVEL 1
Communicates information clearly.	Communicates information with a high degree of effectiveness.	Communicates information with considerable effectiveness.	Communicates information with some effectiveness.	Communicates information with a limited degree of effectiveness.
Uses proper conventions of language, grammar, and punctuation.	Uses proper conventions of language, grammar, and punctuation with a high degree of effectiveness.	Uses proper conventions of language, grammar, and punctuation with considerable effectiveness.	Uses proper conventions of language, grammar, and punctuation with some effectiveness.	Uses proper conventions of language, grammar, and punctuation with a limited degree of effectiveness.

Application	LEVEL 4	LEVEL 3	LEVEL 2	LEVEL 1
Demonstrates knowledge of newspaper article conventions, format, and elements (headline, W5H, lead, inverted pyramid, conclusion).	Demonstrates thorough knowledge of newspaper article conventions, format, and elements (headline, W5H, lead, inverted pyramid, conclusion).	Demonstrates considerable knowledge of newspaper article conventions, format, and elements (headline, W5H, lead, inverted pyramid, conclusion).	Demonstrates some knowledge of newspaper article conventions, format, and elements (headline, W5H, lead, inverted pyramid, conclusion).	Demonstrates limited knowledge of newspaper article conventions, format, and elements (headline, W5H, lead, inverted pyramid, conclusion).
Uses images, words, and phrases that are true to role, audience, and format.	Shows a high degree of effectiveness in choosing persuasive images, words, and phrases that are true to role, audience, and format.	Shows considerable effectiveness in choosing persuasive images, words, and phrases that are true to role, audience, and format.	Shows some effectiveness in choosing persuasive images, words, and phrases that are true to role, audience, and format.	Shows limited effectiveness in choosing persuasive images, words, and phrases that are true to role, audience, and format.

photocopy for students to fill out

Lesson: Using Quotations

*Both the **Paraphrasing** and the creative **Graffiti Walk** activities provide a different pedagogical approach to help students deepen their understanding of the Holodomor using quotations.*

Lesson #1: Paraphrasing
Lesson #2: Graffiti Walk

Lesson #1: Paraphrasing

Grade Level:
Grades 8 to 12

Curriculum Fit / Specific Expectations / Learning Outcomes:
Select expectations you wish to cover from either English language arts, social studies, history, politics, law, social justice, genocide, or religious studies and prepare an assessment to share with the students at the outset.

Materials Required:
Copies of the worksheet on pp. 205-207

Set-up Required:
N/A

☑ **PRE TASK AND POST TASK ACTIVITIES.**

- This activity may be either a pre-task or post-task activity to viewing a film on the Genocidal Famine or a reading on the historical background of the Holodomor, Part II, pp. 21-28. Students paraphrase quotations about the Holodomor and suggest the purpose or aim of the speaker.

Worksheet #1: Paraphrasing Quotations

The quotations before you are statements made by participants, observers, researchers and victims of the Ukrainian Genocide. Paraphrase — restate in your own words — what the person was trying to say about the seriousness of the situation in Ukraine in the 1930s. Identify the role of the person making the statement: participant, observer, victim, or researcher.

1. "Walter Duranty helped to turn the monster Stalin into a world figure and a hero of the leftist Western intelligentsia by defending the bloodbath of the Soviet Union from its critics in the now famous: *"You can't make an omelet without breaking eggs."*

   Lance Morrow, journalist from 1975-1995

   Role: ______________________________

   Paraphrasing: ______________________________

   ____

   ____

   ____

   ____

   ____

2. "Peasants present by themselves the basic force of the national movement. Without peasants there can be no strong national movement. This is what we mean when we say that the national question, is actually, the peasants' question."

   Joseph Stalin, General Secretary of the Communist Party of the Soviet Union (1922-1953)

   Role: ______________________________

   Paraphrasing: ______________________________

   ____

   ____

   ____

   ____

   ____

3. "I remain convinced that for Stalin to have complete centralized power in his hands, he found it necessary to physically destroy the second-largest Soviet republic, meaning the annihilation of the Ukrainian peasantry, Ukrainian intelligentsia, Ukrainian language, and history as understood by the people; to do away with

photocopy for students to fill out

Ukraine and things Ukrainian as such. The calculation was very simple, very primitive: no people, therefore, no separate country, and thus no problem. Such a policy is Genocide in the classic sense of the word."

James Mace, Holodomor scholar

Role: ____________________

Paraphrasing: ____________________

____

____

____

____

4. Q. "Among writers, some say that the (genocide) famine of 1933 was deliberately organized by Stalin and the whole of your leadership."
A. "Enemies of communism say that! They are the enemies of communism! People who are not politically blind… I twice travelled to Ukraine…Of course I saw nothing of the kind there. Those allegations are absurd. Absurd."

Viacheslav Molotov, Foreign Minister of the Soviet Union

Role: ____________________

Paraphrasing: ____________________

____

____

____

____

5. "The famine was brought about in Ukraine in order to reduce the number of Ukrainians, resettle in their place people from other parts of the USSR, and in this way kill all thought of independence."

Prokopenko, Communist Party member and government official, 1934

Role: ____________________

Paraphrasing: ____________________

____

____

____

____

____

6. "...[Our reporting] served Moscow's purpose of smearing the facts out of recognition and declaring a situation which, had we reported simply and clearly, might have worked up enough public opinion abroad to force remedial measures. And every correspondent each in his own measure, was guilty of collaborating in this monstrous hoax on the world."

Eugene Lyons, Moscow United Press *correspondent, 1928-1934*

Role: ____

Paraphrasing: ____

____

____

____

____

7. "The Terror-Famine of 1932-33 was a dual-purpose by product of collectivization, designed to suppress Ukrainian nationalism and the most important concentration of prosperous peasants at one throw."

Norman Davies, British historian, 1996

Role: ____

Paraphrasing: ____

____

____

____

____

Lesson #2: Graffiti Walk

Tamara Kowalczyk

*The **Graffiti Walk** instructional strategy encourages higher-order thinking among students. In this activity students read and respond to a selection of quotations on the Holodomor. Students interpret and analyze the quotations and the impressions of their classmates, and thus, have an opportunity to deepen their understanding of the topic studied. This activity is especially well suited to kinesthetic learners and can easily be differentiated to suit the needs of students in diverse classrooms.*

Grade Level:
Grades 7 to 12

Curriculum Fit / Specific Expectations / Learning Outcomes:
Select outcomes you wish to cover from either English language arts, social studies, history, politics, law, social justice, genocide, or religious studies and prepare an assessment to share with the students at the outset.

Materials Required:

- A selection of quotations on the topic of the Holodomor. See suggested quotations in this activity and Part II, pp. 65-74.
- Chart paper
- Marker for each student

Set-up Required:

- Choose five to six of the suggested quotations provided on pp. 210-211 or selected from Part II, pp. 65-74.
- Print each quotation on a separate sheet of chart paper.
- Place quotations in stations around the classroom, ensuring sufficient space between stations. Quotations may also be hung on the wall and/or dispersed on desks around the classroom.

  NOTE: Whiteboards or chalkboards may be used instead of chart paper provided there is ample space between each station to prevent overcrowding.
- Print out instructions that follow the suggested quotations. Place somewhere in the room for easy reference by students.
- Divide students into groups of four to six.

☑ **PRE-TASK ACTIVITY**

- It is suggested that the first time a graffiti walk is used as an activity, the teacher, with the entire class, select one quotation and model what is to be done with it.

☑ **TASK 1**

- Students are instructed to move with their group from station to station at timed intervals until each group has visited all stations.
- At each station, students read the quotation and the responses contributed by students in previous groups.
- Students record their comments directly on the sheet of chart paper. Comments may be about their interpretation of the quotation, their opinion about what was said, inferences they have made, questions that came to mind, connections to previously learned course content, connections to ideas, topics, news, and/or events beyond the classroom, or their thoughts on what their classmates have written.

☑ **TASK 2**

- Groups return to their first station to analyze the responses. Within their group, students allocate the following roles:
  - group leader—ensures everyone has the opportunity to participate and that opinions are respected, maintains order
  - time keeper—ensures the discussion is on topic and manages the group's discussion time
  - recorder—records the group's ideas, arguments, and evidence
  - presenter—presents the group's arguments to the class
- Students identify common themes and interesting ideas among the comments, and develop questions based on their findings for class discussion.
- Each group presents a summary of their comments, analysis, and questions to the rest of the class.
- **Using brainstorming technique, teacher aids students to find 5 focus items from the class presentations.**

Variations:

- *Differentiation*
  Quotations may be substituted with photographs, statements, facts, video clips, audio clips, visual media, and/or questions developed by the teacher.

- *Individual variation*
  Students may be asked to respond to quotations without discussing or collaborating with others in their group.

- *Group variation*
  Students within each group may be asked to collaborate when generating their responses to the quotations. Students may change roles and responsibilities within their groups at each station.

photocopy for students to fill out

☑ POST-TASK ACTIVITY

Students may choose a quotation on the Holodomor that most closely reflects their conclusions, based on their thoughts, analysis, and class discussion.

INSTRUCTIONS

- Students record their comments directly on the sheet of chart paper.
- Comments may be about:
    - their interpretation of the quotation
    - their opinion about what was said
    - inferences they have made
    - questions that came to mind
    - connections to previously learned course content, connections to ideas topics, news, and/or events beyond the classroom
    - their thoughts on what their classmates have written

☑ SUGGESTED QUOTATIONS ON THE HOLODOMOR

Quotations for grades 7-12

"Food is a weapon."

Maxim Litvinov, Soviet Commissar of Foreign Affairs, 1921

"But — to put it brutally — you can't make an omelette without breaking eggs…"

Walter Duranty, New York Times *Correspondent, Moscow, 1933*

"Peasants present by themselves the basic force of the national movement. Without peasants there can be no strong national movement. This is what we mean when we say that the national question is, actually, the peasants' question."

Joseph Stalin, General Secretary of the Communist Party of the Soviet Union (1922-1953)

"Famine has not taught the peasants a lesson."

Stanislav Kosior, First Secretary of the Communist Party of Ukraine (1928-1938), March 1933

"To go against the dominant thinking of your friends, of most of the people you see every day, is perhaps the most difficult act of heroism you can perform."

Theodore H. White, political journalist, historian and novelist

"Death solves all problems. No man, no problem."

Joseph Stalin, General Secretary of the Communist Party of the Soviet Union, 1950

Quotations for grades 10-12

"A Famine that came about without drought and without war."

Alexander Solzhenitsyn, Russian dissident, The Gulag Archipalego, *1973*

"If we do not start rectifying the situation in Ukraine now, we may lose Ukraine."

Joseph Stalin, General Secretary of the Communist Party of the Soviet Union and Chairman of the Council of Ministers, 1932

"The child of a Ukrainian kulak deliberately starved to death by the Stalinist regime is worth no less than a Jewish child in the Warsaw ghetto starved to death by the Nazi regime."

Stéphane Courtois, French historian and editor of Le livre noir du communisme: Crimes, terreur et repression, *1997*

"Ukrainians, with their profound religiosity, individualism, tradition of private property, and devotion to their plots of land, were obviously not suitable material for building communism and this fact was noted by the high-ranking Soviet officials."

Vasyl Ovsiienko, Ukrainian dissident, member of the Ukrainian Helsinki Group, 2007

"Huge events like the Ukraine famine of 1933, involving the deaths of millions of people, have actually escaped the attention of the majority of English russophiles."

George Orwell, English novelist and journalist, 1945

"Ukrainian nationalism is our chief danger."

Stanislav Kosior, First Secretary of the Communist Party of Ukraine, Izvestiia, *December 2, 1933*

"...[Our reporting] served Moscow's purpose of smearing the facts out of recognition and declaring a situation which, had we reported simply and clearly, might have worked up enough public opinion abroad to force remedial measures. And every correspondent each in his own measure, was guilty of collaborating in this monstrous hoax on the world."

Eugene Lyons, correspondent for the Moscow United Press, *1928-1934*

photocopy for students to fill out

Lesson: Writing Persuasive Paragraphs

Tamara Kowalczyk

*The **Persuasive Paragraph** (essay) activity is an excellent way for students to improve their critical thinking and writing skills. This assignment requires students to make a firm judgment or take a stand on a particular issue and/or question. Students must develop solid arguments supported by evidence to back up their position and are charged with critically examining their own arguments by anticipating and rebutting potential critiques of their position. The activity may be used for summative assessment on the Holodomor.*

Grade Level:
Grades 7 to 12

Curriculum Fit / Specific Expectations / Learning Outcomes:
Select outcomes you wish to cover from either English language arts, social studies, history, politics, law, social justice, genocide, or religious studies and prepare an assessment to share with the students at the outset.

Materials Required:

- DVD of *Harvest of Despair* or *Genocide Revealed (Educational version)*
- Copies of quotations in Part III, pp. 210-211, depending on the grade level
- Copies of the Graphic Organizer and Checklist in this lesson

Set-up Required:

- Equipment to view DVD

☑ **PRE-TASK ACTIVITY**

- Discuss with students the components and structure of a persuasive paragraph (i.e., thesis, arguments, evidence, opposing argument, rebuttal, conclusion). Check for understanding.
- It is suggested that the teacher model one example with the entire class.
- Inform students they will be answering the following question in their persuasive paragraph about the Holodomor: "Who should be held responsible for the Holodomor?" Another question relevant to the subject can also be considered.
- Hand out the Graphic Organizer to students pp. 214.
- Hand out the Checklist to students p. 215.
- Have students read a selection of background resources from Part II.

☑ **TASK**

- Students complete the Graphic Organizer.
- Students share their completed Graphic Organizer with a peer and/or the teacher to receive feedback.
- Students write their persuasive paragraph, incorporating the feedback they have received.
- Students use the Checklist to ensure their paragraph is complete before submitting it for evaluation.

Variations

- *Differentiation*
  Students may be provided with a choice of topics for their persuasive paragraph on the Holodomor.

- *Essay*
  Students could write a persuasive essay rather than a paragraph answering the question.

"Village home (khata)," Kyiv Oblast, 1932.

Graphic Organizer: Persuasive Paragraph/Essay

After reviewing the varying roles figures played during the Ukrainian Genocidal Famine, write a persuasive paragraph/essay to answer the following question: Who should be held responsible for the Holodomor? Use this form to help you organize your ideas. Share this work with a classmate or teacher to obtain feedback. Write your persuasive paragraph incorporating the feedback you received.

THESIS:	
ARGUMENT 1:	EVIDENCE:
ARGUMENT 2:	EVIDENCE:
ARGUMENT 3:	EVIDENCE:
ARGUMENT 4:	EVIDENCE:

photocopy for students to fill out

Checklist: Persuasive Paragraph/Essay

- ☐ I have stated my thesis clearly.
- ☐ The body of my paragraph includes arguments that are supported by concrete facts.
- ☐ My arguments are organized from the strongest to the weakest.
- ☐ I have included the strongest argument that someone with an opposing opinion may present.
- ☐ I have provided evidence to invalidate this opposing argument (rebuttal).
- ☐ I end my paragraph with a compelling concluding statement that reiterates my main idea.
- ☐ I have edited my work.

photocopy for students to fill out

Confiscation of kurkul's property during the Holodomor, Donetsk Oblast, early 1930s.

Lesson: RAFT Holodomor Activity

Tamara Kowalczyk

*RAFT is an acronym for **Role, Audience, Format, and Topic**. The RAFT Activity encourages students to think historically and is an excellent way for teachers to differentiate their assessment practices. In this activity students explore a historical perspective to learn more about the people and ideas of a specific historical period. Students produce a product in a format of their choice while taking on the role of a historical person. In creating it, they must address the topic or question asked and gear their product towards a specified audience. Students will enjoy exchanging their products with classmates, as the varied formats and topics will ensure an interesting and varied range of products and ideas. This activity is well suited to learners with various learning preferences, as students have creative options.*

Grade Level:
Grades 6 to 12

Curriculum Fit / Specific Expectations / Learning Outcomes:
Select outcomes you wish to cover from either English language arts, social studies, history, politics, law, social justice, genocide, or religious studies and prepare an assessment to share with the students at the outset.

Materials Required:

- Copies of RAFT Assignment, p. 218
- Essay on the Holodomor, pp. 21-28
- Rubric for each student, p. 219

Set-up Required:
N/A

teacher tip

Create additional roles, audiences, formats, and topics on the Holodomor, if desired.

☑ **PRE-TASK ACTIVITY**

- Discuss with students that history is made up of individuals and groups with diverse opinions, perspectives and experiences. It is important to understand and empathize with persons throughout history in order to develop a more thorough understanding of the events and/or time periods studied.
- Have students read a selection of background resources from Part II or the Appendix.

☑ **TASK**

- Distribute the RAFT Activity on p.218 and the rubric on p. 219.
- Explain that students are to take on the role of a historical person who lived through the Holodomor, and review the expectations and criteria for assessment.
- Students choose a role suggested and create a product that addresses the specified topic while keeping their audience in mind. For example, students who choose Option 1 take on the role of a kulak political prisoner who writes a song for his fellow prisoners about coping with daily life as a concentration camp inmate. Only five students per role should be accepted.

☑ **POST-TASK ACTIVITY**

Students present their RAFT assignment to their classmates.

Variation

Students can prepare an outline of their ideas and submit them for peer and/or teacher feedback prior to proceeding with the assignment.

☑ **ASSESSMENT**

- RAFT Rubric, p. 219

Roman Koval's Holodomor monument in Winnipeg, Manitoba, 1984.

RAFT Holodomor Activity

It is March of the year 1933. You are living in Soviet Ukraine. Assume the identity of one of the historical figures below (role) and explore the topic and the person's perspective using the specified format.

	ROLE	AUDIENCE	FORMAT	TOPIC
1	A political prisoner constructing the White Sea Canal	Fellow prisoners	Song or poem	Coping with daily life as a concentration camp worker in the Soviet Union.
2	A Ukrainian *kurkul* (*kulak*)	Self or family	Soliloquy	Choosing whether to join a collective farm or face the consequences.
3	A *Komsomol* leader (Communist Youth League)	Junior *Komsomol* members	Speech or pamphlet	Encouraging *Komsomol* members to continue their activism in support of the Communist Party and collectivization.
4	A foreign journalist based in the Soviet Union	Self	Journal	Interactions with the starving farmers and Soviet officials about taking their goods.
5	A factory worker in Kharkiv	Family members outside the Ukrainian SSR	Letter	Life in the city
6	Ukrainian farmer in the Kyiv region	Self and Family	Monologue	Explain to family why there is no food to eat after a decent harvest.
7	Priest in Poltava	Former parishioners	Speech	Destruction of the Ukrainian Orthodox Church
8	Writer in Chernihiv	General Public	Newspaper article	Explain why he cannot write because of censorship due to his national background.

In your RAFT product, be sure to include the following about your role:

- an introduction or description of yourself, including a name (e.g., Ivan, Oksana)
- your feelings and beliefs
- a description of the events in Ukraine prior to the Holodomor
- a detailed description of the current state of events in Ukraine (including your experiences, the experiences of your neighbours, family, your role, etc.)

You will share your final product with your classmates. Be sure to back up your information with references.

photocopy for students to fill out

Assessment Rubric: RAFT

Knowledge/ Understanding	LEVEL 4	LEVEL 3	LEVEL 2	LEVEL 1
Demonstrates knowledge and understanding of key historical concepts, facts, and terminology.	Demonstrates thorough knowledge and understanding of key historical concepts, facts, and terminology.	Demonstrates considerable knowledge and understanding of key historical concepts, facts, and terminology.	Demonstrates some knowledge and understanding of key historical concepts, facts, and terminology.	Demonstrates limited knowledge and understanding of key historical concepts, facts, and terminology.
Uses evidence to develop empathetic understanding of a historical actor.	Uses evidence to develop empathetic understanding of a historical character with a high degree of effectiveness.	Uses evidence to develop empathetic understanding of a historical character with a considerable degree of effectiveness.	Uses evidence to develop empathetic understanding of a historical character with some degree of effectiveness.	Uses evidence to develop empathetic understanding of a historical character with a limited degree of effectiveness.

Thinking	LEVEL 4	LEVEL 3	LEVEL 2	LEVEL 1
Analyzes ideas and information.	Analyzes ideas and information with exceptional depth.	Analyzes ideas and information with considerable depth.	Analyzes ideas and information with some depth.	Analyzes ideas and information with limited depth.
Synthesizes ideas and information.	Synthesizes ideas and information with a high degree of effectiveness.	Synthesizes ideas and information with considerable effectiveness.	Synthesizes ideas and information with some effectiveness.	Synthesizes ideas and information with a limited degree of effectiveness.

Communication	LEVEL 4	LEVEL 3	LEVEL 2	LEVEL 1
Communicates position and ideas.	Communicates position and ideas with a high degree of clarity.	Communicates position and ideas with considerable clarity.	Communicates position and ideas with some clarity.	Communicates position and ideas with limited clarity.
Use of diction, tone, and language suits the purpose and audience.	Diction, tone, and level of language suit the purpose and audience with a high degree of effectiveness.	Diction, tone, and level of language suit the purpose and audience with considerable effectiveness.	Diction, tone, and level of language suit the purpose and audience with some effectiveness.	Diction, tone, and level of language suit the purpose and audience with a limited degree of effectiveness.

Application	LEVEL 4	LEVEL 3	LEVEL 2	LEVEL 1
Draws appropriate conclusions in the chosen role.	Draws appropriate conclusions in the chosen role with a high degree of effectiveness.	Draws appropriate conclusions in the chosen role with considerable effectiveness.	Draws appropriate conclusions in the chosen role with some effectiveness.	Draws appropriate conclusions in the chosen role with a limited degree of effectiveness.
Uses persuasive images, words, and phrases true to role, audience, and format.	Chooses persuasive images, words, and phrases true to role, audience, and format with a high degree of effectiveness.	Chooses persuasive images, words, and phrases true to role, audience, and format with considerable effectiveness.	Chooses persuasive images, words, and phrases true to role, audience, and format with some effectiveness.	Chooses persuasive images, words, and phrases true to role, audience, and format with limited effectiveness.

photocopy for students to fill out

Lesson: Four Corners Debate, Making Ethical Decisions

Tamara Kowalczyk

The Four Corners *instructional strategy encourages students to think critically and helps them develop the ability to make sound decisions. Four Corners can be used to advance historical thinking in the history classroom as students are called on to consider and understand the ethical dimensions of history. In this activity, students listen to controversial statements read by the teacher and indicate their position on the issue by standing in the appropriate corner of the room, labelled "strongly agree" to "strongly disagree." Students with kinesthetic, logical, and interpersonal learning preferences will find this cooperative learning activity particularly beneficial. Teachers should choose and modify statements to gear them to the age and abilities of their students.*

Grade Level:
Grades 6 to 12

Curriculum Fit / Specific Expectations / Learning Outcomes:
Select outcomes you wish to cover from either English language arts, social studies, history, politics, law, social justice, genocide, or religious studies and prepare an assessment to share with the students at the outset.

Materials Required:

- Statement(s) to read out to students. See suggestions in post-task activities.
- Four signs (strongly agree, agree, disagree, strongly disagree)
- Masking tape
- Optional: board, projector and computer to display statement(s) in the classroom
- Copies of Debate Worksheet for each student, p. 223

Set-up Required:

- Select one of the controversial statements suggested in the post-task activities or develop one of your own controversial statements on the Holodomor.
- Write the words "strongly agree," "agree," "disagree," and "strongly disagree" on four separate sheets of paper and post one sign in each corner of the room.
- Options: Statements may be read out loud, written on the board, and/or projected onto a screen.

☑ **PRE-TASK ACTIVITIES**

- Select an activity, DVD or reading from Part II or III for background information.
- Discuss with students the possibility of different people having divergent yet justifiable perspectives on a specific topic and the need to remain respectful and tolerant of others' points of view, especially when considering sensitive topics.
- Read out the chosen controversial statement.
- Students quietly consider the statement and decide whether they "strongly agree," "agree," "disagree," or "strongly disagree" based on what they have learned about the Holodomor. Students write their position on a piece of scrap paper or in their notebooks.

Variations

- Students may be provided with the statement in advance to explore arguments and evidence for different viewpoints. A graphic organizer may be provided to help students organize their thoughts.
- Students may be asked to present their opinion on more than one statement.

☑ **TASK**

- Instruct students to move to the corner that reflects their opinion about the controversial statement.
- Once students have reached their respective corners they find a partner with whom to discuss their position and their reasoning.
- In their corner, students choose one of the following roles:
  - group leader — ensures everyone has the opportunity to participate and that opinions are respected
  - time keeper — ensures the discussion is on topic and manages the group's discussion time
  - recorder — records the group's ideas, arguments, and evidence
  - presenter — presents the group's arguments to the class
- All students in each corner discuss and record their position and justification as a group. Students use the Debate Worksheet on p. 223 to organize their arguments.
- Each group presents their position to the rest of the class. Classmates may ask questions and challenge the arguments and/or evidence presented by other groups.
- After the presentations, students may decide to change corners and provide an explanation for doing so.

NOTE: It is possible that a particular corner (position) will have few or no students. The teacher may wish to represent that position and/or play the role of devil's advocate.

Variation

Students may be asked to present their opinion on more than one statement.

☑ **POST-TASK ACTIVITY**

- Students submit a paragraph or short essay based on the class debate.
- Students reflect on the different perspectives voiced in class in a journal entry.

Suggested Controversial Statements

Grades 6-12

- It is important to study genocides that occurred in the past.
- It is important to commemorate genocides that have occurred throughout history.
- It is possible to achieve justice for the crimes committed during the Holodomor. Explain.
- Genocide can be prevented.
- Walter Duranty's Pulitzer Prize should be revoked.
- It is permissible to lie to protect others.

Grades 10-12

- "Food is a weapon."
  Maxim Litvinov, Soviet Commissar of Foreign Affairs
- Onlookers allowed the Holodomor to happen. If more people had intervened millions of lives could have been saved. Onlookers should be held responsible along with the perpetrators.
- Reconciliation after genocide is possible.
- People today should be held accountable for the actions of their predecessors.
- Anyone is capable of genocide.
- "To go against the dominant thinking of your friends, of most of the people you see every day, is perhaps the most difficult act of heroism you can perform."
  Theodore H. White

Worksheet: Four Corners Debate

Controversial issues frequently have many interpretations. Advocates of each viewpoint often cite arguments and evidence to support their position. In preparation for the "Four Corners Debate" on the Holodomor, use this form to organize the arguments and evidence both for and against the statement provided by your teacher. Make a decision about where you stand based on the arguments and evidence you develop.

STATEMENT:

Evidence that supports the statement:	Evidence that opposes the statement:

My position:

Reasoning:

photocopy for students to fill out

Unit: Human Rights and Genocide

Valentina Kuryliw

This unit presents the Ukrainian Holodomor of 1932-1933 as a case study. The activities are cumulative, with progressive stages helping students to explore many different aspects of the Genocidal Famine.

The learning activities encourage inquiry, analysis, problem solving and planning skills, as well as cooperation and team building. The case study can be used to set up debates, discussion or further research of the Genocidal Famine in Ukraine 1932-33.

Grade Level:
Grades 10-12

Curriculum Fit:

- Ontario Grade 10 Course: "Canadian History Since WWI" in *Canadian and World Studies*, 2013 revised. By the end of this course, students will:
  - C3.2 Analyse responses of Canada and Canadians to some major international events and/or developments that occurred during this period and assess the significance of these responses, including their significance for Canadian identity and heritage.
  - E3.3 Assess the significance of public acknowledgements and/or commemoration in Canada of past human tragedies and human rights violations, both domestic and international.
  - C3.2 Describe responses of Canada and Canadians to some major international events and/or developments that occurred between 1929 and 1945, including their military response to World War II and explain the significance of these responses for Canadian identity and/or heritage.
  - E3.4 Describe some of the ways in which Canada and Canadians have, since 1982, acknowledged the consequences of and/or commemorated past events, with a focus on human tragedies and human rights violations that occurred in Canada, and explain the significance of these commemorations for identity and/or heritage in Canada.
- Ontario Grade 10 Course: "Civics" in *Canadian and World Studies*, 2013 revised. By the end of this course, students will:
  - C2.2 Describe ways in which some events, issues, people, and/or symbols are commemorated or recognized in Canada (e.g., by war memorials and Remembrance Day services, through citizenship awards such as the Order of Canada, by depicting them on postage stamps or currency, in museums, on public plaques, or through observations such as Human Rights Day, etc.). Students analyze the significance of these recognitions.

- Students work individually and in small groups with a real case of international significance that requires them to apply human rights standards developed by the UN Convention.
- They will analyze the Famine and the issues of political power, economic development, human rights and other issues related to it using articles, eyewitness accounts and documents.
- They will summarize the rights and responsibilities of global citizens based on the analysis and comparison of the United Nations Universal Declaration of Human Rights and the UN Convention on the Prevention and Punishment of Genocide. With the knowledge of human rights standards they will analyse whether the facts in the case study constitute a human rights violation or a group rights violation.
- They will complete a form to the International Criminal Court requesting an investigation of violations, or will decline to do so and give reasons.
- They will demonstrate an understanding of a citizen's role and a global citizen's role in responding to non-democratic movements through personal or group actions.
- They will assess the effectiveness of responses to the violations.
- They will evaluate the civic action of governments, individuals and NGOs that made a difference in global affairs, especially the father of the UN Convention on the Prevention and Punishment of Genocide — Raphael Lemkin.

Materials Required for this Unit:

- UN Universal Declaration of Human rights: **http://www.un.org/en/documents/udhr/**
- Other genocides recognized by Canada: Armenian, Rwandan, Holocaust, Srebrenica (Bosnian Genocide)
- Documentary film, for example:
  - *Harvest of Despair* (55 min.) **www.youtube.com/watch?v=VXkgGdZC6uQ**
  - *Genocide Revealed,* Educational Version (26 min.) **yurij@yluhovy.com**
  - *The Soviet Story* (11 min. introduction) **www.soviethistory.com**
  - *Holodomor, Voices of Survivors* (30 min.) **www.ucrdc.org**
- Background article and discussion questions regarding the Genocide. Handout of essay, "The Holodomor,1932-1933" by Valentina Kuryliw in Part II, pp. 21-28.
- DVD *"Holodomor—Let Their Memory Be Eternal"* by Canad Inns, a 26-minute production featuring 12 Holodomor survivors. (Canad Inns, Winnipeg, distribute the DVD) - **mcindy@canadinns.com**; or the DVD *Holodomor: Voices of Survivors* (**www.ucrdc.org** to order).

- UN Convention on the Prevention and Punishment of the Crime of Genocide. See excerpts Part II, p. 59 and pp. 62-63.
- Teacher background information websites:
  - **http://www.education.holodomor.ca/introduction/basic-facts/**
  - **http://www.faminegenocide.com**
  - **http://www.infoukes.com/history/famine**

☑ **ASSESSMENT / EVALUATION TECHNIQUES**

Create a diagnostic, formative, or summative evaluation for this unit.

Teachers select from the four activities in this unit that they would like their students to explore.

ACTIVITY 1

Viewing and reflecting on a documentary: *Harvest of Despair* or *Genocide Revealed*

Film is an excellent way to introduce the topic: Genocidal Famine in Ukraine 1932-33.

teacher tip

It is recommended that the documentary film "*Harvest of Despair*" be shown in 2 parts:
Part 1. Background information, events leading up to the Holodomor (30 min.)
Part 2. Ukrainian Genocide (30 min.)

Materials Required:

- The documentary *Harvest of Despair*, available on DVD or online **http://www.youtube.com/watch?v=VXkgGdZC6uQ**
  or
- *Genocide Revealed* **www.yluhovy.com**
- Copies for each student group of Worksheet #1, pp. 228-229 and, if relevant, Worksheet #2, p. 230
- When discussing the answers to questions in the worksheets, the class could be divided into groups of five to six students, with each group reporting their findings to the entire class.

ACTIVITY 2

Background Article on the Holodomor

Material Required:

- Worksheet #3 for background essay, pp. 231-232

- Copies for each student of background essay "The Holodomor, 1932-1933," Valentina Kuryliw, Part 11, pp. 21-28

The findings presented in group reports may be recorded on a chart. Conclusions will be drawn during the class discussion based on student findings. Each group is to hand in one page on conclusions reached.

ACTIVITY 3
Eyewitness accounts of Holodomor survivors

Material Required:

- Worksheet #4, pp. 233-234, for each student and #5 for each group, p. 235
- DVD: *Holodomor—Let Their Memory Be Eternal* distributed by Canad Inns, a 26-minute production featuring 12 Holodomor survivors or *Holodomor: Voices of Survivors*
- Eyewitness accounts reproduced from Part II, pp. 77-80 for group work
- Essay "The Holodomor, 1932-1933" by Valentina Kuryliw, Part II, pp. 21-28
- Brief Timeline of Events, available in Part IV, pp. 267-268

After completing Worksheet #4 individually, pp. 233-234, students may form groups of no more than six students to work collaboratively on Worksheet #5, p. 235.

ACTIVITY 4
Analysis of Historical Documents

Material Required:

- A copy of Worksheet #6 for each group, pp. 237-238
- Historical documents provided in Part II, pp. 81-93
- Brief Timeline of Events, available in Part IV, pp. 267-268
- Assessment Rubric, p. 236

Students will work in groups consisting of no more than six students. Each group may receive the same historical document for the assignment, or groups may work on different historical documents.

Educators may wish to switch the sequencing of Activity 3 and Activity 4. If they feel that their students need a break from watching documentaries, they may want to assign Activity 4 earlier.

Worksheet #1: Harvest of Despair (First Half)

PART 1 OF THE DOCUMENTARY

After viewing part one of the film (30 minutes) discuss and answer these questions as directed by the teacher.

1. What events led to the Genocidal Famine?

2. What was the response of the farmers to these events? Do you think this response was legal? Justified?

3. According to the film, how many people died as a result of the Famine? What percent of the population?

4. What evidence exists that the Famine was human-made?

5. List the actions of Soviet Government officials which led to the Famine in Ukraine.

photocopy for students to fill out

6. Select one eyewitness in the film. Describe the conditions under which that family lived. Describe their testimony.

____

____

____

____

7. Who would you name as victims, perpetrators, accomplices, bystanders, rescuers?

____

____

____

____

8. What evidence is there that the Famine-Genocide was directed specifically against the Ukrainian people?

____

____

____

____

____

photocopy for students to fill out

Worksheet #2: Harvest of Despair (Second Half)

PART 2 OF THE DOCUMENTARY

After viewing the second part of the film Harvest of Despair, *discuss and answer these questions individually or in groups as directed by the teacher.*

1. Western nations knew about the starvation of millions in Ukraine. What was their response? Was it an effective response to the violations?

2. Why was there a "media cover-up" inside and outside the Soviet Union?

3. Who were Malcolm Muggeridge and Walter Duranty? How did they portray the Famine in Ukraine in 1933? What role did Muggeridge and Duranty play in the media coverage?

Worksheet #3: Background Essay

"THE HOLODOMOR, 1932-1933"

*Read **"The Holodomor, 1932-1933"** by Valentina Kuryliw, pp. 21-28. Answer the questions below. The questions may be used as a guide for a class discussion. The results of the discussion could be checked orally or handed in for marking.*

1. What groups did the Soviet authorities specifically target in Ukraine?

___

___

2. According to the article, what is the estimated number of victims of this tragedy?

___

___

3. Why is the Ukrainian Holodomor considered to be one of the worst tragedies of the 20th century?

___

___

___

4. How did Stalin deal with the farmers in Ukraine?

___

___

___

5. List the actions of Soviet authorities that escalated into the Genocidal Famine in Ukraine.

___

___

___

6. What reason is given for these actions against the population of Ukraine?

___

___

photocopy for students to fill out

photocopy for students to fill out

7. How did foreign journalists deal with the Famine in Ukraine in 1932-1933? Why was this the case?

8. Explain how Canadians were affected by events in Ukraine in 1932-1933.

9. Why was it possible to cover up the Famine for over 50 years?

10. Why has the discussion about the Holodomor surfaced in recent years?

11. What does the term "Holodomor" mean?

12. Why was it important for Canada to recognize the Ukrainian tragedy as a genocide? When did this occur? What is Holodomor Memorial Day?

13. Do you think it is possible to hide a genocide like the Ukrainian Holodomor from the world today? Explain your answer.

14. Bonus question: List other genocides that have occurred since 1933 in which food was used as a weapon.

Worksheet #4: Viewing Eyewitness Accounts

VIEWING DVDs

View the DVD ***Holodomor—Let Their Memory Be Eternal****, featuring the accounts of 12 Holodomor survivors or the CD* ***Holodomor: Voices of Survivors*** *and answer the following questions:*

a) Gather 10 facts about the Holodomor from the accounts of the survivors.

1. ______________________________

2. ______________________________

3. ______________________________

4. ______________________________

5. ______________________________

6. ______________________________

7. ______________________________

8. ______________________________

9. ______________________________

10. ______________________________

b) According to survivors, who were the:

Perpetrators? ______________________________

Henchmen? ______________________________

Victims? ______________________________

c) What evidence was given that the Famine was deliberate?

____

____

____

photocopy for students to fill out

d) How did some people survive?

____

____

____

____

e) Select an incident described by a survivor that was especially distressing:

____

____

____

____

f) Select an incident described by a survivor that was especially memorable or uplifting:

____

____

____

____

photocopy for students to fill out

g) Describe the survivors.

____

____

____

____

Worksheet #5: Analyzing Eyewitness Accounts

ANALYZING ACCOUNTS

Students may separate into groups of up to six students.

- *All groups will receive copies of the essay "The Holodomor, 1932-1933," "Timeline of Events" and an Assessment Rubric.*
- *Three groups will receive copies of the first eyewitness account.*
- *The three remaining groups will receive copies of the second eyewitness account.*

Each group is to read the eyewitness account of the Famine and pick out the five most important facts in the account. Using information from the article "The Holodomor, 1932-1933," the Timeline and the eyewitness account, each group is to prepare an article for a newspaper published in 1933 explaining what was happening in Ukraine.

Be sure to include the following in your article:

a) name of newspaper and date of article
b) article headline
c) author of article
d) drawing, photo or illustration, if possible
e) main points to be made (who/what, when, where, why and how)

Where possible use terms such as: *victims, perpetrators, bystanders, observers, rescuers.* Articles are to be handed in for evaluation. A class newspaper may be produced.

Assessment
Use the Assessment Rubric provided by your teacher.

photocopy for students to fill out

Assessment Rubric: Newspaper Article

Newspaper Article Using Eye Witness Accounts

Knowledge/ Understanding	LEVEL 4	LEVEL 3	LEVEL 2	LEVEL 1
Uses factual evidence to support conclusions drawn in article.	Uses factual evidence to support conclusions drawn in article with a high degree of effectiveness.	Uses factual evidence to support conclusions drawn in article with considerable effectiveness.	Uses factual evidence to support conclusions drawn in article with some effectiveness.	Uses factual evidence to support conclusions drawn in article with limited degree of effectiveness.
Demonstrates knowledge and understanding of key ideas, concepts, terminology, and themes.	Demonstrates thorough knowledge and understanding of key information, ideas, concepts, terminology, and themes.	Demonstrates considerable knowledge and understanding of key information, ideas, concepts, terminology, and themes.	Demonstrates some knowledge and understanding of key information, ideas, concepts, terminology, and themes.	Demonstrates limited knowledge and understanding of key information, ideas, concepts, terminology, and themes.

Thinking	LEVEL 4	LEVEL 3	LEVEL 2	LEVEL 1
Analyzes ideas and information.	Analyzes ideas and information with exceptional depth.	Analyzes ideas and information with considerable depth.	Analyzes ideas and information with some depth.	Analyzes ideas and information with limited depth.
Synthesizes ideas and information.	Synthesizes ideas and information with a high degree of effectiveness.	Synthesizes ideas and information with considerable effectiveness.	Synthesizes ideas and information with some effectiveness.	Synthesizes ideas and information with a limited degree of effectiveness.

Communication	LEVEL 4	LEVEL 3	LEVEL 2	LEVEL 1
Communicates information.	Communicates information with a high degree of clarity.	Communicates information with considerable clarity.	Communicates information with some clarity.	Communicates information with a limited degree of clarity.
Uses proper conventions of language, grammar, and punctuation.	Uses proper conventions of language, grammar, and punctuation with a high degree of effectiveness.	Uses proper conventions of language, grammar, and punctuation with considerable effectiveness.	Uses proper conventions of language, grammar, and punctuation with some effectiveness.	Uses proper conventions of language, grammar, and punctuation with a limited degree of effectiveness.

Application	LEVEL 4	LEVEL 3	LEVEL 2	LEVEL 1
Demonstrates knowledge of newspaper article style conventions, format, and elements (headline, byline, 5Ws, lead, inverted pyramid, caption).	Demonstrates thorough knowledge of newspaper article style conventions, format, and elements (headline, byline, 5Ws, lead, inverted pyramid, caption).	Demonstrates considerable knowledge of newspaper article style conventions, format, and elements (headline, byline, 5Ws, lead, inverted pyramid, caption).	Demonstrates some knowledge of newspaper article style conventions, format, and elements (headline, byline, 5Ws, lead, inverted pyramid, caption).	Demonstrates limited knowledge of newspaper article style conventions, format, and elements (headline, byline, 5Ws, lead, inverted pyramid, caption).
Uses persuasive images, words, and phrases true to role, audience, and format.	Uses persuasive images, words, and phrases true to role, audience, and format with a high degree of effectiveness.	Uses persuasive images, words, and phrases true to role, audience, and format with considerable effectiveness.	Uses persuasive images, words, and phrases true to role, audience, and format with some effectiveness.	Uses persuasive images, words, and phrases true to role, audience, and format with limited effectiveness.

photocopy for students to fill out

Worksheet #6: Analysis of Historical Document

Work in groups of five to six students. Choose roles (recorder, presenter, etc.) among yourselves. Analyze the historical document using the questions below. The presenter reports the findings to the class, which will be recorded on the blackboard or on chart paper.

Each group may receive the same document to work on, or use different documents from the same time period.

teacher tip

The questions below apply to different grade levels. However, higher grades must complete the preceding stage(s) before answering their own grade-level questions.

Stage 1: Grades 6 - 8

1. Who is the author of the document?
2. Is it a single individual or a group of people?
3. What can we learn about the author's position, social class, nationality, and political views from the document?
4. When and where was the document written?
5. For whom was the document intended?
6. What do we learn about the times from this document? List five items.
7. Do you believe in what was written? Is it credible? Why or why not?
8. Is the language of the document easy to understand?
9. Is it addressed to more than one individual? Explain.
10. What main ideas are expressed in the document?

photocopy for students to fill out

Stage 2: Grades 9 - 10

1. What is the purpose of this document? What is it?
2. Is it a convincing document that logically outlines its position?
3. Does it entertain?
4. Is it emotionally charged? If so, select words that illustrate this.
5. What is the genre of the document? (formal/official, letter, etc.)
6. Is it grammatically correct with proper punctuation, etc.?
7. What are your general impressions about the document?

Stage 3: Grades 11 - 12

1. A critical analysis of the document. How important is this document? Be skeptical - is it telling the truth? What evidence is presented to support its claims? What other points of view might there be on the subject under discussion?

2. What can you learn about the society in which it was produced? List five things. What were their values/beliefs? What was important to them?
3. What does this document mean to you? What have you learned? Be sure to examine it by looking at concepts like *perpetrators, victims, bystanders, rescuers, henchmen*.

Follow-up assignment for individual students:

Write a one-page essay using the information taken from the historical document, explaining what you learned about the Ukrainian Genocide in 1932-33. Use the terms *perpetrator, victim, rescuer, bystander* when relevant, or prepare a drawing, painting or poster about the Holodomor that reflects your understanding of this event.

Ukrainian village in Kyiv oblast, 1929.

Lesson: Rights and Responsibilities

Grade Level:
Grades 9 to 12

Materials Required:

- Students should use materials and assignments from previous activities.
- Copies of the UN Universal Declaration of Human Rights for each group
- Implications of the UN Universal Declaration of Human Rights: **http://www.un.org/en/universal-declaration-human-rights/**

Set-up Required:
Form student groups

☑ **PRE-TASK ACTIVITY**

- Brainstorm a definition of "genocide."
- Ask students for examples of genocides that they know of in different areas of the world and the types of governments involved. The examples can be organized in chart form using columns.
- Discuss the question, "Why do genocides usually occur under such governments?"

☑ **TASK**

- Review the purpose of the UN Universal Declaration of Human Rights, and apply it to the 1932-1933 Famine in Ukraine.
- In small groups, students read the UN Universal Declaration of Human Rights and work from earlier activities to decide whether there were violations of human rights during the Famine and determine what rights were violated, if any.
- Groups present their findings. They then assess if there is consensus among the groups and identify different positions. One group is assigned to record the results of these discussions, which are then distributed to all the students.

Lesson: Effective Civic Action

Grade Level:
Grades 9 to 12

Materials Required:

- Copies of the handout in this lesson for each student or student group
- Copies for each student of the UN Convention Part II, p. 59 and online version, see URL below

Set-up Required:
UN Convention on the Prevention and Punishment of the Crime of Genocide
http://www.icrc.org/ihl.nsf/full/357?OpenDocument

☑ **PRE-TASK ACTIVITY**

- Teachers should discuss the UN Convention on the Prevention and Punishment of the Crime of Genocide with students, showing excerpts of the document.
- Teachers should discuss Raphael Lemkin's contribution to the concept of genocide, Part II, pp. 57-58.
- Students then read excerpts from Raphael Lemkin's "Soviet Genocide in the Ukraine," Part II, pp. 60-61.

☑ **TASK**

In groups or individually answer the questions in the handout provided on p. 241.

☑ **POST-TASK ACTIVITY**

What more would you want to know about individuals and non-government organizations dealing with genocide that have made a difference in global affairs?

Dead body on the street in Kharkiv, 1933.

Worksheet: Effective Civic Actions

Read the material provided by your teacher. In groups or individually consider the following questions:

1. What reason does Lemkin give for the Soviet attack on the Ukrainian population?

2. What is meant by "Russification"? What are its implications?

3. How, according to Lemkin, did the Soviets plan to destroy the Ukrainian nation?

4. List the 4 steps by which this was attempted. How was each carried out?

5. According to Lemkin, why was it necessary to destroy a large number of Ukrainian farmers?

6. How did the Soviets plan and carry out the Famine in Ukraine?

7. How, according to Lemkin, does the Ukrainian genocide differ from the attack on the Jews during the Second World War?

8. What evidence has Lemkin presented that the Genocide was indeed an attempt to destroy a culture and a nation?

9. What are your feelings about Lemkin's ideas on the "Soviet Genocide in Ukraine"?

10. What do you think of Raphael Lemkin's contribution to ensure genocide is viewed as a criminal act in international courts? Explain why.

11. How has the UN helped in either the prevention or punishment of the crime of genocide? How can this be improved?

photocopy for students to fill out

Lesson: International Criminal Court (ICC)

This lesson focuses on how people around the world responded to non-democratic actions by individuals, groups, or governments. Students will review ICC and UN documents to complete their assigned tasks.

Grade Level:
Grades 9 to 12

Materials Required:

- Copy of a "Request to Investigate" form to the International Criminal Court: **https://www.icc-cpi.int/get-involved/Documents/App%20form%20NEW%20PP%202016%2022%2003%2016.pdf**
- Additional web-sites with information about the International Criminal Court:
  - **http://www.icc-cpi.int/en_menus/icc/situations%20and%20cases/situations/icc0112/Documents/QandAMaliEng.pdf**
  - **https://www.icc-cpi.int**
  - Copies of Roman Serbyn's "The Holodomor and Article II of the UN Convention," Part II, pp. 62-64

☑ PRE-TASK ACTIVITY

- Students should have some knowledge of the Holodomor.
- Students review the UN Convention on the Prevention and Punishment of the Crime of Genocide and list any acts that occurred during the Ukrainian Famine that they think violate the Convention.

☑ TASK

- Select one act from the UN Convention, Part II, p. 59 (by Roman Serbyn). Based on their review of the UN document, have students complete the request form to send to the International Criminal Court.

☑ POST-TASK

- Students research the history, location and functions of the ICC and collect 2 facts about each.
- Students may research other methods for global citizens to respond to non-democratic movements through personal or group actions and discuss these in small groups. Small groups report their suggestions to the whole class.
- Students personally rate the various methods, including appeals to the International Criminal Court, on their effectiveness in preventing or punishing genocide in non-democratic and democratic countries.

PART IV

Appendix

IN THIS SECTION

Resource Lists:

Top Picks

Educational Websites

General Holodomor Websites

Documentaries

Print Materials

Supplementary Materials

Image Credits

"Children of the Holodomor," by Nina Marchenko. Oil on canvas panel of the Holodomor Monumental Triptych, 1998-2000. From "The Holodomor through the Eyes of Ukrainian Artists." Founder and trustee Morgan Williams.

In this Appendix you will find **Resource Lists,** including **Top Picks,** to a list of **Educational Websites**, **General Holodomor Websites**, **Documentaries**, and **Exhibits,** available on the Holodomor, as well as a list of some of the best and most recent **Print Materials** (mainly books) on the Holodomor.

The **Appendix** also includes **Supplementary Materials**, such as Raphael Lemkin's complete 1953 speech "The Soviet Genocide in the Ukraine," short stories for students, a brief two-page Timeline of Events before and during the Holodomor, and a newspaper article suggesting a connection between the Holodomor and events in present-day Ukraine. This section ends with **Image Credits** for images and photos used in this learning resource.

Q. ***"Why is the Holodomor unique among genocides and great crimes against humanity?"***

A. ***" Because its last chapter has yet to be written."***

From a presentation in 2014 at Columbia University by Walter Zarycky, Director of the Center for US-Ukrainian Relations.

"The famine was brought about in Ukraine in order to reduce the number of Ukrainians, resettle in their place people from other parts of the USSR, and in this way kill all thoughts of independence."

Prokopenko, Communist Party member and government official within the Ukrainian SSR, in 1934.

Resource Lists

TOP PICKS

Selected by Valentina Kuryliw and Lana Babij

The listings below are examples of resources in a given category suitable for classroom instruction.

NOTE: As of 2016, demographers have arrived at 4 million direct unnatural deaths during the Holodomor. Research is ongoing, this book used "millions."

Educational Websites on the Holodomor

1. **Holodomor Research and Education Consortium**
   A project of the Canadian Institute of Ukrainian Studies, University of Alberta
   www.education.holodomor.ca and *www.holodomor.ca*

   This website contains research-based, reliable content and curricular materials on the Holodomor for grades 6-12. Educational materials found here include background information for teachers and students, memoirs of survivors, primary documents, newspaper articles, excerpts from literature, as well as a variety of suggested lesson plans and assignments. Emphasis is placed on developing historical and critical thinking skills using a variety of strategies that complement curricula expectations in a number of provinces. The site has an excellent list of resources and links.

2. ***Nadiya – Hope*; Holodomor Supplemental Resource for Teachers**
   Edmonton Catholic Schools, Alberta
   www.education.holodomor.ca/supplemental-resource-for-teachers-nadiya-hope/
   www.ecsd.net/AboutUs/Overview/Holodomor/Pages/default.aspx

   Developed by educators throughout Canada for use in K-12 and for school events, this site draws together dozens of lesson plans, PowerPoint presentations, and background materials on the Holodomor and is grouped by grade level. Although some of the materials are designed for use in Catholic schools, all the resources can be adapted as needed.

3. **Manitoba. Diversity Education: Holodomor Education and Awareness**
   Manitoba Education and Training
   www.edu.gov.mb.ca/k12/cur/multic/holodomor.html
   www.edu.gov.mb.ca/k12/diversity/educators/index.html

   The official site of the Manitoba Ministry of Education describes how the Holodomor has been incorporated into the Manitoba curriculum, provides teaching resources, and offers links to sites on the Holodomor and other genocides.

4. **Classroom Resources for Teachers**
Connecticut Holodomor Awareness Committee
www.holodomorct.org and *www.holodomorct.org/links.html*

This site provides general information and includes an "Information Links" page that offers a categorized and regularly updated list of carefully selected print and media titles and direct links to a wide range of Holodomor resources.

5. **"Exposing the Ukrainian Holodomor – How starvation was used as a political weapon,"** 2017. (Unit 2, Chapter 5). Free curriculum-based teaching resource from "Voices into Action," 2017.
www.voicesintoaction.ca/Learn/Unit2/Chapter5/

This is a resource for educators prepared by the Saskatchewan Holodomor Awareness and Education Committee for Voices into Action. Unit 2 of the online resource provides information on five genocides. Chapter 5 is dedicated to the study of the Holodomor.

Documentaries on the Holodomor

1. ***Genocide Revealed.***
Educational Version, 2013. Directed by Yurij Luhovy. The 26- and 52- minute versions are on a single DVD for classroom use.
To purchase the DVD: http://www.yluhovy.com

This internationally acclaimed documentary on the Holodomor features rare historical footage, survivor accounts, commentaries by historians and declassified Soviet archival documents.

2. ***Harvest of Despair: The 1932-33 Man-Made Famine in Ukraine*.**
Directed by Slavko Nowytski and Yurij Luhovy. Toronto, 1984. 55 min.
To purchase the DVD: www.ucrdc.org/Films.html or *contact info@ucrdc.org*

Harvest of Despair is a feature-length documentary containing excellent background information on the Famine and its cover-up. Produced in the 1980s, it remains one of the best overall presentations on the history of the Holodomor within the context of world events, with an emphasis on how the world reacted.

3. ***The Soviet Story.***
Directed by Edvins Snore, 2008, 85 min.
To purchase the DVD: iTunes, Amazon

The opening 11 minutes of the film describe the 1932-33 Holodomor and can serve as a powerful introduction to the topic. The film outlines Stalin's murderous regime from its inception through its early complicity with the Nazis and describes the impact of this legacy today.

4. ***Holodomor: Voices of Survivors.***
Produced and directed by Ariadna Ochrymovych, Toronto, 2015, 30 min.
To purchase the DVD, contact: *www.ucrdc.org*

This 30-minute film is appropriate for grades 7-12. It presents the personal stories of 25 Ukrainian-Canadian survivors who were children in the 1930s, many of whom were orphaned and suffered severe illnesses and trauma. The film is interwoven with drawings that illustrate their experiences, rare archival footage, Soviet propaganda posters, and photos.

Books

1. Applebaum, Anne. *Red Famine: Stalin's War on Ukraine.* Toronto: Doubleday, 2017.

2. Conquest, Robert. *The Harvest of Sorrow: Soviet Collectivization and the Terror-Famine.* New York: Oxford University Press, 1986.

3. Klid, Bohdan and Alexander Motyl, eds. *The Holodomor Reader: A Sourcebook on the Famine of 1932-1933 in Ukraine*. Edmonton and Toronto: CIUS Press, 2012.

4. Liber, George O. *Total Wars and the Making of Modern Ukraine, 1914-1954*. Toronto: University of Toronto Press, 2016.

5. Naimark, Norman. *Stalin's Genocides*. Princeton, NJ: Princeton University Press, 2010.

6. Pyrih, Ruslan, ed. *Holodomor of 1932-33 in Ukraine: Documents and Materials*. Translated by Stephen Bandera. Kyiv: Kyiv Mohyla Academy Publishing House, 2008.

7. Romanyschyn, Oleh, Orest Steciw and Andrew Gregorovich, eds. *Holodomor: The Ukrainian Genocide 1932-1933*. Toronto: League of Ukrainian Canadians & Ucrainica Research Institute, 2014.

8. Snyder, Timothy. *Bloodlands: Europe Between Hitler and Stalin*. New York: Basic Books, 2010.

Articles on the Holodomor

1. Werth, Nicolas. "The Great Ukrainian Famine of 1932-1933: A Case Study" in the *Online Encyclopedia of Mass Violence*, published 19 April, 2008, modified Feb. 2015.

2. Lemkin, Raphael. "Soviet Genocide in the Ukraine" 1953.
Lemkin, who coined the word "genocide" and worked on the UN Convention on Genocide, asserts that events in Ukraine in the early 1930s were "the classic example of Soviet genocide." He concludes "This is not simply a case of mass murder. It is a case of genocide, of the destruction, not of individuals only, but of a culture and a nation."
www.education.holodomor.ca/teaching-materials/role-of-lemkin/

EDUCATIONAL WEBSITES

1. **Holodomor Research and Education Consortium**
   A project of the Canadian Institute of Ukrainian Studies, University of Alberta
   www.education.holodomor.ca and *www.holodomor.ca*

   This website contains research-based, reliable content and curricular materials on the Holodomor for grades 6-12. Educational materials found here include background information for teachers and students, memoirs of survivors, primary documents, excerpts from literature, newspaper articles, as well as a variety of suggested lesson plans and assignments. Emphasis is placed on developing historical and critical thinking skills using various strategies, which complement the new curricula expectations in a number of provinces.

2. **Manitoba – Diversity Education – Holodomor Education and Awareness**
   Manitoba Education and Training
   www.edu.gov.mb.ca/k12/cur/multic/holodomor.html

   The official site of the Manitoba Ministry of Education describes how the Holodomor has been incorporated into the Manitoba curriculum, provides teaching resources, and offers links to sites on the Holodomor and other genocides.

3. ***Nadiya – Hope*; Holodomor Supplemental Resource for Teachers**
   Edmonton Catholic Schools, Alberta
   www.education.holodomor.ca/supplemental-resource-for-teachers-nadiya-hope/
   www.ecsd.net/AboutUs/Overview/Holodomor/Pages/default.aspx

   Developed by educators throughout Canada for use in K-12 and for school events, this site draws together dozens of lesson plans, PowerPoint presentations, and background materials on the Holodomor and is grouped by grade level. Although some of the materials are designed for use in Catholic schools, all the resources can be adapted as needed.

4. ***Share the Story***
   Ukrainian Canadian Research and Documentation Centre; Ukrainian Canadian Congress; Ukrainian World Congress
   www.sharethestory.ca

   The website includes a collection of interviews with survivors of the Holodomor living in Canada. "Share the Story" offers 80 short video clips and transcripts from the interviews that are an excellent resource for students.

5. ***Ukrainian famine memoirs***
   The Montreal Institute for Genocide and Human Rights Studies (MIGS), Concordia University
   www.concordia.ca/research/migs/resources/ukrainian-famine-memoirs.html

This site features 32 brief written eyewitness testimonies translated from Ukrainian into English. Recommended for use as a primary source in classrooms.

6. **Ukrainian Education Virtual Resources Portal**
Saskatchewan Ministry of Education. Prairie Spirit School Division No. 206
www.spiritsd.ca/ukrainian/eng_high_holodomor.htm

This site provides links to a basic Holodomor PowerPoint presentation for middle grades. The 14 slides are provided in both English and Ukrainian versions; background information and a list of additional resources are also included.

7. **Holodomorct.org**
Connecticut Holodomor Awareness Committee
www.holodomorct.org and *www.holodomorct.org/links.html*

This website provides general information and an "Information Links" page that includes a categorized and regularly updated list of carefully selected print and media titles and direct links to a wide range of Holodomor resources.

8. **"Turning a Blind Eye: A Unit of Study"**
Lana Babij, Lidia Choma and Borys Krupa. Rev. 2013
www.holodomorct.org/HOLODOMOR-CLASSROOM-RESOURCES.html

This resource is intended for high school and college levels, centering on comparative news analysis. It is based on Stanford's "Reading like a historian" model and linked to specific Common Core standards. This resource includes primary sources consisting of sets of conflicting news reports, with secondary sources for background information. Readings are provided on the Holodomor, the Great Leap Forward Famine, the Darfur Crisis, and Media Challenges Today. Suggested further activities and additional resource options are also provided.

9. **"Holodomor: Famine Genocide in Ukraine 1932-1933"**
PowerPoint presentation PDF by Maria Kiciuk and Oksana Kulynych, 2012
www.holodomorct.org/Holodomor-FamineGenocideinUkraine1932-193312-12.pdf
Addendum: *www.ridnashkola.org/Holodomor/HOLODOMOR-P.P.ADDENDUM.pdf*

This site consists of 45 slides, which include suggested activities and resources for further study of the Holodomor.

10. ***Genocide Never Again [Ukrainian Genocide]***
Teacher and student workbook by Vera Bej, Ihor Mirchuk, and Christine R. Shwed, 2007
www.ncua.inform-decisions.com/eng/files/UkrGenocide_Teacher_Student_Workbook.pdf

This workbook for grades 7-12 that includes 12 worksheets explicitly matched by "eligible content" to applicable Pennsylvania standards. This workbook is multidisciplinary and addresses social studies, math, music, literary and visual arts, and is supplemented by a liberal use of photos, graphics, and full colour reproductions.

11. ***The Ukrainian Genocide/Holodomor, 1932-1933; A Curriculum and Resource Guide for Educators***
Myron B. Kuropas and James Mace, updated 2011
http://cis.uchicago.edu/oldsite/sites/cis.uchicago.edu/files/resources/100113-ukraine-holodomor-curriculum.pdf

Developed by the state of Illinois, which mandates the study of "the Famine-Genocide in Ukraine," this curriculum and resource guide contains an overview of the subject, a section on "food as a political weapon," a glossary, and an extensive bibliography as well as several pages of activities and questions for either the junior high or senior high school level.

12. ***Curriculum Guide for Teaching Genocides with a Focus on the Holodomor, the Famine Genocide in Ukraine***
Motria Melnyk, 2011
http://cis.uchicago.edu/oldsite/sites/cis.uchicago.edu/files/resources/110128-ukraine-genocide.pdf

This curriculum guide applies Stanton's classic "eight stages of genocide" and provides an overview of seven genocides in the 20th century, using the Holodomor as a case study. Also included are related classroom exercises and activities for grades 6-9.

13. ***Model Curriculum for Human Rights and Genocide***
California Department of Education, California State Board of Education
www.cde.ca.gov/ci/hs/im/documents/modelcurrichrgenoc.pdf

14. **"Exposing the Ukrainian Holodomor – How starvation was used as a political weapon,"** (Unit 2, Chapter 5) Free curriculum-based teaching resources from "Voices Into Action," 2017.
www.voicesintoaction.ca/Learn/Unit2/Chapter5/

This is a teaching resource for educators prepared by the Saskatchewan Holodomor Awareness and Education Committee for "Voices into Action." Unit 2 of the online resource provides information on five genocides. Chapter 5 is dedicated to the study of the Holodomor.

ONLINE RESOURCES

1. **Holodomor Survivors and Share the Story**
   Ukrainian Canadian Research and Documentation Centre; Ukrainian Canadian Congress; Ukrainian World Congress
   www.holodomorsurvivors.ca/Survivors.html and *www.sharethestory.ca*

   These sites contain interviews with Holodomor survivors living in Canada, who share their memories and experiences of the Famine, during which many of them were children. The interviews are an excellent primary source, and the site also provides other information and scholarly articles.

2. **Gareth Richard Vaughan Jones – Hero of Ukraine**
   www.garethjones.org/

   This website on the life and writings of this British/Welsh journalist Gareth Jones includes his articles and writings about the Famine–Genocide in the 1930s, for which he was criticized by Soviet authorities and some of his colleagues. He was killed a few years later under mysterious circumstances. The site also presents valuable articles on Holodomor photo documentation.

3. **The Ukraine Famine**
   Webpage on the HistoryWiz website.
   www.historywiz.com/ukrainefamine.htm

   HistoryWiz is for "lovers of history." The section on the Ukrainian Famine includes some useful links for further information, along with a brief "multimedia" exhibit on the Holodomor called "The Terror Genocide" by Jennifer Brainard.

4. **The Artificial Famine/Genocide (Holodomor) in Ukraine 1932-33**
   Webpage on the Infoukes website.
   www.infoukes.com/history/famine/

   This site is notable for a few interesting articles on Holodomor denial and deniers.

5. **USSR 1932-1934: Soviet Genocide/Famine in Ukraine (Holodomor)**
   Webpage for the Prevent Genocide International website.
   www.preventgenocide.org/edu/pastgenocides/soviet/ukraine/resources/

   This website is a global education and action network for the prevention of genocide and crimes against humanity, which includes a page on the Holodomor that offers a list of references.

6. **The Great Famine Project (MAPA): Digital Atlas of Ukraine**
   Ukrainian Research Institute, Harvard University
   www.gis.huri.harvard.edu/ and *www.gis.huri.harvard.edu/historical-atlas/the-great-famine.html*

For information on the Holodomor presented in a unique visual form, see the Great Famine Project of the MAPA: Digital Atlas of Ukraine program. The Atlas uses Geographic Information Systems (GIS) for illustrating and explaining economic, historical, political, and social transformations within Ukraine. The Great Famine Project presents various types of data in graphic and map form, to better understand the nature and effects of the Holodomor.

7. **"The Great Hunger"**
CBC Radio "Ideas"
Part 1: *www.cbc.ca/radio/ideas/the-great-hunger-part-1-ukraine-1.2913833*
Part 2: *www.cbc.ca/radio/ideas/the-great-hunger-part-2-ireland-1.2913835*

These two episodes first aired on the CBC Radio program "Ideas" in 2009. Part 1 examines the Holodomor in Ukraine and Part 2 examines the Great Famine in Ireland.

PRINT MATERIALS

The books listed here are a good starting point for teachers and students wishing to learn about the Holodomor and are also recommended as reference materials for student assignments and projects.

1. Altman, Linda Jacobs. "Forced Famine in Ukraine," *Genocide: The Systematic Killing of a People.* New York: Enslow Publishers Inc., 2008 (pp. 43-50).
   A very good overview, especially for the young adult reader, this book contains ten short chapters that present different examples of genocide, along with extensive references for further reading. The book received strong positive reviews for use by students in grades 6 and older.

   Preview of selected pages from this chapter:
   https://books.google.ca/books?id=9jui9D_JVVEC&printsec=frontcover&source=gbs_ge_summary_r&cad=0#v=onepage&q&f=false

2. Applebaum, Anne. *Red Famine: Stalin's War on Ukraine*. Toronto: Doubleday, 2017.
   Applebaum's compulsively readable narrative captures the horror of ordinary people struggling to survive extraordinary evil, who perished in the millions because Stalin set out to destroy the Ukrainian peasantry after a series of rebellions to his policy of agricultural collectivization, and it presents how Russia, the successor to the Soviet Union, may foreshadow a new threat to the political order in the twenty-first century.

3. Borysenko, V. K. *A Candle in Remembrance: An Oral History of the Ukrainian Genocide of 1932-1933.* New York: Ukrainian National Women's League of America, 2010.
   A collection of brief testimonies resulting from research conducted in Ukraine, this book includes an informative, well-documented introduction as well as historical and contemporary photographs.

4. Cawthorne, Nigel. *The Crimes of Stalin: The Murderous Career of the Red Tsar.* London: Arcturus Publishing Ltd., 2011.

5. Chalupa, Andrea, *et al. Orwell and the Refugees: The Untold Story of Animal Farm.* Kindle Edition, 2012.
   Responding to the book *Animal Farm*, Chalupa explains Orwell's inspiration for writing his book and connects the concept of *Animal Farm* to the Ukrainian Famine.

6. Charny, Israel W. *Encyclopedia of Genocide.* Santa Barbara, California: ABC-CLIO, 1999.
   The sections titled "Ukrainian Genocide," Vol. II, pp. 565-567, and "On the Ukrainian Famine and the Definition of Genocide," Vol. II, pp. 382-383, present an extended quotation by eminent genocide scholar Leo Kuper asserting that the Ukrainian Famine was a genocide.

7. Chorbajian, Levon and George Shirinian, eds. *Studies in Comparative Genocide.* London: Palgrave Macmillan, 1999.
   The chapter "The Ukrainian Famine of 1932-33" by Frank Sysyn is recommended reading.

8. Colley, Margaret S. *More Than a Grain of Truth: The Biography of Gareth Richard Vaughan Jones.* Nottingham, England: Nigel Lindsay Colley Publisher, 2005.

9. Conquest, Robert. *The Harvest of Sorrow: Soviet Collectivization and the Terror-Famine.* New York: Oxford University Press, 1986.
   A classic account of the Holodomor, *The Harvest of Sorrow* is still one of the best sources of information by one of the pioneers in Holodomor studies.

10. Courtois, Stéphane, et al. *The Black Book of Communism: Crimes, Terror, Repression.* Cambridge, Massachusetts: Harvard University Press, 1999.
    Particularly recommended are sections 7-9 of Part I: "A State against Its People: Violence, Repression, and Terror in the Soviet Union," by Nicolas Werth; (pp.146-179).

11. Hetman, David, and Ivan Yukhnovskiy. *The Holodomor 1932-1933: genocide against the Ukrainian people.* Kyiv: Olena Teliha Publishers, 2008.
    This book contains photos of an exhibit of posters on the Holodomor in a large booklet format, presented by the Ukrainian Institute of National Memory. Also included are photos and documents from various archives in Ukraine that are suitable for students.

12. Hunczak, Taras and Roman Serbyn, eds. *Famine in Ukraine 1932-1933: Genocide by Other Means.* New York: Shevchenko Scientific Society, 2007.
    A valuable collection of articles, demographic analysis, newly translated archival decrees, correspondence, and survivor testimony.

13. Isajiw, Wsevolod W., ed. *Famine Genocide in Ukraine 1932-1933: Western Archives, Testimonies and Research.* Toronto: Ukrainian Canadian Research and Documentation Centre, 2003.

14. Ivshyna, L., ed. *Day and Eternity of James Mace.* Kyiv: Ukrainian Press Group Ltd., 2005.

This book contains articles by American historian James Mace, a pioneer in the study of the Ukrainian Genocide in the West and in Ukraine.

15. Kardinalowska, Tatiana. *The Ever-Present Past: The Memoirs of Tatiana Kardinalowska.* Transcribed by Assya Humesky and translated by Vera Kaczmarska. Toronto/ Edmonton: CIUS Press, 2004.

An exceptional and extremely readable testimony of the cataclysmic times witnessed by the author—the Ukrainian Revolution, the subsequent Civil War and Ukrainian-Soviet War, and the first fifteen years of Bolshevik rule in Ukraine, including the periods of Ukrainization and then Stalinist terror. To obtain a copy, visit: *https://ciuspress.com/catalogue/memoir-and-biography/84/the-ever- present-past*

16. Klid, Bohdan and Alexander Motyl, eds. *The Holodomor Reader: A Sourcebook on the Famine of 1932-1933 in Ukraine.* Toronto: CIUS Press, 2012.

The *Holodomor Reader* is a wide-ranging collection of key texts and source materials, many of which have never before appeared in English on the genocidal famine. The Holodomor is introduced in an extensive interpretive essay, and the material is presented in six sections: scholarship; legal assessments, findings, and resolutions; eyewitness accounts and memoirs; survivor testimonies, memoirs, diaries, and letters; Soviet, Ukrainian, British, German, Italian, and Polish documents; and works of literature.

To purchase the book: *www.ciuspress.com/catalogue/history/324/the-holodomor-reader*

To view excerpts online: *http://holodomor.ca/the-holodomor-reader-a-sourcebook-on-the-famine-of-1932-1933-in-ukraine/*

17. Krawchenko, Bohdan and Roman Serbyn, eds. *Famine in Ukraine, 1932–1933.* Edmonton: CIUS Press,1986.

This pioneering volume was one of the first scholarly efforts to analyze the famine. To purchase the book: *www.ciuspress.com/catalogue/history/18/famine-in-ukraine%2C-1932%2D1933*

18. Kuromiya, Hiroaki. *The Voices of the Dead: Stalin's Great Terror in the 1930s.* New Haven, CT: Yale University Press, 2007.

19. Liber, George O. *Total Wars and the Making of Modern Ukraine, 1914-1954.* Toronto: University of Toronto Press, 2016.

The chapters on the 1920s and 1930s deal with the background, planning, and execution of the Holodomor and use current archival information and analysis.

20. Luciuk, Lubomyr. ed. *Holodomor: Reflections on the Great Famine of 1932-1933 in Soviet Ukraine.* Kingston, Ontario: Kashtan Press, 2008.

21. Luciuk, Lubomyr, ed. *"Tell Them We Are Starving," The 1933 Soviet Diaries of Gareth Jones.* Kingston, Ontario: Kashtan Press, 2015.
This book provides scans and transcriptions of the three pocket notebooks that Welsh journalist Gareth Jones compiled during a three-week stay in the USSR in March 1933. His research resulted in the publication of articles about the Famine in 1933, which the Soviets and many of his colleagues denied.

22. Luciuk, Lubomyr. *Not Worthy: Walter Duranty's Pulitzer Prize and the New York Times.* Kingston, Ontario: Kashtan Press, 2004.

23. Mace, James. *Communism and the Dilemma of National Liberation: National Communism in Soviet Ukraine 1918-1933.* Cambridge, Massachusetts: Harvard Universiisty Press, 1983.

24. Mace, James. "I Was Chosen by Your Dead," *The Day* (Kyiv), Feb.18, 2003.

25. Marples, David. *Heroes and Villains: Creating National History in Contemporary Ukraine.* Budapest: Central European University Press, 2008.
This work offers compelling examples from archival documents on the significance of "the national question" for understanding the Holodomor.

26. Martin, Terry. *The Affirmative Action Empire: Nations and Nationalism in the Soviet Union, 1923-1939.* Ithaca, NY: Cornell University Press, 2001.
Chapter 7, "The National Interpretation of the 1933 Famine" (pp. 273- 308), is recommended reading, although related material is found throughout the book.

27. McVay, Athanasius D. and Lubomyr Luciuk, eds. *The Holy See and the Holodomor: Documents from the Vatican Secret Archives on the Great Famine of 1932-1933 in Soviet Ukraine.* Kingston, Ontario; Kashtan Press, 2011.

28. Naimark, Norman. *Stalin's Genocides.* Princeton, NJ: Princeton University Press, 2010.
In this gripping book, Naimark explains how Stalin became a pitiless mass killer. He looks at the most consequential and harrowing episodes of Stalin's systematic destruction of his own populace — the liquidation and repression of the so-called kulaks, the Ukrainian Famine, the purge of nationalities, and the Great Terror — and examines them in light of other genocides in history.
To purchase the book: *www.press.princeton.edu/titles/9278.html*

29. Pidhainy, Semen, ed. *The Black Deeds of the Kremlin: A White Book, Volume 1, Book of Testimonies,* Toronto, Ontario: Ukrainian Association of Victims of Russian Communist Terror, 1953.
In 1953, on the occasion of the twentieth anniversary of the Famine of 1932–1933 in Ukraine, Ukrainian émigrés published an English-language collection of eyewitness accounts and testimonies detailing Soviet crimes they had experienced less than 20 years earlier, which constitute some of the earliest recorded oral histories of the Holdomor.
Volume 2, The Great Famine in Ukraine in 1932-1933, Detroit, MI: Democratic

Organization of Ukrainians Formerly Persecuted by the Soviet Regime, 1955.
A second volume, published in 1955, was dedicated to collectivization and the Famine.

30. Pyrih, Ruslan, ed. *Holodomor of 1932-33 in Ukraine: Documents and Materials.* Translated by Stephen Bandera. Kyiv: Kyiv Mohyla Academy Publishing House, 2008.
A collection of 73 archival Soviet and Ukrainian documents and the correspondence of Stalin, Molotov and Kaganovich on the Ukrainian Famine in the 1930s. An excellent primary source. To view excerpts online:
www.education.holodomor.ca/educational-resources-list/pyrih-documents/

31. Romanyschyn, Oleh, Orest Steciw, and Andrew Gregorovich. *Holodomor: The Ukrainian Genocide 1932-1933.* Toronto: League of Ukrainian Canadians, Ucrainica Research Institute, 2014.
A series of informational graphic posters on the Holodomor compiled in a book.

32. Shapoval, Yurij. "Letters from Kharkiv," *The Day newspaper,* no. 35, (20 Nov. 2007).
An article describing the Holodomor through the eyes of Italian diplomats.

33. Snyder, Timothy. *Bloodlands: Europe Between Hitler and Stalin.* New York: Basic Books, 2010. (pp. 21-58).
Bloodlands is a new kind of European history, presenting the mass murders committed by the Nazi and Stalinist regimes as two aspects of a single history, in the time and place where they occurred: between Germany and Russia, when dictators Hitler and Stalin both held power in 1933 to 1945. Required reading for anyone seeking to understand the Holodomor in its context within this central tragedy of modern history. Pages 21-58 are particularly recommended.

34. Viola, Lynne. *The War Against the Peasantry 1927 – 1930: The Tragedy of the Soviet Countryside*. New Haven, CT: Yale University Press, 2005.

HISTORICAL FICTION

1. Dimarov, A., Y. Hutsalo, and O. Zvychayna. *A Hunger Most Cruel: The Human Face of the 1932-1933 Terror-Famine in Soviet Ukraine.* Translated by Roma Franko. Toronto: Language Lantern Publications, 2003.
This is a book of short stories on the Genocidal Famine suitable for students.

2. Grossman, Vasily. *Everything Flows.* Translated by Robert Chandler, Elizabeth Chandler and Anna Aslanyan. New York: New York Review Books, 2009.

3. Kaaberbol, Lene and Agnete Friis. *Death of a Nightingale.* Translated by Elisabeth Dyssegaard. New York: Soho Press Inc., 2013.

4. Mak, Olha. *Stones Under the Scythe.* Translated by Vera Kaczmarskyj. Bloomington: iUniverse Inc., 2011.

A novel suitable for young adults about a young man looking for refuge in the city of Kharkiv during the Holodomor.

5. Motyl, Alexander J. *Sweet Snow.* Somerville, Massachussetts: Cervena Barva Press, 2013.
   A novel suitable for mature students.

6. Orwell, George. *Animal Farm.* New York: Penguin. 1945.
   A novel suitable for students at the grade 6 level and higher.

7. Samchuk, Ulas. *Maria*. Translated by Roma Franko. Toronto: Language Lanterns Publications Inc. 2011.
   A novel about the life of a woman in a Ukrainian village before and during the Holodomor; suitable for high school students.

8. Skrypuch, Martha Forchuk. *Enough*. Markham, Ontario: Fitzhenry & Whiteside, 2000.
   An illustrated children's book for younger grades.

9. Skrypuch, Martha Forchuk, ed. *Kobzar's Children: A Century of Untold Ukrainian Stories.* Markham, Ontario: Fitzhenry & Whiteside, 2006.
   "The Rings" is a short story reproduced in this book with recommended student activities, suitable for youth.

10. Smith, Tom Rob. *Child 44.* New York: Grand Central Publishing, 2008.
    A gripping WW2 detective story suitable for mature students and adults.

DOCUMENTARIES

1. Genocide Revealed.
Educational version. Directed by Yurij Luhovy (Montreal, 2013). The 26- and 52-minute versions are on a single DVD for classroom use.
To purchase the DVD: www.yluhovy.com

This internationally acclaimed documentary on the Holodomore features rare historical footage, survivor testimonies, commentaries by historians and declassified Soviet archival documents.

2. Harvest of Despair: The 1932-33 Man-Made Famine in Ukraine.
Directed by Slavko Nowytski and Yurij Luhovy. Toronto, 1984. 55 min.
To purchase the DVD: www.ucrdc.org/Films.html or contact *info@ucrdc.org*

A feature-length documentary containing excellent background information on the Famine and on its cover-up. Produced in the 1980s, the documentary remains one of the best overall presentations on the history of the Holodomor in the context of world events, with an emphasis on how the world reacted.

3. ***The Soviet Story.***
Directed by Edvins Snore, 2008, 85 min.
To view video: www.youtube.com/watch?v=tlslHXPN2Fo or *www.vimeo.com/73284941*

The opening 11 minutes of the film describe the 1932-33 Genocidal Famine and can serve as a powerful introduction to the topic. The film outlines Stalin's murderous regime from its inception through its early complicity with the Nazis and describes the impact of this legacy today.

4. ***Holodomor: Voices of Survivors.***
Produced and directed by Ariadna Ochrymovych, 2015, 30 min.
To purchase the DVD, contact: www.ucrdc.org

This 30-minute film is appropriate for grades 7-12. It presents the personal stories of 25 Ukrainian-Canadian survivors who were children in the 1930s, many of whom were orphaned and suffered severe illnesses and trauma. The film is interwoven with drawings that illustrate their experiences, rare archival footage, Soviet propaganda posters, and photos.

5. ***Eternal Memory: Voices From the Great Terror.***
New York: Wellsprings Films, 1997, 81 min.
To view online: https://www.youtube.com/watch?v=H9e9B5NsA_M

Award-winning documentary, produced and directed by a team of American and Canadian filmmakers and narrated by Meryl Streep.

6. ***The Living*** (Ukr: *Zhyvi*).
Directed by Serhiy Bukovsky, Ukraine, 2008. English subtitles, 75 min.
To view the trailer: https://www.youtube.com/watch?v=15Urz6CdOu4
To purchase the DVD, contact: sy2165@columbia.edu, Ukrainian Film Club of Columbia University.

Conversations with several Holodomor survivors are woven into a gripping reconstruction of the investigative reporting by the young Welsh journalist Gareth Jones as he attempts to alert the world to the devastating Famine in Ukraine in the winter of 1932-33. The faith and resilience of "the living" poignantly counterbalance the harrowing legacy of their experience. Bukovsky previously directed *Spell Your Name*, about the Holocaust in Ukraine.

7. ***Holodomor.***
Canad Inns, Winnipeg, 2008, 26 min.
To purchase the DVD, contact Cindy Carswell: www.CanadInns.com/contact-us/

This 26-minute account of the Holodomor, as seen through the eyes of twelve eyewitnesses now living in Canada, is an excellent resource for schools.

8. ***In Memory of Konstantyn Bokan*** (English version).
Produced in cooperation with the Ucrainica Research Institute, Toronto, 2015. 9 min.
To view the video online: www.youtube.com/watch?v=wyATD6Nd0S8&feature=youtu.be

In this brief video, the author constructs a vignette based on an extremely rare series of photos taken during the Holodomor by Mykola Bokan, an amateur photographer who documented the deaths of his family members from starvation. Supplemented by many other photos from the period and a simple to understand narrative, this video can be useful for grades 7+.

9. ***Holodomor: Ukraine's Genocide.***
Produced by Bobby Leigh (Beverly Hills, California: Moksha Films, 2012), 22 min.
To obtain the DVD and view a short version: http://www.holodomorthemovie.com/

The film uses recent archival evidence, academic commentary and eyewitness accounts to describe the execution of the Famine genocide.

EXHIBITS

1. ***Holodomor: Genocide by Famine***
Produced by the League of Ukrainian Canadians in cooperation with the Kyiv Memorial Society in Ukraine and the Ucrainica Research Institute. 2008.
To download the 2-part set visit: www.holodomoreducation.org/index.php/id/202
This informational exhibit features 101 colour posters presented on a CD.

2. ***National Museum "Memorial to Holodomor Victims,"*** Kyiv, Ukraine.
en.wikipedia.org/wiki/National_Museum_%22Memorial_to_Holodomor_victims%22
The museum in Kyiv is an unforgettable experience that is both moving and uplifting. Its website has original photographs of the Famine period.

3. ***Revelations from the Russian Archives: Ukrainian Famine***
U.S. Library of Congress. Washington, D.C.
www.loc.gov/exhibits/archives/ukra.html
Created in the early 1990s, the exhibition was the first public display of previously secret archival documents from the former USSR.

SURVIVOR ACCOUNTS AND MEMOIRS

These online and print sources consist almost entirely of survivor memoirs or accounts.

1. Dolot, M. ***Execution by Hunger: The Hidden Holocaust.*** New York: W. W. Norton & Company, 1987.
The author, a teenager during the Famine in Ukraine, presents a harrowing eyewitness account of the Holodomor as it was implemented and experienced in his village.

2. Szpuk, Andy. ***Sliding on the Snow Stone.*** The UK: That Right Publishing LLC., 2011.
   This is a memoir in which the author recounts his childhood years during the Famine. In later chapters, Szpuk describes his experiences running from both the Nazis and the Russian army with his father.

3. ***Holodomor: Voices of Survivors.*** Produced and directed by Ariadna Ochrymovych, 2015, 30 min.
   To purchase the DVD, visit: www.ucrdc.org
   This 30-minute film is appropriate for grades 7-12. It presents the personal stories of 25 Ukrainian-Canadian survivors who were children in the 1930s, many of whom were orphaned and suffered severe illnesses and trauma. The film is interwoven with drawings that illustrate their experiences, rare archival footage, Soviet propaganda posters, and photos.

4. ***Holodomor Survivors Tell Their Stories.*** Ukrainian Canadian Research and Documentation Centre and the Ukrainian Canadian Congress.
   www.holodomorsurvivors.ca
   This excellent primary source features 60 interviews with Canadians who were children in 1932-1933 and survived the Holodomor. The video accounts are in Ukrainian with English subtitles.

5. ***The Ever-Present Past: The Memoirs of Tatiana Kardinalowska.*** Kardinalowska, Tatiana. Transcribed by Assya Humesky and translated by Vera Kaczmarskyj. Toronto/Edmonton: CIUS Press, 2004.
   Suitable for high school students.

6. ***Share the Story.*** Ukrainian Canadian Research and Documentation Centre, Ukrainian Canadian Congress, and the Ukrainian World Congress.
   www.sharethestory.ca
   It features 80 short vignettes of survivors who were children during the Holodomor in 1932-1933. An excellent resource for students.

7. ***Holodomor.*** Canad Inns, 2008, 26 min.
   To obtain the DVD contact Cindy Carswell: www.CanadInns.com/contact-us/
   This 26-minute account of the Holodomor as seen through the eyes of twelve eyewitnesses, now living in Canada, is an excellent resource for schools.

8. ***Ukrainian famine memoirs.*** Montreal Institute for Genocide and Human Rights Studies (MIGS), Concordia University.
   www.migs.concordia.ca/links/UkrainefaminememoirsfromMartaD.Olynyk.htm
   The site features 32 brief written testimonies translated from Ukrainian into English that were originally published in Holod 33: Narodna knyha-memorial (Famine 33: People's Memorial Book). Kyiv: Radiaskyi Pysmennyk, 1991. The testimonies are recommended for use as primary sources in classrooms.

9. ***The Ukrainian Holodomor.*** 3 survivor transcripts.
www.theage.com.au/multimedia/ukrainefamine/transcripts/transcript_viktor.pdf http:// www.theage.com.au/multimedia/ukrainefamine/transcripts/transcript_tanya.pdf www. theage.com.au/multimedia/ukrainefamine/transcripts/transcript_bozenna.pdf
These three brief accounts are included in a collection of materials on the Holodomor held by the Australian newspaper *The Age*.

10. ***Oral History Project of the Commission on the Ukraine Famine.*** Washington: U.S. G.P.O., 1990. Compiled by James E. Mace and Leonid Heretz.
www.catalog.hathitrust.org/Record/002468069
The three volumes contain hundreds of eyewitness and survivor testimonies translated into English.

11. **U.S. Commission on the Ukraine Famine. *Investigation of the Ukrainian Famine, 1932-1933: Report to Congress.*** Washington: U.S. GPO. 1988.
Each of the reports linked below includes the testimony of scores of Famine survivors.
First Interim Report: http://catalog.hathitrust.org/Record/001299877
Final Report, Appendix I also includes a selection of oral histories from the three volumes of the Oral History Project listed above
http://babel.hathitrust.org/cgi/pt?id=umn.31951d00831044s;view=1up;seq=263

12. Pidhainy, Semen, ed. ***The Black Deeds of the Kremlin: A White Book****, Volume 1, Book of Testimonies,* Toronto, Ontario: Ukrainian Association of Victims of Russian Communist Terror, 1953.
In 1953, on the occasion of the twentieth anniversary of the Famine of 1932–1933 in Ukraine, Ukrainian émigrés published an English-language collection of eyewitness accounts and testimonies detailing Soviet crimes they had experienced less than 20 years earlier, which constitute some of the earliest recorded oral histories of the Holdomor.
Volume 2, The Great Famine in Ukraine in 1932-1933, Detroit, MI: Democratic Organization of Ukrainians Formerly Persecuted by the Soviet Regime, 1955.
A second volume, published in 1955, was dedicated to collectivization and the Famine.

13. Borysenko, V K. ***A Candle in Remembrance: An Oral History of the Ukrainian Genocide of 1932-1933.*** New York: Ukrainian National Women's League of America, 2010.
A collection of testimonies resulting from research conducted in Ukraine, this book includes an informative, well-documented introduction as well as historical and contemporary photographs.

FEATURE FILM

Bitter Harvest. Produced by Ian Ihnatowycz, directed by George Mendeluk, 2017. 1h 43 min. *For more information: http://www.imdb.com/title/tt3182620/*
To purchase the DVD: Amazon and other outlets.

Supplementary Materials

SPEECH: "SOVIET GENOCIDE IN THE UKRAINE"

Raphael Lemkin (1953)

'Love Ukraine'
You cannot love other peoples
Unless you love Ukraine.
- Volodymyr Sosyura, poet

The mass murder of peoples and of nations that has characterized the advance of the Soviet Union into Europe is not a new feature of their policy of expansionism, it is not an innovation devised simply to bring uniformity out of the diversity of Poles, Hungarians, Balts, Romanians — presently disappearing into the fringes of their empire. Instead, it has been a long-term characteristic even of the internal policy of the Kremlin — one which the present masters had ample precedent for in the operations of Tsarist Russia. It is indeed an indispensable step in the process of 'union' that the Soviet leaders fondly hope will produce the 'Soviet Man', the 'Soviet Nation' and to achieve that goal, that unified nation, the leaders of the Kremlin will gladly destroy the nations and the cultures that have long inhabited Eastern Europe.

What I want to speak about is perhaps the classic example of Soviet genocide, its longest and broadest experiment in Russification — the destruction of the Ukrainian nation. This is, as I have said, only the logical successor of such Tsarist crimes as the drowning of 10,000 Crimean Tatars by order of Catherine the Great, the mass murders of Ivan the Terrible's 'SS troops' — the Oprichnina; the extermination of National Polish leaders and Ukrainian Catholics by Nicholas I; and the series of Jewish pogroms that have stained Russian history periodically. And it has had its matches within the Soviet Union in the annihilation of the Ingerian nation, the Don and Kuban Cossacks, the Crimean Tatar Republics, the Baltic Nations of Lithuania, Estonia and Latvia. Each is a case in the long-term policy of liquidation of non-Russian peoples by the removal of select parts.

Ukraine constitutes a slice of Southeastern USSR equal in area to France and Italy, and inhabited by some 30 million people. Itself the Russian bread basket, geography has made it a strategic key to the oil of the Caucasus and Iran, and to the entire Arab world. In the north, it borders Russia proper. As long as Ukraine retains its national unity, as long as its people continue to think of themselves as Ukrainians and to seek independence, so long Ukraine poses a serious threat to the very heart of Sovietism. It is no wonder that the Communist leaders have attached the greatest importance to the Russification of this independent member of their 'Union of Republics', have determined to remake it to fit their pattern of one Russian nation. For the Ukrainian is not and has never been, a Russian. His culture, his temperament, his language, his religion — all are different. At the side door to Moscow, he has refused to be collectivized, accepting deportation, even death. And so it is peculiarly important that the Ukrainian be fitted into the Procrustean pattern of the ideal Soviet man.

Ukraine is highly susceptible to racial murder by select parts and so the Communist tactics there have not followed the pattern taken by the German attacks against the Jews. The nation is too populous to be exterminated completely with any efficiency. However, its leadership, religious, intellectual, political, its select and determining parts, are quite small and therefore easily eliminated, and so it is upon these groups particularly that the full force of the Soviet axe has fallen, with its familiar tools of mass murder, deportation and forced labour, exile and starvation.

The attack has manifested a systematic pattern, with the whole process repeated again and again to meet fresh outbursts of national spirit. The first blow is aimed at the intelligentsia, the national brain, so as to paralyse the rest of the body. In 1920, 1926 and again in 1930–1933, teachers, writers, artists, thinkers, political leaders, were liquidated, imprisoned or deported. According to the /Ukrainian Quarterly/ of Autumn 1948, 51,713 intellectuals were sent to Siberia in 1931 alone. At least 114 major poets, writers and artists, the most prominent cultural leaders of the nation, have met the same fate. It is conservatively estimated that at least 75% of the Ukrainian intellectuals and professional men in Western Ukraine, Carpatho–Ukraine and Bukovina have been brutally exterminated by the Russians.

Going along with this attack on the intelligentsia was an offensive against the churches, priests and hierarchy, the 'soul' of Ukraine. Between 1926 and 1932, the Ukrainian Orthodox Autocephalous Church, its Metropolitan Lypkivsky and 10,000 clergy were liquidated. In 1945, when the Soviets established themselves in Western Ukraine, a similar fate was meted out to the Ukrainian Catholic Church. That Russification was the only issue involved is clearly demonstrated by the fact that before its liquidation, the Church was offered the opportunity to join the Russian Patriarch at Moscow, the Kremlin's political tool.

Only two weeks before the San Francisco conference, on 11 April 1945, a detachment of NKVD troops surrounded the St. George Cathedral in Lviv and arrested Metropolitan Slipyj, two bishops, two prelates and several priests. All the students in the city's theological seminary were driven from the school, while their professors were told that the Ukrainian Greek Catholic Church had ceased to exist, that its Metropolitan was arrested and his place was to be taken by a Soviet-appointed bishop. These acts were repeated all over Western Ukraine and across the Curzon Line in Poland. At least seven bishops were arrested or were never heard from again. There is no Bishop of the Ukrainian Catholic Church still free in the area. Five hundred clergy who met to protest the action of the Soviets, were shot or arrested.

Throughout the entire region, clergy and laity were killed by hundreds, while the number sent to forced labour camps ran into the thousands. Whole villages were depopulated. In the deportation, families were deliberately separated, fathers to Siberia, mothers to the brickworks of Turkestan and the children to Communist homes to be 'educated'. For the crime of being Ukrainian, the Church itself was declared a society detrimental to the welfare of the Soviet state, its members were marked down in the Soviet police files as potential 'enemies of the people'. As a matter of fact, with the exception of 150,000 members in Slovakia, the Ukrainian Catholic Church has been officially liquidated, its hierarchy imprisoned, its clergy dispersed and deported.

These attacks on the Soul have also had and will continue to have a serious effect on the Brain of Ukraine, for it is the families of the clergy that have traditionally supplied a large part of the intellectuals, while the priests themselves have been the leaders of the villages, their wives the heads of the charitable organizations. The religious orders ran schools, and took care of much of the organized charities.

The third prong of the Soviet plan was aimed at the farmers, the large mass of independent peasants who are the repository of the tradition, folklore and music, the national language and literature, the national spirit, of Ukraine. The weapon used against this body is perhaps the most terrible of all — starvation. Between 1932 and 1933, 5,000,000 Ukrainians starved to death, an inhumanity which the 73rd Congress decried on 28 May 1934.

There has been an attempt to dismiss this highpoint of Soviet cruelty as an economic policy connected with the collectivization of the wheat-lands, and the elimination of the kulaks, the independent farmers, was therefore necessary. The fact is, however, that large-scale farmers in Ukraine were few and far-between. As a Soviet politician Kosior declared in Izvestiia on 2 December 1933, 'Ukrainian nationalism is our chief danger', and it was to eliminate that nationalism, to establish the horrifying uniformity of the Soviet state that the Ukrainian peasantry was sacrificed.

The method used in this part of the plan was not at all restricted to any particular group. All suffered — men, women and children. The crop that year was ample to feed the people and livestock of Ukraine, though it had fallen off somewhat from the previous year, a decrease probably due in large measure to the struggle over collectivization. But a famine was necessary for the Soviet and so they got one to order, by plan, through an unusually high grain allotment to the state as taxes. To add to this, thousands of acres of wheat were never harvested, and left to rot in the fields. The rest was sent to government granaries to be stored there until the authorities had decided how to allocate it. Much of this crop, so vital to the lives of the Ukrainian people, ended up as exports for the creation of credits abroad.

In the face of famine on the farms, thousands abandoned the rural areas and moved into the towns to beg food. Caught there and sent back to the country, they abandoned their children in the hope that they at least might survive. In this way, 18,000 children were abandoned in Kharkiv alone. Villages of a thousand had a surviving population of a hundred; in others, half the populace was gone, and deaths in these towns ranged from 20 to 30 per day. Cannibalism became commonplace.

As W. Henry Chamberlain, the Moscow correspondent of the *Christian Science Monitor*, wrote in 1933: The Communists saw in this apathy and discouragement, sabotage and counter-revolution, and, with the ruthlessness peculiar to self-righteous idealists, they decided to let the famine run its course with the idea that it would teach the peasants a lesson.

Relief was doled out to the collective farms, but on an inadequate scale and so late that many lives had already been lost. The individual peasants were left to shift for themselves; and much higher mortality rate among the individual peasants proved a most potent argument in favor of joining collective farms.

The fourth step in the process consisted in the fragmentation of the Ukrainian people at once by the addition to the Ukraine of foreign peoples and by the dispersion of the Ukrainians throughout Eastern Europe. In this way, ethnic unity would be destroyed and nationalities mixed. Between 1920 and 1939, the population of Ukraine changed from 80% Ukrainian to only 63%. In the face of famine and deportation, the Ukrainian population had declined absolutely from 23.2 million to 19.6 million, while the non-Ukrainian population had increased by 5.6 million. When we consider that Ukraine once had the highest rate of population increase in Europe, around 800,000 per year, it is easy to see that the Russian policy has been accomplished.

These have been the chief steps in the systematic destruction of the Ukrainian nation, in its progressive absorption within the new Soviet nation. Notably, there have been no attempts at complete annihilation, such as was the method of the German attack on the Jews. And yet, if the Soviet programme succeeds completely, if the intelligentsia, the priests and the peasants can be eliminated, Ukraine will be as dead as if every Ukrainian were killed, for it will have lost that part of it which has kept and developed its culture, its beliefs, its common ideas, which have guided it and given it a soul, which, in short, made it a nation rather than a mass of people.

The mass, indiscriminate murders have not, however, been lacking — they have simply not been integral parts of the plan, but only chance variations. Thousands have been executed, untold thousands have disappeared into the certain death of Siberian labour camps.

The city of Vinnitsa might well be called the Ukrainian Dachau. In 91 graves there lie the bodies of 9,432 victims of Soviet tyranny, shot by the NKVD in about 1937 or 1938. Among the gravestones of real cemeteries, in woods, with awful irony, under a dance floor, the bodies lay from 1937 until their discovery by the Germans in 1943. Many of the victims had been reported by the Soviets as exiled to Siberia.

Ukraine has its Lidice too, in the town of Zavadka, destroyed by the Polish satellites of the Kremlin in 1946. Three times, troops of the Polish Second Division attacked the town, killing men, women and children, burning houses and stealing farm animals. During the second raid, the Red commander told what was left of the town's populace: 'The same fate will be met by everyone who refuses to go to Ukraine. I therefore order that within three days the village be vacated; otherwise, I shall execute every one of you.'

When the town was finally evacuated by force, there remained only 4 men among the 78 survivors. During March of the same year, nine other Ukrainian towns were attacked by the same Red unit and received more or less similar treatment.

What we have seen here is not confined to Ukraine. The plan that the Soviets used there has been and is being repeated. It is an essential part of the Soviet programme for expansion, for it offers the quick way of bringing unity out of the diversity of cultures and nations that constitute the Soviet Empire. That this method brings with it indescribable suffering for millions of people has not turned them from their path. If for no other reason than this human suffering, we would have to condemn this road to unity as criminal. But there is more to it than that.

This is not simply a case of mass murder. It is a case of genocide, of destruction, not of individuals only, but of a culture and a nation. If it were possible to do this even without suffering we would still be driven to condemn it, for the family of minds, the unity of ideas, of language and of customs that form what we call a nation that constitutes one of the most important of all our means of civilization and progress.

It is true that nations blend together and form new nations — we have an example of this process in our own country — but this blending consists in the pooling of benefits of superiorities that each culture possesses. And it is in this way that the world advances. What then, apart from the very important question of human suffering and human rights that we find wrong with Soviet plans is the criminal waste of civilization and of culture. For the Soviet national unity is being created, not by any union of ideas and of cultures, but by the complete destruction of all cultures and of all ideas save one — the Soviet.

Source: *Raphael Lemkin Papers,* The New York Public Library, Manuscripts and Archives Division, Astor, Lenox and Tilden Foundation, Raphael Lemkin ZL-273. Reel 3. First published in L.Y. Luciuk (ed), *Holodomor: Reflections on the Great Famine of 1932–1933 in Soviet Ukraine* (Kingston, Ontario: Kashtan Press, 2008).

The first monument to victims of the Holodomor in Kyiv, St. Mykhailivsky Square, 2013.

BRIEF TIMELINE OF EVENTS

1900 Ukraine is divided between the Austro-Hungarian and Russian Empires prior to World War 1. The majority of Ukrainians live in the Russian Empire.

1914 WW1 begins. 5,000 Ukrainians (Galicians, Ruthenians) who emigrated from the Austro-Hungarian Empire are interned in Canada.

1915 **TO 1916** The Armenian Genocide inside the Ottoman Empire.

1917 **MARCH** The Russian Revolution and the breakup of the Russian Empire. Ukraine establishes a government, the Central Rada.

NOV. 7 The Bolshevik/Communist takeover in Petrograd, Russia.

1918 **JAN. 22** Ukraine declares independence as the Ukrainian People's Republic.

TO 1920 Ukraine attempts to remain independent, while fighting the Red Army (Bolshevik/Communists), the White Army (Russian monarchists), the Poles and the Romanians on Ukrainian soil.

MARCH The Treaty of Brest-Litovsk, a separate treaty on the Eastern Front to end the war between Germany and her allies, and Russia and the Central Rada of Ukraine. Leon Trotsky, representing the Bolshevik Government of Russia, recognized Ukrainian independence.

1919 Ukraine is left out at the negotiations on self-determination of nations at the Treaty of Versailles. Ukraine is refused recognition as a separate country.

TO 1921 Civil War rages in the Russian Empire, including Ukraine.

1920 The Bolsheviks gain control of Ukraine with the aid of the Red Army.

1921 **TO 1923** Famine rages in Ukraine. More than 700,000 Ukrainians starve to death in this Famine. Food is confiscated and taken out of Ukraine to feed the Volga region and Russian cities while Ukrainians starve.

The New Economic Policy (NEP) is brought in by the Bolsheviks to rebuild the economy. It allowed for small farm holdings, permitting Ukrainian farmers to continue farming their private land and running small businesses.

1922 Ukraine is formally incorporated into the Soviet Union as a republic, the Ukrainian SSR, with Kharkiv, in eastern Ukraine, as the new capital.

1924 Lenin dies and a power struggle for control of the USSR results between Leon Trotsky and Joseph Stalin.

1925 Ukrainization policy leads to a cultural renaissance. The Ukrainian language is encouraged and some Ukrainian intellectuals join the Communist Party of Ukraine.

1928 Stalin gains control of the Soviet Union and Communist Party, introduces the first Five Year Plan, with collectivization of agriculture and industrialization.

1929 The Soviets authorities launch an attack on the potential leaders of resistance in Ukraine. A show trial is conducted of a fictitious Union for the Liberation of Ukraine which was accused of promoting an independent Ukraine.

During de-kulakization, over a half million Ukrainian farmers with their families are sent to Siberia, executed or sent to concentration camps. Uprisings against the Soviet government occur, especially in Ukraine.

1930 The Ukrainian Autocephalous Orthodox Church (independent from the Moscow Patriarch) is liquidated and the hierarchy are imprisoned or executed.

1932 Famine in Ukraine. 40% of the harvest in Ukraine is handed over to the government. Little is left for farmers on which to survive. They flee to cities and to Russia and Belarus in search of food.

APRIL 23 The Communist Party ends Ukrainization and liquidates all non-governmental literary organizations in Ukraine.

AUGUST 7 The "Law of Five Stalks of Grain" allows for the death penalty or imprisonment for taking even a handful of grain from the fields. Unproductive villages are blacklisted and deprived of food (over one third of villages in Ukraine).

1933 There is widespread starvation in Ukraine, the Kuban, and the Caucasus. A secret decree blames Ukrainian nationalism for grain problems. The Ukrainian language is forbidden in Kuban. The Ukrainian leadership is purged, replaced by non-Ukrainians, and the policy of Russification begins. The borders of Ukraine and Kuban are closed, preventing starving farmers from searching for food. Those caught stealing are sent to the gulag or sent home to starve. Moscow denies there is a famine and rejects offers of relief.

Hitler comes to power in Germany. The United States formally recognizes the USSR and establishes diplomatic relations.

1934 The USSR is invited to join the League of Nations.

"THROUGH THE EYES OF A CHILD" ART SUPPLEMENT

Halia Sawycky-Dmytryshyn

The following information supplements the lesson "Through the Eyes of a Child" found on pp. 135-142 in Part III. This section may be particularly useful to teachers unfamiliar with art theory, art education principles and the basics of art production.

1. CHILDREN'S STAGES OF DEVELOPMENT OF ART EXPRESSION

Art is a language — a visual language common to all. Perhaps even the cave paintings etched with lumps of coloured clay by ancient man on the walls of his primitive dwellings were meant to be understood and appreciated by all who viewed them — a millennia before verbal and written language.

All young children understand and involve themselves in this visual language, given the opportunity and their natural inclination to do so. The range of abilities of each child is wide and varied but each has potential. As they grow and mature, children pass through recognizable stages in their development of artistic expression.

Children's stages of art development

a. *Manipulation/Discovery Stage* – the scribble stage (2-4 years of age)
b. *Schematic/Symbolic Stage* – pictures of almost recognizable form (4-8 years of age)
c. *Transitional Stage* – the beginning of realism (8-9 years of age)
d. *Realism/Realizational Stage* – reasoning (9 years of age and older)

Effective art programs take into account these different stages of art development. Young children create spontaneously, often motivated by the mere presence of colourful art material. Older children, however, strive for realism, and as they develop, they are encouraged to observe, draw and paint by looking at the world around them. Teachers can provide many opportunities for children to draw/sketch from real life. Scenes from nature (trees, clouds, insects, etc.), objects (cars, buildings, clothes, books, etc.), and people (teachers, friends, classmates, siblings, etc.) provide excellent models for students to further their developing language of art.

2. ART EDUCATION PRINCIPLES

Ideally, art education is an on-going process, introduced early and continued throughout the school years. Each classroom art teacher at subsequent grade levels continues art development by building on children's previous knowledge and skills by planning a program rich in information, visual stimulation and materials in a comfortable, nurturing environment.

Children learn and gain new skills through planned activities and projects based on the following art principles:

a. *Elements of Art* - building blocks of art: line, shape, colour, texture, value, form and space.

b. *Principles of Art* - the design, balance, pattern, rhythm, movement, emphasis and harmony.

c. *Art Appreciation* - viewing, enjoying, evaluating artwork of others based on the understanding of art elements, principles and their structure. (This is usually a function of maturity.)

d. *Art History* - studying, learning the story of art through time, from cave drawings to modern art and about the artists behind the work.

Providing children with a variety of different art materials and open-ended tasks, with many opportunities to draw, cut, paste, mix paint, pinch clay, sculpt, build, assemble, take apart, weave, paint and construct, allows children to make countless observations, theorize, hypothesize, reach conclusions, and make many decisions regarding colours, materials, sizes, patterns, values and construction. These activities require thinking, planning and evaluating to implement.

These kinds of activities reinforce learning and teach new skills to be used in innovative and creative ways. They help children integrate complex information and develop problem-solving skills. Creative thinking and the expression of ideas through artwork production will flourish in a supportive, encouraging and stimulus-rich environment.

REGARDLESS OF THE SUBJECT MATTER, INTEGRATING SCHOOL CURRICULA AND THEMES WITH ART EDUCATION IS A VALUABLE STRATEGY IN TEACHING.

It helps reinforce previous learning by requiring students to imagine and give visual form to their observations and feelings about concepts, problems, theories, etc., based on curricular subjects. Integration should further the creative process by combining subject matter with art. Planned activities on specific topics should reflect the values of art elements and principles. This enriched course of study then becomes a rewarding teaching/learning experience for both teacher and students.

MOTIVATION

Motivation can generally be defined as the inner drive that causes an individual to want to do something. One of the teacher's tasks is to do just that — to inspire, to invite, to encourage students to want to say, express, write and paint about the way they think and feel about the subject. To motivate is the teacher's most important role. There are many ways to motivate students. For this project, motivational strategies consist of two components: verbal strategies and visual strategies.

1. Verbal Motivational Strategies

Narrative — Information is presented through story telling with voice inflection, dramatic emphasis, gesture, role-playing speech.

Brainstorming — The teacher presents a question, an open-ended statement or an idea and children respond one at a time. All answers are accepted and recorded either on a chalkboard or on chart paper for all the class to see. The recording person may be the teacher, another teacher, an assistant or a student in the room.

There are no right or wrong answers. All children have a chance to respond if they wish. This strategy is excellent because it tells the teacher what the children already know about the subject and the questions they may have; what they think and feel about the subject; and what gaps in comprehension need to be addressed. Since questions and answers are recorded, the written information may later be posted in the classroom for children to read and use as required. Since these are the children's own ideas and answers, the record will be meaningful to the class.

List Making — Make a chart of the brainstormed ideas to be used later for other activities, such as chanting.

Chanting — Children are able to read the brainstormed text over and over again as a whole class. Songs, poems, class rules or routines chanted or sung in unison by groups or individually reinforce oral and written language structures. Brainstormed ideas when repeated often help with learning retention because they are the students' own ideas and may be more meaningful to them. This strategy is most effective in the lower grades. See example in the "Overview Presentation" section.

Question & Answer Discussion — A basic tool whereby the teacher poses a question and invites children to respond. This allows the teacher to learn what information the children possess, what they think and feel and what information on the topic needs to be included. Unlike brainstorming, this information does not need to be recorded. Further dialogue and discussion expands ideas and generates new ones.

Cloze — A basic strategy where words or phrases in a sentence are omitted and students must fill in the blanks with words or phrases so as to create a sentence that makes sense. Cloze is a technique that fosters anticipating and predicting language. The answers may be open-ended or have one correct response. For example, "The wheat was the colour of _________."

Categorizing — A basic thinking and concept development activity, grouping ideas according to some criteria. For example, ideas about how things are alike or different from each other can give new perspectives on the topic.

2. Visual Motivational Strategies

Pictures

- Illustrate relationships to the topic. They may come from magazines, newspapers, and books based on many subjects in all sorts of groupings and arrangements. For example: fruit (common, tropical, exotic), grains (wheat), or crops (sunflowers) growing in Canada, USA, Ukraine, etc. Others examples: people from different parts of the world doing all sorts of work, celebrating, dressed in costumes or work clothes, children, livestock, animals, pets and machinery (tools, equipment).

- Provide invaluable support material for the Overview discussion. The pictures, however, are not presented to shape or form the children's ideas, but rather to focus their attention on the picture and have them make up their minds as to whether the pictures support the topic. For example, one question posed early in the "Overview" section of the lesson is "What do you think people in Ukraine grew in their fields in the 1930s?" If a picture of a pineapple is held up, the response will probably be: "No, no, no. Of course they didn't grow pineapples on their farms. Everybody knows pineapples grow in warm climates like Hawaii." This information is subconsciously reviewed in children's minds. They already have this knowledge, however, this method focuses their attention on the question. "What do you think people in Ukraine grew in their fields in the 1930s?" Their minds eliminate the inappropriate answers like an instant Rolodex and pick out the correct foods. "No, no, no teacher, they didn't grow pineapples, that's silly. They grew wheat, corn, cabbage, etc..." Not only one appropriate answer will be expressed, but one by one, many answers may be expressed.

Pictures stimulate the children's thinking in order to identify incompatible information. Even though time for discussion is short, this method ensures that children gain new knowledge through their own process of gathering information and elimination or acceptance of information generated by a whole class discussion.

If relevant information is not forthcoming, it will have to be provided by the teacher, but had images of a wheat field or Ukrainian farmers working the land been held up in front of the class initially, their thinking and image-forming process would have been directed. Such pictures can be shown later, after all information has been gathered and discussed, and as reference material during the painting process.

Posters of Artwork

- Posters and art reproductions of other artists' impressions of the Genocidal Famine are also displayed in the context of the Art Elements and Principles discussion. "How did the artist use the shapes and colours in his painting to express the feeling of hunger, agony, starvation, pain and/or sadness?"

Objects

- Dolls dressed in traditional Ukrainian costumes with intricate patterns and designs on their clothing. Teacher's questions: "What lines were repeated to produce the pattern in the embroidery of the blouses?" "What shapes can we see on the shirt—triangles, rectangles...?" All this provides children with ideas and images for their own work later on.

Books

- Books can be read from, shown, alluded to, or quoted from. Books record history and indeed, all events of life. The author's words provide knowledge, information and lend credence to past events. In the children's picture book *Enough* by author Marsha Forchuk Skrypuch, the artwork of Michael Marchenko can be used as examples of illustrations.

Teaching Boards

- Large visual teaching boards made of foam core should be created containing material important to the presentation of the Genocidal Famine. These should be displayed during the entire workshop:
  - *Agony of a Nation* by Stephen Oleskiw
  - a quotation from the above publication
  - *Enough* by Marsha Forchuk Skrypuch
  - posters of past Genocidal Famine commemorations printed by the Ukrainian Canadian Congresses of Winnipeg and Toronto
  - pictures and postcards of Holodomor monuments
  - copies of art on the Famine produced by artists around the world
  - symbols, flags, tridents and maps of Ukraine
  - paintings and pictures of the Famine made by other children
  - small portraits of children, mothers, fathers, families in Ukraine
  - brainstorming list (for reading, chanting, etc.)
  - anything else that provides a stimulus, if time allows
  - small plastic baggies stapled to the board may hold additional materials in place
  - several smaller teaching boards (constructed in the same manner as described above) could contain visuals and material on Art Elements and Principles

Pocket Charts and Word Cards

- A chart with fixed pockets for moveable words or sentences is a very useful aid for lower grades. It may also be used in higher grades to emphasize certain points. For example, during the Overview, the following quotation by Mendel Khataevich from the book *Agony of a Nation* by Stephen Oleskiw was posted:

  > *"There was a RUTHLESS STRUGGLE going on between the UKRAINIAN PEASANTRY and the RUSSIAN COMMUNIST PARTY... a struggle to the Death. This year (1933) was a test of our strength. It took a FAMINE to show them "WHO IS THE MASTER HERE." It cost MILLIONS of lives, but the COLLECTIVE SYSTEM is here to stay. WE HAVE WON THE WAR."*

  This quote can be typed and enlarged to poster size and stapled on the teaching board. Certain important words and phrases from the quote can be highlighted, and printed on separate construction paper cards (3"x12") and placed in plastic baggies (also stapled to the teaching board) next to a small pocket chart (also affixed to the teaching board). During the Overview, the quote can be read, and the word cards can be presented one at a time. Ask students the meaning of the words and phrases and what feelings the words evoke. Each word card is pondered and put in a pocket chart to be read again later. The whole quote becomes more meaningful and significant because of the word-by-word presentation and thoughtful analysis.

ART ELEMENTS (AE) AND ART PRINCIPLES (AP)

The practical part of the workshop can begin with some simple exercises. The chalkboard

along with teaching boards and information, which display visuals, line, shapes, colours, textures, patterns, are useful tools.

Example of Discussion

The teacher draws a line on the chalkboard, and asks,

"What is this?"
"A line," ventures a brave soul in the front row.
"Yes, a line. But what kind of line?"

"A straight line," someone pipes up.

"That is correct, a straight line. What is this line called?" asks the teacher, drawing another line on the chalkboard.

"A wavy line," someone responds.

"And this?" Drawing a diagonal.

"A diagonal," someone responds.

Teacher continues to draw different lines.

"Golden wheat dancing in the wind," Matthew Clark, St. Demetrius Catholic School, Toronto, 2000.

"This is a zigzag. And this one is called a .....?"

"Spiral!"

"Good for you! How about this?" the teacher continues, "If we join some of these lines together, what does it become?"

Obviously the answers identify a triangle, rectangle, square, etc.

"How about this? If I continue with this curved line and join it to this, now you have what? Yes, circles, ovals. Now add these together to form more complex forms." At this point the teacher draws some animals on the chalk board using the above shapes. For example, a spiral, plus thin rectangles, plus a little triangle, plus small circles become.... Voila!

"A snail!" children exclaim and clap and cheer.

This is a very basic early childhood strategy, but an important one. This strategy works just as well for upper-level students and adults as it does for kindergarteners. Whenever you draw or put together a few simple lines and shapes to produce animals or other objects, many young and older people will be surprised, not because these drawing are works of art or that they are intricate, but because they are so simple, made from basic lines that join together to make shapes. It is the wonder of this simple exercise in basic art elements that opens children's eyes to a new way of looking at the world around them. It encourages them to look more closely at objects, to become more aware of shapes and structures.

As we proceed, one or two students are asked to go to the window and look outside at the tree in the schoolyard and to tell the rest of the class what words can be used to describe the shape of the tree. Already they know to look for lines. Before they would have used other words to describe the tree, such as "It's kinda tall with all these leaves everywhere."

Now, one student answers, "It has straight lines for its trunk, side by side."

The teacher asks, "What do you call lines that run side by side like this?" and draws a few of those lines on the chalk board.

"Parallel," someone shouts out in the back.

"Yes, parallel."

"What shape are the leaves?" the teacher can ask.

"They are kind of oval shaped."

"Yes, they're oval. Are the ovals pointed on one end? Yes, this point at one end modifies the shape of the oval enough to give that leaf its characteristic shape."

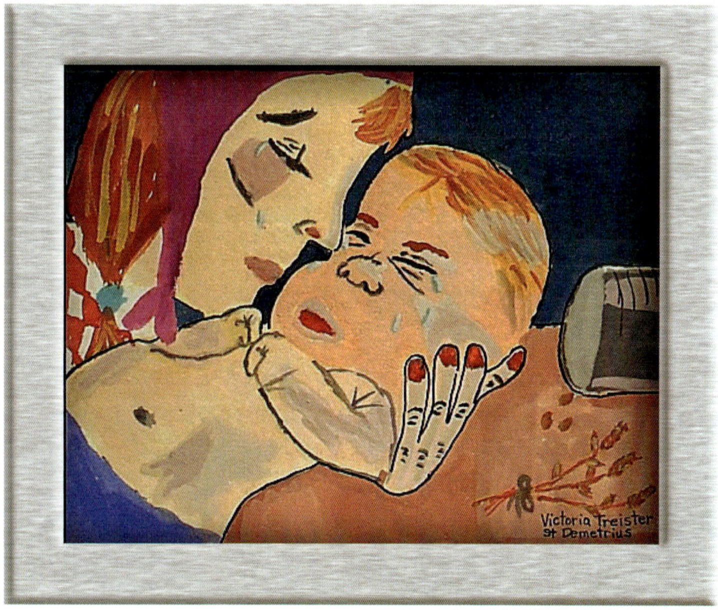

Student painting by Victoria Treister, St. Demetrius Catholic School, Toronto, 2000.

"I wonder if trees like this grew in Ukraine during the Famine. What shapes would you use to draw, say, sunflowers, which grow abundantly in Ukraine? What shapes would you use to draw a small child, a mother, and workers in the field and the enemy? What lines and shapes would be used for the *vyshyvka* (embroidery) in the shirt? Straight lines, zigzag, triangles?" Children are asked to come to draw some of these shapes on the chalk board.

"What other shapes do you see outside your window?" the teacher may ask. "What about that box on your teacher's desk? What designs does it have? It is a long oval shape with a thinner curved tail shape."

"That's called a paisley design."

"Might someone's grandmother in Ukraine have worn a paisley scarf like your grandmother has?"

"Hmm. Maybe I can use this design in my painting."

"My aunt has a shawl with red poppies on it," someone else volunteers.

"Colours? Look all around you. What do you see? Shades, tints, values, dark, light, dull, bright colours."

Student painting by Oksana Hrychyk, St. Sofia Catholic School, Mississauga, 2000.

The discussion continues: "What about design? The principle elements – patterns (single and repetitive) – how would you incorporate these elements in your paintings? Where would you find these elements? In clothing, on wood, stones, in trees, leaves, on homes, in fields… Can you put all of these things into your paintings? Will there be space, time? What would it look like if you tried to put everything we talked about today into your paintings? You need to decide what the focus of your painting will be."

What subjects or ideas to paint is the first decision students will have to make. What elements can they use to draw those subjects? How will they make their subjects look sad? How will they make their fields look empty? What lines will show that? What shapes do they need to use? What colours will help them with their ideas? Should the paper be large and all the shapes in the pictures tiny? How big should the body be if it is in the front (foreground) of the picture? What size should the objects be if they are way in the back (background)?

By the end of the session children have reviewed and discussed some of these basic elements:

- They have learned about lines – straight, short, thin, parallel, zigzag, spiral, horizontal.
- They have learned that lines join to make basic shapes – circle, square, triangle, trapezoid, hexagon.
- They have learned that shapes joined together combined in various ways form objects, houses, trees, cats, books, human beings.
- They have learned that objects have texture, can be rough, smooth, glass-like, bumpy.
- They have learned that colour is everywhere and in everything around them.

- They have learned that everything around them is put together – designed in ways that have movement or are static, have balance, patterns.
- They have learned that designs inspire awe, admiration, pleasure, order and delight, if put together well with harmony, balance, etc. They will also have learned that designs without harmony, balance, colours may confuse, jar, cause disorder, frighten and anger.
- They have learned that they need to look, see, touch, to experience and appreciate the world around them.
- They have learned that they can express these feelings verbally and/or visually.

Student painting by Marta Mekylyta, St. Demitrius Catholic School, Toronto, 2000.

Art is a language everyone can learn

There are so many things to think about, so many decisions to make. They know a little better now what they must do to start their painting. Thoughts again are swirling, ideas humming. They are almost ready to paint but not quite yet. There is still one step, one more tool to be provided before that time: the artists' materials they will use.

ART MATERIALS

Paint

Quality paints, which provide good coverage, are opaque, bright, and long lasting. These are large round tempera water cake paints, which fit into trays holding six to eight colours (for more colours use large muffin tins). These tempera cake paints come in many vibrant colours and do not require mixing, which cuts down on mess. They are very easy to clean up with simple tap water (let trays stand to dry), and can be stacked for easy storage and transport.

Black and white paints are kept in separate individual cups. White paints are available at all times for mixing new colours. Black paint is reserved and used later during the painting process for details, for those who needed black backgrounds or outlining.

Brushes

Brushes should consist of a variety of good quality flat and round bristle brushes and flat and round sable line brushes, both in large, medium and fine sizes. Two to three brushes per child in a class of 25-35 children should be provided.

Paper

Good quality white construction paper is preferable. The sizes can range from large 12" x 18" (30.5 cm x 45.5 cm) to small 7" x 10" (8 cm x 25 cm) with several sizes in between.

It is a good idea to give students a choice in the size of paper they wish to use. A large white sheet of paper may intimidate some students, especially if they have little or no painting experience. Selecting the paper size helps to alleviate some of this concern.

Paint Mixing Palettes

White, medium-sized Styrofoam meat trays or paper plates should be provided for each child as paint mixing palettes.

Water

Each child should have a small can filled with water for cleaning and rinsing brushes.

Newspaper and Paper Towels

Each worktop should be covered with newspapers to protect desks, and paper towels should be on-hand to blot brushes and wipe up water spills.

Student painting by Natalie Trusz, Josyf Cardinal Slypij Catholic School, Toronto, 2000.

"THE RINGS," A SHORT STORY

Marsha Forchuck Skrypuch

Accounts exist of people who escaped from Soviet-occupied Ukraine and offered eyewitness testimony about the Genocidal Famine. Many were collected and published in 1953 in a book called Black Deeds of the Kremlin: A White Book, Volume 1: Book of Testimonies, *edited by S. O. Pidhainy. Since the fall of the Soviet Union, more first-hand accounts have surfaced. A good online resource is www.education.holodomor.ca/teaching-materials/the-rings/. "The Rings" is based on a number of these first-hand accounts. After the story was written in 1999, other accounts with eerie parallels to this story made the author realize how common the experience of Danylo in "The Rings" really was.*

SOURCE: "The Rings" is reproduced with permission from *Kobzar's Children: A Century of Untold Ukrainian Stories.* Markham, Ontario; Fitzhenry & Whiteside, 2006.

Danylo's sharpest memory was of hunger. When his father had refused to sign the papers handing over their tiny farm to the state, his family earned the label pidkurkul- or poor farmer who sympathizes with the kulaks.

His father knew that the communists would send in the Red Army to confiscate their grain, so he had mixed some wheat with the chaff and hidden it in the loft. He had also put the best wheat, for sowing, up in the rafters. Danylo's mother had hidden a sack of grain in the chimney.

The soldiers who came were a rough and brutal lot. They were not from the village, and they spoke Russian, not Ukrainian. They brought with them a stabber – a device made of a sharp-pronged stick with a bag on the end-to collect evidence of grain.

As one of the soldiers carried an armful of his father's hidden grain to the waiting cart, Danylo rushed forward and grabbed back some stalks of wheat. "Why are you doing this," he cried.

The man said something in Russian that sounded like a curse. Another Red Army soldier opened the pich (oven) and confiscated the fresh loaves of bread baking there. They loaded all the food into the cart and took it away.

A few pieces of stale bread on the rubbish pile had somehow been missed. Danylo's family – his father, his mother, and three younger brothers – survived on these crusts and water for a couple of days. His baby sister Larissa was still at his mother's breast, one less mouth to feed.

Danylo watched as those around him appeared to shrink. His mother remarked one day, as she washed her face, that she could feel every bone in her skull. Later, when Danylo carried the soapy basin outside to empty it, he had found her wedding ring, which had slipped off. She had not noticed. His mother had not been able to get the silver band past her knuckles for years. Danylo dried it on his shirt, and brought it back in to her. From then on, she wore it on a cord of leather around her neck.

When the crusts of bread were gone, one day passed with no food at all, just water. Danylo's feet and stomach began to swell with the first signs of starvation. His father caught and skinned a stray cat, which sustained them a few more days. But Danylo's four year old brother, Anatoly, swelled up and died. Danylo caught a hedgehog, and the remaining family survived on that for a while.

As winter set in, the rats, cats, dogs, and birds in the village disappeared. Danylo learned, like everyone else, that one must eat at least one morsel, each and every day to keep oneself from swelling. If the swelling set in, your feet and belly would get so huge that you wouldn't be able to move. At that point, you could only sit and wait to die. When his mother began to starve, Danylo couldn't bear to look at her body, ballooning out grotesquely, as if it were about to burst. Her swelling caused what little milk she had been able to produce to stop. And so Larissa died. His mother died the next day, then ten-year-old Vasyl, and then seven-year-old Ivan.

Danylo and his father said prayers for the dead. His father reverently removed the cord that held her wedding ring from around his wife's neck. Before putting it around his own neck, he slipped off his own wedding ring and strung it on the cord.

In their small home, Danylo and his father sat with their dead loved ones for hours, perhaps days. What was time, anyway? It wasn't until their corpses began to stink that they dragged their family beyond the threshold. The village authorities had dug a huge pit in the graveyard. Each morning they sent a cart around to all the houses, collecting the bodies. They dumped the bodies into the pit until it was full. And then they dug a new one.

"Perhaps I was a fool not to sign our land away", Danylo's father wondered aloud one day. Then he and his son walked to the collective, intending to sign up. But even from the road, they could see that the workers in the state farm were no better off than the kulaks. The only people who were not starving were the Communist Party members, and they had confiscated the grain in the first place, so Danylo and his father returned home.

They resorted to boiling shoe leather and drinking it as a broth, but this did not stave off the swelling. Word broke that a horse had starved to death in the commune, so Danylo, his father, and the few other surviving villagers walked to the collective, knives in hand, to carve up the horse. Without waiting to cook the meat, Danylo sat down on the ground and cut it into bloody chunks, devouring a morsel on the spot. The horse meat they carried away lasted for several weeks.

When another horse died, on a state farm, Danylo and his father tried to repeat the success. But the Communist Party members foiled their plan. The horse was thrown into a pit and covered with acid. By the time Danylo and his father got there, most of the flesh had sizzled away. His father threw himself on the horse anyway. He cut off a hunk of still-intact flesh from the horse's hind quarter. Danylo tried to pull it away, but his father had already cut off some smaller bits and swallowed some poisoned meat. His father doubled up with pain, almost immediately, and died that night.

Danylo said a prayer for his father. He sat beside the cold body from dusk until dawn. It wasn't until he heard the creaking wheels of the corpse wagon that Danylo broke his meditations. As he dragged his father's corpse over the threshold in the early morning light, a glint of silver shone from the leather cord around his father's neck. With the corpse collectors only yards away, Danylo reached down and undid the cord. As he retied it around his own, he noticed that the two silver wedding rings looked unnaturally large.

Danylo walked through the house one last time, as if to imprint the image on his memory. It was nothing more than a one-room mud shack. Everything of value had long been bartered for scraps of food. There was one small sharp knife, so he took it. The only remaining item was a silver spoon that had been passed down, mother to daughter, for generations. It was his mother's prized possession. Danylo carefully wrapped it in a bit of cloth and placed it inside his shirt. He stepped outside and walked through the frozen strip of land that constituted their family farm. For the sake of this meager property, his whole family had been killed. How could he leave this place? His family had farmed this small patch of earth for uncounted generations. Danylo despaired at the thought of abandoning it. With his family gone, this was all he had in the world, yet he knew that staying guaranteed his death. If he could somehow survive, perhaps he could reclaim it one day.

As he walked down the main street and away from his home for the last time, he was struck by the absolute silence. No bird sang, no child ran in the street.

Danylo's uncle had a farm about ten kilometers away. Danylo and his siblings had been taken here once with his parents for a family wedding, and so he knew the general direction. He set off, hoping that things would be better there. He was so weak with hunger that his legs wobbled, but he had no choice but to forge ahead. He rested frequently, nibbling on bugs and early spring shoots of grass.

When he got to his uncle's home, he realized that things were just as bad there. Going through the motions of hospitality, his aunt offered him stew made of boiled water and grass. Danylo ate it, with his hollow-eyed uncle, aunt, and their children looking on. He thanked them, but he knew he must leave. Their generosity in the midst of such dire need touched his heart.

Twenty kilometers beyond his uncle's farm was a town with a train station, and so Danylo set out for there. Perhaps a train would be his salvation. The town was not much better off than Danylo's village, although not everyone was starving. The street was lined with swollen people. But there were also market stalls selling food, Russian-speaking townsfolk went about their day-to-day business, seemingly oblivious to the misery all around them.

Danylo went up to the first market stall he passed, "How much for that?" he asked, pointing at a loaf of white bread. "More than you have to pay for it," answered the man behind the stall, as he appraised Danylo's homespun clothes. "What do you have that I could afford?" asked Danylo. And he unwrapped his precious bundle and drew out the silver spoon.

The man examined it with cold, appraising eyes. "I'll take that for this," he said, and he held up a small loaf of the cheapest, blackest bread that he had.

Danylo was in no position to argue. He handed over the spoon and grabbed the bread, tearing off one chunk on the spot and devouring it. Almost immediately, he felt a little bit stronger. But Danylo considered how much he had paid for that one loaf of bread, and how little he had to buy more. He knew that he had to come up with a way to get to a safer place.

As days passed, Danylo became adept at stealing bread from the market stalls. He also learned how to evade the grasp of the Communist Party members who scoured the streets, looking for urchins like himself.

Most days, the comrades were content with keeping the ever-encroaching multitude of starving children away from the market stalls, but one day, their ambitions intensified. They methodically swept the streets and caught every last child. Danylo feared for his life as he and the others were herded into a vacant warehouse across from the train station. As the door was closed and bolted from the outside, darkness enveloped the sorry group. Most were too weak and exhausted even to protest. All around Danylo, little ones curled into balls and fell asleep. The windows of the warehouse had been blackened with paint, making it impossible to look out. But Danylo still had his knife with him, so he drew it from his belt and scraped a tiny bit of the window clean, just enough for a single eye.

What he saw amazed him. A Red Army officer was in the middle of the square at a makeshift desk. Behind him was a rack of what looked like Ukrainian folk outfits. The officer had a metal box and sheet of paper on the table in front of him. A lineup of city folk had formed. As the officer marked down something on the paper, he would hand each person what appeared to be money form the metal box, and then the person would walk behind and choose a costume. What in heaven's name were they doing? Danylo wondered. Putting on a play? After more than a dozen people had chosen outfits, Danylo lost interest. Like the other inmates, he found a bare spot on the floor, curled up into a ball, and fell asleep.

He awoke with a start some time later. There was a horrible, frightening, and otherworldly sound outside. It was so awful that Danylo was almost afraid to look out, but his curiosity got the better of him. He crept back up to the peephole and looked out.

There, just thirty feet in front of him, was what could only be a train. It was like a fire-breathing monster, and he shook with fear as the huge creature screeched to a halt. Once his heart had stopped fluttering with fear, Danylo examined this odd contraption as best he could. It was made up of individual wheeled boxes, all linked together like sausages.

One of these boxes was a sleek unit, with huge glass windows on the side. Even from the warehouse, Danylo could see that the windows on the train compartment were either painted or papered over. Strange, Danylo thought. Perhaps it's to transport urchins?

Just then, a door opened on the compartment and a uniformed man jumped out. He fiddled with the lower part of the doorway until a set of metal steps appeared, reaching to the ground. Almost immediately, a number of well-fed adults stepped out of the doorway and onto the platform of the train station.

Danylo knew, just by looking at them, that these people were foreigners. They wore strange clothing, and many of them carried pads of paper and were writing in them, even as they were stepping down to the platform. There was also a Red Army officer mingling with the group.

As if on cue, a group of townspeople appeared. Danylo was shocked to see that these people were dressed in the Ukrainian folk outfits. They all looked healthy and well fed. One young girl walked up to the foreigners and presented them with the traditional welcoming of braided bread and salt. As this performance was being acted out, others set up a table in the square and placed an embroidered cloth over it. They motioned the foreigners to sit down at the table. Then the actors brought out bowls and platters filled with steaming food. Danylo could hardly contain his envy as he watched the well-stuffed foreigners stuff themselves even more. What was this all about?

Shortly after, the people got back on the train, and it pulled away. A few minutes after that, a party comrade came over to the warehouse, removed the bolt, and opened the door wide.

"Phew," the man muttered in Russian. "Don't you Khakhols (an insulting term for Ukrainians) ever bathe?

Danylo and the rest wandered out. Their lack of hygiene was the least of their worries.

As the days passed, other trains came in, but they carried goods, not people. Some of them were filled with wood and coal; some were empty. Danylo watched as children like him hopped into these compartments when the Communist Party members weren't looking. More often than not, the comrades would search the cars before they departed. It was the rare urchin who escaped this way. Danylo knew that he had to get on a train himself one day soon. Any place would be better than here.

Then one day, he saw his chance. The party members were sweeping the streets for every single child again, and so Danylo knew that another passenger train was coming. Would another charade also be performed? The comrades wouldn't dare search a passenger car for urchins; that would be too embarrassing for them, since urchins weren't suppose to exist.

He dashed away from the streets altogether, and hid on the outskirts of town. Then he waited for the train to appear. When it roared in, he skulked back into town, making sure to stay hidden. He needn't have worried. All attention was focused on the spectacle of rosy-cheeked "Ukrainians" and the delicious steaming dishes they were serving.

The door to the train car had been left open, so Danylo waited until the uniformed man wasn't watching. Then he dashed inside. In a flash, he took in his surroundings. There were two rows of cushioned benches and a pot-bellied coal stove at the far end of the car. He hid himself quickly, behind the stove.

A few moments later, he heard a set of footsteps. He was afraid to look out to see if it was a Red Army officer who had followed him on to the train, or simply one of the passengers. He tried to stay still; he tried not to breath.

The footsteps sounded louder and Danylo soon realized that a person was standing in front of the stove. A shiver of fear shot through him, and then he heard the voice of a young girl speak Russian.

"They'll find you there."

Danylo was frozen with fear. He hoped wildly that somehow it wasn't him she was talking to; but the next thing he knew, a hand rested on his shoulder.

"I can see your shoulder as clear as day," she said. "It would be better if you hid under here."

Danylo dared to look out. A well-fed girl about his age stood before him. Her gloved hand pointed to a space underneath one of the benches. Then they could hear voices, close to the open door of the car.

"Hurry!" cried the girl.

Danylo scrambled from behind the stove and rolled under the bench. The girl shoved some luggage underneath the bench to hide him, and then she sat down on the bench above him.

How was it that she had been so willing to help him? Had the girl scraped a bit of paint off her own windows, and recognized the truth where her parents had not? How many others really knew what was going on in Ukraine, but preferred the charade?

Danylo settled himself under the bench and looked around. He noticed that one of the items she had shoved under was a wicker basket lined with checkered cloth. He could smell sausage, and cheese, and bread. As the other passengers got onto the train, Danylo's stomach rumbled loudly. He prayed that no one could hear it.

Moments later, the train roared out of the station, and then Danylo could hear an official checking the passenger tickets. After he left, Danylo closed his eyes and tried to sleep, but the aroma of the food next to his nose was overwhelming. He reached in and drew out a long link of kobasa, a smoked sausage. Almost swooning with hunger, Danylo drew the knife out of his belt and cut off a piece of meat. He bit into it and chewed with pleasure. He took a few more bites and then put it back in the basket. As the hours passed and the memory of the wonderfully fatty kobasa filled his mind, he couldn't stop himself from reaching in and taking another bite. Before he knew it, the whole link was gone. He would have liked to eat the bread and cheese, too, but by sheer force of will, he stopped himself.

It was a good thing he did, because a few hours later, a hand reached down and picked up the basket, momentarily exposing Danylo to anyone who happened to look down. The girl quickly rearranged herself above him, though, covering him back up again.

"Rachel, you little imp," said a man's voice. "You've eaten all our sausage!"

"I'm sorry, Papa," said the girl. "I was starving, and it smelled so good."

"Next time, ask if someone else wants a bit, before you devour the whole thing," the man said in an exasperated voice.

"I will," she said meekly.

The train rumbled on, and night fell. Danylo drifted off to sleep, only to wake up with a jolt hours later, when the train was still. Eating all the kobasa had upset Danylo's stomach and he was doubled over in pain. He had an urgent need to fart, but he was afraid that if he did that, he would wake the people sleeping in the compartment.

The car door was open again, and there were men smoking on the platform outside.

Without giving much thought to a plan, Danylo rolled out of his hiding place and, on legs leaden and numb from being cramped up for so long, hobbled out the car door. A uniformed man on the platform tried to grab his collar as he sped past, but Danylo broke free. He ran and ran, as far from the train as he could get. Then, when his pain would let him run no further, he collapsed on the ground in agony and let out one long, loud fart.

He felt better immediately. Looking around, he saw that he was completely alone. It was the deepest part of night. He hugged his bundle to him and fell asleep.

He woke to the feeling of bright sun shining in through his eyelids. He tried to get up but realized that he was almost numb through with cold. He wriggled his arms and legs to get the circulation back and then stood up and looked around to see where he had landed. The train was long gone, and Danylo was in the middle of nowhere. Not a house, field, or village in sight, just mile upon mile of open steppe. Danylo walled back to the train tracks and waited for another train. In the days that he waited, he ate roots and grass and bugs. And he dreamed of the lovely kobasa.

When a train finally passed by, it didn't stop. Danylo had to run beside it and hoist himself onto an empty freight car. He was so hungry by the time the train pulled into a station that he decided to risk going outside, to see if he could find food. He was no sooner off the train when a Red Army soldier grabbed him by the collar.

"Where are you going?"

Danylo had already seen the fate of urchins who had been caught, so he thought fast for a plausible excuse. "I was visiting friends and am just on my way back home."

The soldier looked Danylo up and down; he didn't buy the story for a moment. "Come with me, he said. He took Danylo to a freight car that had been pulled off the tracks, and shoved him through the open door. It was filled with filthy and emaciated urchins. There was no food or water in the car, nor even a pot to pee in. The soldier locked the door behind Danylo.

Each day, a few children died. The doors were opened to remove the dead children, and the live ones were led out to relieve themselves. Food was brought in, on occasion, but never more often than every other day. Danylo saw that his legs were swelling and he knew that starvation was again setting in. He considered trying to escape on the daily visit to the lavatory, but he knew he wouldn't have the strength. His only hope was to lie still enough and hope that he was mistaken for dead.

He felt himself gripped by the ankles and hands and tossed on top of a mound of corpses. He forced himself not to cry out. He had seen so many dead bodies in his short lifetime that it surprised him how upset he found himself to be. What kind of monsters were these comrades, who considered people like Danylo to be no more than rubbish to be thrown out?

The cart rumbled away from the freight car, and Danylo felt himself swaying back and forth, perched precariously on top of a mass of human bodies. The sweet, sickly smell of rotting flesh enveloped him as the cart pulled away from the train depot, away from the village, and into darkness. Danylo drifted off into uneasy sleep.

The cart came to a jolting stop, and Danylo had to force himself to keep still. Suddenly, he felt the cart tip, and then he and the bodies tumbled out, into a pit. A gust of fresh air enveloped Danylo, and the smell of rotting was momentarily replaced with a sharp whiff of freshly-dug black earth. The scent brought back memories of his family farm. Each spring and summer, that same wonderful scent of rich, black earth was in the air for seeding and harvest.

The lovely scent was soon extinguished, as the weight of corpses from the bottom of the cart fell on top of him, covering him completely.

Danylo lay there amidst the dead for what seemed like hours. He was afraid to dig himself out in case the corpse collectors were still there, yet he was even more fearful of staying where he was. He knew that if he drifted into unconsciousness, he would suffocate. When he could wait no longer, slowly burrowed his way to the top. He remembered that the commissioners in the village sprinkled lye on the mass graves to make them deteriorate faster; so when Danylo sensed he was near the top layer of corpses, he gingerly flipped each body over, making sure not to touch the upper surface and risk burning from the lye. When he finally broke through, he was glad for his foresight. The sharp smell of lye hung in the air.

It was still dark, but Danylo could see that daybreak was close at hand. The dark of the night looked almost bright compared to the hellish darkness at the bottom of the pit. In the moonlight, Danylo looked at his hands and feet and was dismayed to see them ballooning out with starvation. He had very little time. If he didn't find something to eat, he would die.

He could see the silhouette of the huge mound of freshly dug earth. As his eyes adjusted, Danylo could also see that the pit had been dug in a famer's empty field. He realized that he was standing in the midst of a potato field that had lain fallow for a year, but had partly reseeded itself. A few brave seedlings had grown wild and were beginning to rot. What madness was this? Farmers were starving to death in the midst of soil so rich that it practically planted itself.

The mound turned out to be the best place to look. As soon as he found the first potato, he scraped the dirt off it with his knife and then bit into it. The taste of juicy, raw potato filled his mouth. It tasted almost as good as the kobasa from the train. Once he finished the first potato, he dug out a dozen more and hid them in his shirt. His feet were still painfully swollen inside of his shoes, and his hands were so big that it took an effort to make them work. But he knew that the swelling would soon go down, now that he had eaten.

The most important thing, at this point, was to get away from the mass grave and hide before daylight. But Danylo also knew that the weather was changing. If he were to survive the winter, he would have to find warmer clothes. He turned back to the spot in the mass grave from which he had emerged. Here, the bodies covered with lye had been turned over, exposing the unmutilated corpses one layer down. Gingerly, Danylo stepped back in amidst the bodies and looked for warmer clothing. Ghostly faces of hollow-eyed children, men and women old before their time, stared back at him. A sob caught in Danylo's throat as he stood there, hugging himself in sadness. Who mourned for these innocents, piled like so much rubbish in a farmer's field? Danylo vowed to himself to live, not only for his own sake, and for the memory of his family, but also as a tribute to those who died.

The dead were dressed in rags no better than his own, so he opted for quantity, removing several large threadbare coats, layering them one by one. He tied rags about his shoes, both for warmth, and to hold them together.

Then he wandered on weary legs, in the only direction he knew - away.

He wandered, delirious for days, subsisting on bits of potato. Once the potatoes were gone, he used his knife to dig through the frozen earth for roots and bark. When he found a set of train tracks, he followed them. Days later, they began to vibrate beneath his feet. When the train came, it moved slowly enough for him to jump into a freight car as it passed.

Days blended, one into another, as Danylo hopped from train to train. Sometimes he entered a boxcar that was already inhabited by one or two hollow-eyed children in rags.

He learned that the Famine ended at the River Zbruch. He heard tales of the few who had escaped the soldiers' bullets and crossed to the other side. What the other side held was a mystery, but Danylo was sure it had to be better. Otherwise, why would soldiers try to stop them from crossing?

He rode the rails in the direction of the River Zbruch. When he got there, it was a crisp, cold day and he could see soldiers posted amidst the trees along the icy banks. Danylo hopped off the boxcar and hid in the bushes before the train stopped. From his hiding place, he observed the soldiers' movements.

There was a cluster of Red Army soldiers by the station. Danylo watched as the train came to a halt. A soldier walked up to the boxcar he had just vacated and looked inside. Thank goodness he had decided to jump off early! Danylo darted from bush to bush, making his way downriver and away from the station. There were soldiers as far as he could see, but he had no choice but to keep moving. The river itself was almost completely frozen over in spots.

As he got farther away from the station, Danylo kept his eyes on the banks of the river. His biggest challenge was to remain hidden. The land beside the River Zbruch was largely clear, open, and covered with snow, so even his footprints would betray his escape.

During the day, he hid behind the scarce bits of brush that he found. He traveled under the cover of night, placing each step quietly and carefully. As he got farther and farther away from the train station, he saw that there were slightly fewer soldiers, but they were still there. He also noticed that the soldiers paid particular attention to the areas of the river that were narrower, and to the parts that were more or less frozen over.

After days of traveling by night and hiding by day, Danylo could see the changes in the river. It had become much wider. His heart sank. How would he ever get across? As he continued, he saw a small island in the middle of the river. It was only big enough to hold about a dozen trees, but there was a deep brush along the edges. Best of all, the river looked frozen right to the edge of the little island. It was getting darker, and Danylo had not seen a soldier for a few hundred yards. Should he take the chance?

Before he could think too carefully about it, he dashed down to the shore of the river and stepped upon the ice. It held firm. As he looked down at his feet, he saw other footsteps in the snow. Perhaps this was a sign of a successful escape? He kissed his parents' wedding rings for good luck and then dashed out toward the island. He knew he would be in full view for hundreds of yards around: a black spec on the white ice.

But what choice did he have?

When he was so close to the island that he could almost reach out and touch it, he heard a shot behind him. He felt a sharp pain in his shoulder. Danylo threw himself into a bush and rolled into the depths of the island as he heard more shots.

Suddenly, he heard a shrill scream. He lay, not daring to move, waiting for a shower of bullets to pierce his rags. He heard footsteps running away from him, and then another scream. He dared not look up.

From the corner of his eye, he saw a bone-thin women running away from the island and back toward the land of famine. In her arms she held a bundle, stained with blood. Danylo realized that the women and her child must have hidden on the island just before he had. He watched in horror as the grief-crazed mother ran up to the soldier and set the body of her dead child down at his feet. Then she threw herself at the soldier, pounding her fists and flailing her arms. The soldier was so surprised that he dropped his gun and grabbed her by the wrists.

Danylo didn't wait to see more. He scrambled to the other side of the island, then dashed across the ice to the other side of the river.

Danylo had no memory of the next few days. Weak with hunger and delirious from the throbbing pain in his shoulder, he somehow stumbled across the countryside toward freedom.

His next recollection was when he was safe. The village Danylo found himself in was much like that of his childhood, though slightly more prosperous. Most of the houses had thatched roofs, but some had tin roofs, eaves troughs decorated with beautiful, swirling patterns punched into the metal.

The Krawchuk clan, who had adopted Danylo as their own, lived in a blue-washed clay cottage at the outer end of the village's only street. When Danylo had made it to the village, emaciated and near death, Anna Krawchuk was the first to notice him. She had been on her way to the well when she spotted a heap of rags not far from her door. She cradled him in her arms, as if he were her own child, and took him home. She nursed him back to health with sips of rich borscht and kolach (a rich, braided egg bread) dipped in honey.

The bullet had grazed the surface of his shoulder, creating a superficial gash about three inches long. His layers of rags had stuck together with oozing blood and pus. Anna cut away the sloth and dried blood, cleaned the wound with an herb tincture, and then bound it with a cool, damp, bread poultice.

His teeth chattered so badly with cold and fever that Anna made a bed for him on top of the pich and bundled him in a down-filled comforter. For added warmth each night, she had her two sons sleep on either side of Danylo.

Danylo suffered days and days of delirium. The hand-painted border of flowers along the top of the whitewashed walls seemed to spring alive, their leaves stretching out to grab him. The red petals seemed to drip with blood. The delicate lace curtains on the windows fluttered innocently in the breeze by day; but at night they wavered like white knuckled hands, thin to the bone, and fluttered as if in the last moments before death. Danylo clutched his parents' rings and prayed for deliverance.

As soon as he was strong enough, Danylo asked Anna to take him to the graveyard. She seemed to know instinctively what he wanted to do, and so she took along several small handmade candles. To get to the graveyard, they had to walk down the main street and through the center of the village.

They turned left at the chytalnya (reading room) and crossed over a footbridge, and then up a small hill. Even though it was winter, the cemetery seemed beautiful to Danylo. He envied the people who were buried there. They had died, one by one, and each had been grieved for and prayed for individually. He wandered through the rows of gravestones, with Anna following a few feet behind. He methodically brushed snow off the stones as he went, and read each inscription carefully. When he came to one labeled Larissa, a sob escaped his throat.

He fell on his knees in front of the stone, and prayed for the baby sister he had lost. Anna took a few steps forward and gently placed her hand on his shoulder, murmuring prayers. Then she knelt down beside Danylo. She handed him a candle and a match. He set the candle on top of the headstone, and lit it. Then he prayed for the girl in the grave, but mostly he prayed for his own sister. He repeated his tributes until he had prayed for every one of the lost members of his family.

It was dark by the time they walked home.

"Harvest time for a Ukrainian farming family," Kyiv Oblast, 1929.

"WITHOUT DOCTORS AND PRIESTS, WITHOUT GRAVES AND CROSSES"

Olena Zvychayna

Olena Zvychayna gave the following speech[34] at a commemoration held on September 20, 1953, at the Manhattan Centre in New York to mark the 20th Anniversary of the Terror-Famine in Soviet Ukraine.

***

Back then, in the villages they ate human flesh
And baked bread out of crumbled bark . . .
Starving children eyed greedily
Their dead sister's bloated body . . .
And thus, although we had long since abandoned our caves,
In the twentieth century we became cannibals . . .
. . . .
Back then, a peasant coming to the city for bread
Starved on the pavement and joined the dead.

It is with words like these that Yuriy Klen, our late poet of blessed memory, described the famine of 1932-33 in Ukraine.

Back then, all of Soviet Ukraine was a stark, naked stage on which was projected unremittingly the historical film of the tragic famine willfully inflicted on the Ukrainian peasantry by Red Moscow.

Back then, every district centre was a stark, naked stage on which the famine in that region was filmed. Back then, Kharkiv, as benefits the capital of the Ukrainian S.S.R., was the centre of the greatest concentration of those who were condemned to die, the capital of the agonizing death-throes—of the starving peasant masses.

Come with me!

I will lead you along the well-trodden paths of my memory to the place where this flagrant crime was committed in full public view!

Let us board a mighty airplane that will take us, with fantastic speed, into the past, from the year 1953 to 1933, from the New World to the Old World, from New York to Kharkiv.

Let us forget about the burdens placed upon us by our "today." Let us cast off the shackles of our cares and devote our undivided attention to our Dear Departed.

Let us open wide the doors and windows of our souls!

34 "Without Doctors and Priests, without Graves and Crosses" is reprinted from *A Hunger Most Cruel,* by Anatoly Dimarov, Yevhen Hutsalo, and Olena Zvychayna. Translated by Roma Franko, edited by Sonia Morris. Toronto: Language Lantern Publications, 2002.

SCENE I

The Showcase Window

May 1933.

You are with me in Mykolayivsky Square in the centre of Kharkiv. Listen carefully! You will hear that the groan "Bread!" is the leitmotiv of the din in the capital. Look carefully! It is ragged peasants who are groaning; maimed by hunger, they are scattered in large numbers throughout the crowd.

Before us stands the squat, white-columned building of the All-Ukrainian Central Executive Committee—abbreviated as "VUTsVyK." This building resembles a white bird—a bird with widely spread wings that has settled down in the very centre of Kharkiv.

"What are those people up to? The ones who are swarming around the right wing of the VUTsVyk building like bees around honey?" you ask.

"Do you really want to know? Come with me!"

And a moment later, you and I are standing in a restlessly moving crowd of famished people from the district of Kharkiv and . . . we are looking, along with this crowd, at the windows of the building.

"Why, the sumptuous displays of food in these windows can compete most favourably with those in New York!" you say.

And it is true! A huge sturgeon, laid out on a shelf, stretches from one end of the display case to the other. Marinated herrings in small casks vie for top honours with their smoked brothers and sisters whose golden spines are heaped in woven baskets . . . There are eels here that resemble snakes, dried navaga, pink cured slabs of sturgeon, and tender mackerel.

And, next to this window, there is another one filled with meat—and this display is in no way inferior to that of the fish. Here there are mountains of sausages, topped by the Ukrainian variety, appetizing headcheese, and delicately pink hams that draw the voracious stares of the starving residents of Kharkiv and its outlying districts.

And that is not all! In a third window there is an entire sea of cookies, elaborately baked pastries, and other dainties. The butter called "Extra" flaunts itself there, along with candies, sugar, and honey! And, in the very middle of the display, as if it had assumed the position of the master, stands a sack of brilliantly white flour with the coveted red label "000."

"All this looks wonderful!" you say. "But why are all these people just staring and swallowing their saliva instead of going inside to buy something?"

"It's really quite simple. This is the Torhsin, and the food may be bought only with foreign currency or gold."

At that moment, a horrifying, strangled groan forces us to glance down, beneath the window.

It is the groan of a peasant, a man in the prime of life, twisting himself over on his back. His eyes are closed, his lips are parched and cracked, his work-worn hands are calloused and swollen with a serous liquid, and his feet and legs, worn-out, rough, and chapped, are bloated like logs . . . Sighing heavily, the peasant exhales hoarsely, straightens out, stretches his body out tautly, grows rigid, and then . . . becomes oblivious to everything around him.

And just like that, ever so simply, without any dramatic effects, this son of our fertile soil dies of hunger under this elegant window of the Torhsin, under the hospitable wing of the VUTsVyK.

You shift your glance from the calloused hands of this still warm body to the white flour with the coveted red label "000," and . . . you become thoughtful.

I leave you to your thoughts.

The peasants, disfigured by hunger, sit and lie—ghastly and motionless—beneath the showcase windows of the Torhsin, forming a unique wholeness with the products of their labour that fill those windows, products that are displayed strictly for show, and sold only for foreign currency or gold . . .

And now, look over there, at that peasant family that is settling down under the window showcasing the fish. There is the still youthful father in his homespun trousers, the mother with the face of a martyred saint, and their two small whimpering children, their voices broken, thin, and ragged. Oh, it is clear to see that they have walked for a long time, and begged for a long time, imploring the crowds in the city to give them succour! Their bags are empty, their strength is drained . . .

Now the father lies down with his legs tucked tightly under him—the space under the display windows is cramped!—and places his unkempt, tousled head on the mother's knees, and she, clutching both infants to her breast, freezes into a state of complete immobility.

This grouping of four human beings creates a tableau of indestructible unity, an eternal cohesiveness that neither Soviet intransigence nor death itself is able to rend asunder.

It is a typical peasant family; it is the unshakeable foundation of our Nation.

"But isn't the Soviet press aware of all this?" you ask in wrathful indignation. "Where is the press?"

"Right over here!" and I point at a large grey building situated directly across from us, on the other side of the narrow street. "It is in that building that the editorial offices of the newspaper The Communist are housed. You see the sign, don't you? Buy a copy of today's paper and you will see that, choking in its haste to praise the collective system of farming and the achievements of collectivization, it calls upon everyone to destroy the kurkuls as a class, while taking great pains to pretend that it does not see what it really sees . . ."

"But why aren't these unfortunate people taken away to a hospital?" you ask.

"Because it is strictly forbidden to take this 'social scum' to a hospital."

How horrifying, how terrifying for a peasant to starve to death under the wing of a building housing the labour-peasant government of the Ukrainian S.S.R., under showcase windows that so cynically display the stolen products of their labour. And in direct view of the editorial offices of The Communist!

"Are you serious? You've decided to step inside the Torhsin? Well, if you have foreign dollars, the Torhsin is at your service!"

How peaceful and pristine, how dazzling and magnificent it is inside the Torhsin! How elegantly the salesclerks are dressed, and how solicitously polite they all are. And then there is the handsome doorman with his ravishing long beard! How diligently he ensures that not a single hungry peasant should, by chance, cross the threshold!

And just look how thick and solid the masonry walls are! And look at these heavy windowpanes! In here, neither the crying of the children, nor the final sighs and prayers of those who are completing their life's journey on the other side of the thick stone wall, can be heard.

SCENE II

Artificial Orphans

You and I are at Kharkiv's main market, the one that is called Blahovishchensky, or, for short, Blahbaz.

A sea of people . . .

Against the background of this sea, our eyes catch sight of an island of ragged peasants who, sitting and lying in rows, are selling off their last remaining heirlooms: some are selling a tablecloth executed in fine needlework; others—a rushnyk; and still others—a beautiful plakhta. And all these treasures are being bought by shrewd hagglers for a scrap of bread, for a couple of boiled potatoes..

"But why don't they go and find some work, while they still have the strength to do it?" you ask.

"There is a categorical decree forbidding people to hire this 'social scum,'" I reply. "But are you aware that the Blahbaz is where, every day, peasant children are abandoned by their mothers?"

"What? Why?"

"They abandon them in the hope that the Soviet government will take the orphans to a shelter and . . . feed them there . . . Listen to what Hanna Bezlushchenko related to me once:

"'Do you hear what I'm saying?' she asked me. 'I abandoned my little Yustynka at the Blahbaz. I told her—stay right here, my dear little daughter, and wait for me! And I'll go buy some bread. I watched her. My little one was standing obediently in the spot where I had left her. And then I ran away as fast as I could without looking back . . . I walked, I ran, I cried, and my tears clouded the roadway, and all the while she—my dearest little one—stood before my eyes . . .'"

Mothers! Do you feel the overwhelming, unspeakable horror of a moment like that?

Do you see these artificial orphans in their grimy homespun shirts, with their skeletal arms and legs, their large, distended bellies, their sallow faces, and their little eyes crazed with terror? Every one of them is searching in vain in the sea of strange faces for his or her mother's face . . . Every one of them is crying, wailing, shrieking . . . And then, exhausted by their screaming, they instinctively huddle together like little chicks whose mother hen has just been swooped up by a hawk . . .

The artificial orphans of an artificial famine!

SCENE III

"The Union of Town and Country"

This is the phrase coined by Moscow communists to express the "exciting unification" of the village and the city, a union supposedly created by Soviet socialism.

The wheels of our taxi roll along smoothly: you and I are travelling to Tovkachivka . . . I'll tell you later why we are going to Tovkachivka. But in the meantime . . . the hopelessly grey cloth of life in the capital city of the Ukrainian S.S.R. unwinds before your eyes—a cloth that death uses as a background on which to embroider its own distinctive patterns with cross-stitches as black as the chornozem.

A flood of hungry people deluges the city and flows in turbulent streams through its streets and squares. Everywhere, absolutely everywhere, there are piteous farmers with empty bags. Some shout and plead: "Bread! A bit of bread!" Others are silent and sit, spent with fatigue, under the masonry walls—these are the "nearly dead." Still others, indifferent to everyone and everything, occupy "comfortable" places in sheltering corners and concavities in the stone walls—these are the dead.

"Why don't the urban residents organize assistance and relief?" you ask.

"Because officially there is no famine, and asserting that there is a famine, or organizing relief for this 'social scum,' is viewed as counterrevolutionary activity for which you will pay with your life. And, as for private assistance, it also is impossible, because every worker receives only a small, clearly inadequate portion of bread with his ration card. Do you see these queues snaking their way through the city?"

"Yes."

"The 'fortunate' residents of socialist Kharkiv are constantly standing in line to get what is 'given' to them. 'What is it that is given?' This is a question that makes you want to go deaf . . .

"On their ration cards they are 'given' bread, millet, kerosene, kamsa—tiny and terribly salty fish that we greedily swallow whole, together with their intestines, tails, and heads—and some other things like that . . .

"Occasionally they are 'given' shoes, or four metres of fabric for a dress, but they also stand in line for days on end not to get these 'factory goods,' because . . . it is impossible to make enough shoes for everyone! Just look at the dresses the women are wearing. It's true that they're multicoloured, but they are all made out of old clothing that has been dyed, turned inside out, and sewn anew.

"Well, what do you think? How much bread can someone who receives only 300 grams on a ration card spare for a hungry person? A labourer gets a little more, but he needs more . . ."

"But are there people who have enough to eat and who can clothe themselves in a normal manner?"

"Yes! Of course! There are even those who eat and dress luxuriously, but they are government officials, the administrators of the Red Terror and their families. They do not help the hungry as a matter of principle, because they view them as 'social scum' fated for extermination."

"Bread! A bit of bread!"

These groans hang like a cloud over the city. There is no escaping them . . .

A human being from a village begs a human being in the city for a bit of bread, and then dies in full public view without ever receiving any.

And there you have "the union of the town and country," the union about which the creators of Soviet socialism speak with such pride!

SCENE IV

Commerce

A line-up of several thousand starving peasants is twisting, bending, and winding in spirals on the wasteland beyond Tokachivka . . . It is twisting, bending and zigzagging its way forward, striving, like a sentient arrow, to reach its ultimate goal—the kiosk with commercial bread.

"What is commercial bread?"

"What? You don't know? The word comes from 'commerce.' The labour-peasant government of the Ukrainian S.S.R. is engaged in commerce: the grain that it has stolen from the peasants it sells back to hungry peasants as bread for three karbovantsi a kilo . . . That is why the bread is called commercial. And it is the correct name for it. But to have the good fortune to eat that bread, three karbovantsi are not enough. After registering in the evening, you have to guard your spot in the queue all night, and, from six o'clock in the morning, you have to keep a good grip on the person ahead of you; you have to stoically withstand rain, hail, shoves, and curses, and in some cases, you pay for your dream about bread with your very life.

"What are those?" you ask in horror, casting your eyes at a row of motionless bodies near a ravine.

"Those are corpses . . . To be more precise—they are the victims of today's queue for 'commercial bread,'" I reply. "Every time that the queue of hungry people, exhausted by the intolerable wait, comes into contact with bread that has just been delivered, there is a violent assault on the kiosk, an assault resembling a tornado, a hurricane. The stronger peasants push forward with all their might, and the weaker ones fall to the ground; and then the stronger ones, treading on the bodies, get a better spot in the line. Ribs and bones crunch. This 'social scum' is destroying itself—thereby fulfilling the goals of the Red Kremlin. The labour-peasant militia observes what is happening with callous satisfaction: its function is to toss the corpses aside when the current of self-destruction finally ebbs... And then the queue, in 'exemplary' order and clutching the person ahead by the waist, enters the kiosk ten at a time under the watchful eye of the militia: 'Bread! Bread! One kilo—per one pair of hands.'"

Over here is one of those fortunate ones who has finally(!) got his "commerce," and he sits down on the grass to eat it . . . Look how his fingers tear at the loaf; how he gulps, chokes, snorts, and swallows the bread without chewing it . . . But before the 'fortunate' owner of this kilogram of bread can finish his splendid repast, the remaining bread drops helplessly from his weak hands. He writhes, roars from the very bottom of his belly, and vomits, throwing up the bread that he has obtained with such great effort.

In the doorway of the kiosk a militiaman appears and, struggling to speak in Russian, says: "So, citizens, there is bread for only thirteen groups of ten. The rest of you must disperse! We don't want to see hide or hair of you here! Come on now, off you go—on the double!"

He quickly counts off thirteen groups of ten, and the queue of people that so recently was twisting, bending, and zigzagging its way like a sentient arrow striving to reach its goal, is suddenly transformed, as if by a thunderbolt, into an exhausted group of "the nearly dead."

And, in this throng of the "nearly dead," unscrupulous people are already roaming about, offering to buy a kilo of bread . . . for thirty karbovantsi. This black marketeering with black bread is conducted under the protective wing of the labour-peasant militia. This too is "commerce" that expedites the destruction of "social scum."

SCENE V

Without Graves and Crosses

Night.

You and I are observing life in the capital of the Ukrainian S.S.R. from a balcony on the sixth floor. Up above, the stars are barely twinkling. And down below, the dull din of the city can hardly be heard.

A truck with a canvas-covered box swoops in like a black bat to the gates of our building. A few militiamen jump down. The janitor of our building appears and, with his help, the bodies of the dead and the still living are flung into the back of the truck.

A moment later, the truck, after travelling a short distance, comes to a stop in front of a neighbouring building where the same "operation" is repeated.

The dark air of the May night is pierced by the groaning and the wailing of the still living—now buried by corpses. But such minor details of their "operation" do not cause the least bit of concern among the workers of the "labour-peasant militia" that carries out the will of the "labour-peasant" government of the Ukrainian S.S.R.

With full loads stashed under their canvases, these trucks speed away beyond the city boundaries, into the fields, into the forest. There they unload their "cargo" into marshes or ravines, or simply leave the unfortunate wretches in the forest . . .

And this scene is repeated every night . . . After such an "experiment," it is only the odd person who is fortunate enough to struggle back to Kharkiv . . .

It is not candles, but stars that light the way for our peasants in their final moments; it is not doctors, but death the saviour that sets them free from their suffering with a touch as cold as ice; and it is not a priest, but God Himself who accepts their final prayers and . . . their souls . . .

Do we fully comprehend the number 7,000,000? It is a number equivalent to the population of New York; it is all of Austria; it is three Slovakias!

Brothers and sisters! Let us honour the memory of the seven million victims of the artificial famine organized in Ukraine by Red Moscow—the seven million who died among stone walls without doctors and priests, without graves and crosses.

Let us rise and honour their memory with a moment of silence.

GLOSSARY FOR THE SHORT STORY

NOTE: For the convenience of the reader, the plurals of certain Ukrainian words used in the story are anglicized in this glossary, i.e., the "s" ending is used.

bandura a Ukrainian musical instrument similar to a lyre

chornozem rich black soil (Russian: *chernozem*)

decree on the protection of socialist property punishment for any theft from the state sector ranged from confiscation of personal property, a five-year term in a forced labour camp, to execution

halushka/s small boiled dumplings made of dough

hopak a spirited Ukrainian folk dance

karbovanets a dollar in pre-1996 Ukrainian currency

karbovantsi (plural of *karbovanets*)

khokhol/s a derogatory Russian term for Ukrainians

kolhosp/s a collective farm (Russian: *kolhoz*)

Komsomol the youth wing of the Communist Party

kopiyka/s a penny in Ukrainian currency

kozak/s Ukrainian equivalent of "*Cossack*"

kurkul/s a well-to-do peasant/farmer (Russian: *kulak*)

kylym/s a tapestry or patterned rug

l'origan koti an expensive perfume

Myrrad Myrhorod radioactive curative water

NKVD People's Commissariat of Internal Affairs; Soviet state political police

oven bed a sleeping area atop a clay oven

plakhta/s a traditional Ukrainian wraparound skirt woven out of multicoloured yarn

put'ovka/s an expensive pass to a health resort, handed out without cost to high-level government officials and supporters

pysanka an egg intricately designed with wax and steeped in dyes

rushnyk/s embroidered linen ceremonial cloth

sam odyn all by himself, all alone

sarafan/s a traditional Russian long, sleeveless dress

serednyak/s a moderately well-to-do peasant/farmer

Torhsin a store in the Soviet Union that accepted payment only in foreign currency or gold *(Russian: Torgsin)*

TOZ (TSOZ) Association for the Common Cultivation of Land

ARTICLE: "BEHIND UKRAINE'S PROTEST ARE MEMORIES OF MOSCOW'S FAMINE"

Marta Baziuk
Dec. 11, 2013, Globe and Mail

teacher tip

This article is suitable for an analysis activity on p. 194.

Hundreds of thousands of Ukrainians have protested in the streets over the past three weeks, culminating in the current occupation of government buildings and pitched battle with riot police in central Kiev. The ostensible trigger was the last-minute decision of President Viktor Yanukovich to back out of a trade agreement with the European Union, moving instead toward a deal with Russia and its Customs Union.

Commentators have framed the demonstrations in terms of competing economic interests, geopolitical intrigues, Russian-speaking eastern vs. Ukrainian-speaking western Ukraine, and Russian-Ukrainian relations. Yet these analyses don't explain why so many Ukrainians are protesting this time. At the heart of their outrage is an emphatic rejection of what many Ukrainians see as Soviet-style rule. Explaining why they are in the streets, the protesters occasionally mention economics, but more often they say, "to live in a normal, civilized country," "so that our children can live with human dignity," or "to be free to travel, to work and to live our lives."

The Soviet legacy of authoritarianism and terror is not so easily shed. The most devastating chapter was the Holodomor - the Famine of 1932-33, when Soviet authorities forcibly removed grain and foodstuffs from farmers, many who had resisted collectivization. Borders were closed to prevent people from seeking food beyond Ukraine. Many millions of Ukrainians were starved to death. Joseph Stalin launched an assault on Ukrainian cultural leaders as well, murdering and exiling thousands of artists, intellectuals, and clergy. The Holodomor was a demographic and cultural catastrophe for Ukraine, exacerbated by Soviet Russification policies.

Oksana Zabuzhko, one of Ukraine's best-known writers, believes that today's corrupt Ukrainian state is a direct consequence of the 1933 genocide, when the most ruthless prospered. "Those who stole the most during the Holodomor made out the best. And indeed, in independent Ukraine, those adept at stealing managed to take hold of the collective farm," Ms. Zabuzhko told me. "That is, all of Ukraine, from which they've plundered, carrying the wealth back to 'their own house.' Our current leadership, the third generation, is not capable of having a different, state-centered 'managerial' mentality. And whether the house in question is a hut with a pigsty or an offshore account on the Cayman Islands is purely a quantitative, not a qualitative, difference."

For three generations, to mention the word "famine" was taboo; the Soviets denied that the Holodomor had taken place until the end of the USSR. Only then did archives become accessible that illuminated its scope and intentionality.

Yet the administration of President Viktor Yanukovich is engaged in diminishing the significance of the Holodomor. This year, staff at the Institute of National Memory in

Kiev produced a book, the central thesis of which echoes Soviet-era Cold War propaganda - that the Holodomor was conceived as a means to discredit the USSR. Similarly, Russia refuses to accept the Holodomor as a Ukrainian rather than a general Soviet tragedy, and leaked diplomatic documents have shown that Russian officials have threatened post-Soviet countries should they recognize the Holodomor as a genocide.

Fear, and in particular, fear before authority, is the most enduring impact of the Holodomor, according to psychiatrist Semyon Gluzman, president of the Ukrainian Psychiatric Association and former Soviet dissident. In an interview weeks before the protests, he said: "It lingers in the consciousness of our Ukrainian people, who are still not free." It would take another generation, he added, for Ukrainians to be rid of it.

The first generation to come out of the shadows of the Holodomor has arrived. Born after the fall of the Soviet Union, they are as likely to have spent time in Paris or Munich as in Moscow. They differ from their parents in other ways. They are completely at home with social media, and they expect information to be shared, and shared quickly. When government forces beat peaceful protesters on Kiev's maidan, or main square, authorities claimed that these special forces had been clearing out hooligans impeding the assembly of a huge Christmas tree (or rather, New Year tree, the term used since Soviet times). But video of the brutal assault was already on the internet for all to see. At least three websites are streaming live feeds as events in Kiev unfolded.

Whatever the short-term outcome of the protests, young Ukrainians will continue to press for change in their country. With a sense of identity informed by the tragedy of their country's past, they are impatient for Ukraine to cast off its lingering Soviet ways. They see no reason why Moscow should determine their fate. They will not be satisfied until their country's institutions guarantee democracy, rule of law, and human rights - which just happen to be criteria for joining the European Union.

"Euromaidan: Revolution of Dignity," Kyiv, December 1, 2013.

Image Credits

Images on the Ukrainian Famine of 1932 –1933 are scarce due to the ban on travel for foreigners within the Soviet Union at that time. Nearly all photographs showing starvation during the Holodomor were taken secretly by foreigners and smuggled out of Ukraine. For example, Alexander Wienerberger, who was working in Kharkiv, Ukraine in 1933, secretly managed to not only take a series of photographs but to get them out of Ukraine. Today they are part of the Cardinal Innitzer Collection in Vienna with copies at Ukrainian museums. Most of the images below come from the National Museum "Memorial to Holodomor Victims" in Ukraine (Kyiv). These images can be found at http://memorialholodomor.org.ua/eng/holodomor/archive/foto-arkhiv/

Some images in this publication have been given full credits on the pages where they appear. The following is a list of additional images and credits:

PART I

(Dedication page) Iwan and Nadia Mychajlowskij, parents of Valentina Kuryliw. Private Collection.

(Dedication page) The Law of Five Stalks of Grain. Logo by Oleh Lesiuk. Ukrainian Canadian Congress.

(Dedication page) James Mace. *Kyiv Daily* (Den Kyiv) newspaper, No. 30, 2003.

P.4 – Holodomor monument. Edmonton, Alberta, 1983. Designed by Ludmilla Temertey. Photo by Venera Kinda, 2015.

PART II

P. 17 – *Ukraine within Europe.* Map from Johnson Cartographics Inc., 2013.

P. 18 – *Ukraine's Changing Borders in the 20th Century.* Map from Johnson Cartographics Inc., 2013.

P. 20 – Chernobyl Reactor No. 4 with its enclosing sarcophagus. Photo by Redrat72, Wikimedia, 2007.

P. 21 – *Ukrainian Lands at Start of First World War, 1914.* Map from Johnson Cartographics Inc., 2013.

P. 22 – Joseph Stalin, c.1942. *The History of the Civil War in the USSR, Vol.1.* Library of Congress, Prints and Photographs Division.

P. 22 – "Zdaiut khlib (Giving up grain)." Kyiv Oblast, 1932. 1932-1933 archives, National Museum "Memorial to Holodomor Victims," Kyiv.

P. 23 – "Small amount of goods a kurkul was allowed to take," Kharkiv. 1932-1933 archives, National Museum "Memorial to Holodomor Victims," Kyiv.

P. 23 – "Young girl." Kharkiv Oblast, 1933. The Cardinal Theodor Innitzer collection, National Museum "Memorial to Holodomor Victims," Kyiv.

P. 24 – *Holodomor Famine Genocide Area in Ukraine and the Kuban*. Map from the exhibit/ CD "Holodomor: The Ukrainian Genocide," Ucrainica Research Institute and the League of Ukrainian Canadians, Toronto, 2008.

P. 25 – "Village scene (starving women)." Kharkiv Oblast, 1933. The Cardinal Theodor Innitzer collection, National Museum "Memorial to Holodomor Victims," Kyiv.

P. 25 – "Confiscation of hidden grain." Donetsk Oblast, early 1930s. 1932-1933 archives, National Museum "Memorial to Holodomor Victims," Kyiv.

P. 27 – Walter Duranty. 1937. Ukrainian Wikipedia.

P. 27 – "Journalist and broadcaster Malcolm Muggeridge in 1929 October." Trinity Mirror/Mirrorpix/Alamy Stock Photo.

P. 28 – "Armed guard guarding wheat." Kharkiv Oblast, 1933. 1932-1933 archives, National Museum "Memorial to Holodomor Victims," Kyiv.

Pp. 29-33 – Photos in Timeline of Events:

- P. 29 – Central Rada, 1911. *The Historical and Cultural Monuments in Ukraine.* Wikimedia Commons.
- Symon Petliura. Wikimedia Commons.
- Vladimir Lenin. 1920. *Soyuzfoto*. Wikimedia Commons.
- Ukrainian delegation in Brest-Litovsk. 1918. F. Bruckmann. Wikimedia Commons.
- Newspaper cover page. *The Daily Mirror.* June 30, 1919.
- P. 30 – Propaganda poster 1935. Gustav Klutsis. Wikipedia. (The poster reads "Long Live the Workers and Peasant Red Army - Loyal Guard of the Soviet Borders!").
- "A boy from village Blahovishchenka, Zaporizhia." Wikimedia Commons.
- Flag-map of Ukrainian Soviet Socialist Republic, 1922-1927. Dmytrij. Wikimedia Commons.
- Poster promoting Ukrainization. Kharkiv, 1921. Wikimedia Commons.
- Leon Trotsky, 1918. Wikipedia.
- P. 31 – Wheat fields with Ukrainian farmer. Kyiv Oblast, 1929. National Museum "Memorial to Holodomor Victims," Kyiv.
- OGPU emblem/medal, 1930. Retrieved from Nikita Vasilevich Petrov and Konstantin V. Skorkin, *Kto Rukovodil NKVD, 1934-1941* ("Who ruled NKVD, 1934-1941"), Moscow: Zvenia, 1999.
- St. Michael's Cathedral. Kyiv, 2003. Valentina Kuryliw.
- "Collection point for grain." Kyiv Oblast. 1932-1933 archives, National Museum "Memorial to Holodomor Victims," Kyiv.
- P.32 – "Hunger drives the farmers to migrate." Kharkiv Oblast, 1933. A.

Wienerberger. The Cardinal Theodor Innitzer collection, National Museum "Memorial to Holodomor Victims," Kyiv.

- Viacheslav Molotov. Dutch National Archives, The Hague.
- The Law of Five Stalks of Grain. Logo by Oleh Lesiuk. Ukrainian Canadian Congress.
- "Blacklisting of village." Kyiv Oblast, 1932. 1932-1933 archives, National Museum "Memorial to Holodomor Victims," Kyiv.
- "Taking away the wheat" (wheat convoy). Kharkiv Oblast. 1932-1933 archives, National Museum "Memorial to Holodomor Victims," Kyiv.
- P. 33 – Pavel Postyshev. 1935. Photo exhibit in Moscow movie theatre. Wikimedia.
- "Starving villagers - Village Scene." Kharkiv Oblast, 1933. The Cardinal Theodor Innitzer collection in the 1932-1933 archives, National Museum "Memorial to Holodomor Victims," Kyiv.
- League of Nations logo from 1920-1946. Wikipedia.
- Raphael Lemkin. August 28, 1959. United States Holocaust Memorial Museum.

P. 34 – Mykhailo Hrushevsky. Early 1930s. Wikimedia Commons.

P. 35 – Symon Petliura. Wikimedia Commons.

P. 35 – Leon Trotsky. 1918. Wikipedia.

P. 35 – Report cover. Treaty of Peace (Versailles), 1919. Auckland War Memorial Museum archives.

P. 36 – "Village Girls in Ukraine." Wikipedia Commons.

P. 36 – "Anti-Religious lesson." Kharkiv Oblast, 1932. National Museum "Memorial of Holodomor Victims," Kyiv. (Writing on chalkboard reads "Religion is opium, down with priests").

P. 37 – "Kurkul's house being emptied." Kharkiv Oblast, 1932. 1932-1933 archives, National Museum "Memorial to Holodomor Victims," Kyiv.

P. 38 – Trial for the Union for the Liberation of Ukraine. Kharkiv, 1930. Wikipedia Commons.

P. 38 – White Sea Canal concentration camp. 1933. Wikipedia.

P. 39 – Bolshevik newspaper. *Pravda*, March 16, 1917. Wikipedia.

P. 39 – The Saviour Tower at the Kremlin in Moscow. Milan Nykodym. Wikimedia Commons.

P. 40 – Newspaper. List of blacklisted villages. *Zoria*, January 27, 1933. Retrieved from *Ukrainska Pravda* (Ukrainian Truth) website.

P. 41 – League of Nations logo from 1920-1946. Wikipedia Commons.

P. 41 – Law of Five Stalks of Grain. Logo by Oleh Lesiuk. Ukrainian Canadian Congress.

P. 47 – *Direct Famine Losses in Ukraine by Region, 1932-1934.* The Great Famine Project of the MAPA: Digital Atlas of Ukraine program. Harvard Ukrainian Research Institute, Harvard University (HURI).

P. 49 – "Corpses in the streets of Kharkiv arouse the sympathy of the famished." Kharkiv, 1933. A. Wienerberger. The Cardinal Theodor Innitzer collection, National Museum "Memorial to Holodomor Victims," Kyiv.

P. 50 – *How the Genocide Was Organized.* Panel from the exhibit/CD "Holodomor: the Ukrainian Genocide." Ucrainica Research Institute and the League of Ukrainian Canadians, Toronto, 2008.

P. 51 – Maxim Litvinov. Retrieved from Isaac McBride, *Barbarous Soviet Russia*. New York: T. Seltzer,1920, p. 102.

P. 52 – Walter Duranty, 1937. Ukrainian Wikipedia.

P. 52 – Book cover. Ray Gamache, *Gareth Jones, Eyewitness to the Holodomor.* Cardiff: Welsh Academic Press, Ashley Drake Publishing Ltd., 2013.

P. 53 – Franklin D. Roosevelt. December 27, 1933. History.com.

P. 53 – Edouard Herriot. George Grantham Bain Collection, Library of Congress.

P. 53 – Richard B. Bennett. Library and Archives Canada.

P. 54 – Sidney & Beatrice Webb. During their trip to the Soviet Union in 1932. Library of the London School of Economics and Political Science, UK.

P. 54 – George Bernard Shaw. December 1934. Wikimedia Commons.

P. 54 – Book cover. George Orwell, *Animal Farm.* New York: Harcourt, Brace and Company, 1946. Book Cover Archive website. Designed by Shepard Fairey.

P. 54 – Book cover. Robert Conquest, *The Harvest of Sorrow.* Edmonton: University of Alberta Press, 1986.

P. 55 – Viktor Yuschenko. October 26, 2000. Wikimedia Commons.

P. 55 – Viktor Yanukovych. September 11, 2012. Estonian Foreign Ministry. Wikimedia Commons.

P. 56 – Petro Poroshenko. Claude Truong-Ngoc/Wikimedia Commons/CC BY-SA 3.0.

P. 56 – "Child lighting a candle on Holodomor Memorial Day." 2014. Private Collection.

P. 57 – Raphael Lemkin. August 28, 1959. United States Holocaust Memorial Museum.

P. 57 – Book cover. Raphael Lemkin. *Axis Rule in Occupied Europe*. The Lawbook Exchange, Ltd., 2008.

P. 58 – "Ratification of the UN Convention on the Prevention and Punishment of the Crime of Genocide." 1950. UN Photo Collection.

P. 58 – Professor Roman Serbyn. Wikimedia/Fondapol – Fondation pour l'innovation politique/CC BY-SA 2.0.

P. 59 – "Starving children rummaging for food in the rubble." Kharkiv, 1933. A. Wienerberger. The Cardinal Theodor Innitzer collection, National Museum "Memorial to Holodomor Victims," Kyiv.

P. 64 – Painting. "Starvation in Ukraine 1933." William Kurelek. Mixed media 1977. The Ukrainian Institute of Modern Art, Chicago.

P. 74 – "Harvest time for a Ukrainian farming family." *Selianka Ukrainy.* (The Ukrainian Villager), 1929, No. 11, p. 16.

P. 76 – Gouache on board. "No One Wanted to Die." Mykola Chervotkin, 1989. From the collection "Holodomor: Through the Eyes of Ukrainian Artists." Founder & trustee Morgan Williams.

P. 77 – Sviatoslav Karavasky. The University of Chicago Library archives.

P. 77 – "Destroyed bells of church." 1932-1933 archives, National Museum "Memorial to Holodomor Victims," Kyiv.

P. 77 – "Playtime in the village." *Selianka Ukrainy.* (The Ukrainian Villager), 1928, No.1, p.2.

P. 78 – "Torgsin" (pawn shop). Putivl, 1933. *National Historic - Cultural Guidebook of Putivl.*

P. 79 – "Village home (khata)." Kyiv Oblast, 1932. 1932-1933 archives, National Museum "Memorial to Holodomor Victims," Kyiv.

P. 79 – Book cover of *Ukraine: 1933 A Cookbook.* Linocut by Mykola Mykhaylovych.

P. 79 – "Children digging for frozen potatoes." Donetsk Oblast, 1933. 1932-1933 archives, National Museum "Memorial to Holodomor Victims," Kyiv.

P.80 – Oil on canvas. "The Road of Sorrow." Nina Marchenko. 1998-2000. From the collection, Holodomor: "Through the Eyes of Ukrainian Artists." Founder & trustee Morgan Williams.

P. 81 – Political poster. *Law of Five Stalks of Grain.* V. Govorokov. 1933. Retrieved from V. Sedliar, Kobzar. Kyiv: Dukh i Litera, 2011.

P. 82 – "Confiscation of hidden grain." Donetsk Oblast. 1932-1933 archives, National Museum "Memorial to Holodomor Victims," Kyiv.

P. 84 – Linocut. "Millions of Ukrainian Peasants, Our Grandfather, Perished from the Holodomor Organized by the Communist Regime." Oleksandr Nikolayets. 1988. From the collection "Holodomor: Through the Eyes of Ukrainian Artists." Founder & trustee Morgan Williams.

P. 87 – "Seizure of kulak grain." Donetsk Oblast, 1932. 1932-1933 archives, National Museum "Memorial to Holodomor Victims," Kyiv.

P. 88 – "Hunger drives villagers to migrate." Kharkiv Oblast, 1933. The Cardinal Theodor Innitzer collection, National Museum "Memorial to Holodomor Victims," Kyiv.

P. 89 – "Cemetery, mounds of graves." Kharkiv Oblast, 1933. The Cardinal Innitzer collection, National Museum "Memorial to Holodomor Victims," Kyiv.

P. 92 – "Starving children rummaging for food in the rubble." Kharkiv, 1933. A. Wienerberger. The Cardinal Theodor Innitzer collection, National Museum "Memorial to Holodomor Victims," Kyiv.

P. 95 – Gouache on board. "Stalin and the Bones of Ukraine." Yevhen Luniov, 1989. From the collection, "Holodomor: Through the Eyes of Ukrainian Artists." Founder & trustee Morgan Williams.

P. 97 – "Journalist and broadcaster Malcolm Muggeridge in 1929 October." Trinity Mirror/Mirrorpix/Alamy Stock Photo.

P. 97 – W. Duranty. 1937. Ukrainian Wikipedia.

P. 98 – Book cover. Marsha Skrypuch. *Kobzar's Children*. Markham, ON: Fitzhenry & Whiteside, 2006.

Pp. 100 to 102 – Student art provided by teacher, Halia Sawycky-Dmytryshyn.

P. 105 – Book cover. Barbara Coloroso. *Extraordinary Evil: A Brief History of Genocide*. Toronto: Penguin Canada, 2008.

P. 108 – Documentary jacket. *The Harvest of Despair,* 1984. Ukrainian Famine Research Committee, Toronto.

P. 108 – Holodomor monument. Edmonton, Alberta, 1983. Designed by Ludmilla Temertey. Photo by Venera Kinda, 2015.

P. 109 – Ukrainian flag and trident crest. Wikimedia Commons/Ssolbergj/CC BY-SA 4.0

P. 109 – Viktor Yuschenko. October 26, 2000. Wikimedia. Private collection.

P. 110 – Canadian flag and crest. Wikipedia.

P. 113 – Manitoba flag and crest. Wikipedia.

P. 114 – Alberta flag and crest. Wikipedia.

P. 115 – Ontario flag and crest. Wikipedia.

P. 116 – Saskatchewan flag and crest. Wikipedia.

P. 117 – Commemoration of Holodomor Memorial Day at St. Mary's Ukrainian Catholic Church in Mississauga, Ontario. 2012. Valentina Kuryliw.

P. 118 – Quebec flag and crest. Wikipedia.

Pp. 120 to 122 – Notable people photos:

- Vsevolod Balytksy. Soviet Communist Party Members, 1898-1991. Wikipedia.
- Poster. "People of Truth." William Henry Chamberlin. The U.S. Committee for Ukrainian Holodomor Genocide Awareness 1932-1933.
- Robert Conquest. LikeSuccess.com.
- Walter Duranty, 1937. Ukrainian Wikipedia.
- Edouard Herriot. George Grantham Bain collection, Library of Congress.
- Cardinal Theodor Innitzer. Alchetron.com.
- Book cover. Ray Gamache. *Gareth Jones: Eyewitness to the Holodomor.* Cardiff: Welsh Academic Press, Ashley Drake Publishing Ltd., 2013.
- Lazar Kaganovich. *New World Encyclopedia*. Creative Commons CC-BY-SA 3.0.
- Stanislav Kosior. Bolshevik archives. Wikipedia.
- Raphael Lemkin. August 28, 1959. United States Holocaust Memorial Museum.
- Vladimir Lenin. 1920. *Soyuzfoto*. Wikimedia Commons.
- Newspaper. James Mace. *Den Kyiv* (Kyiv Daily). No. 30, 2003.
- Viacheslav Molotov. Dutch National Archives, The Hague.
- Pavlik Morozov (1918-1932). Official portrait, wearing the Young Pioneer's red scarf. Retrieved from the *Russian American* newspaper website.
- "Journalist and broadcaster Malcolm Muggeridge in 1929 October." Trinity Mirror/Mirrorpix/Alamy Stock Photo.
- Pavel Postychev. Russian State Library, digital source.
- George Bernard Shaw. December 1934. Wikimedia Commons.
- Mykola Skrypnyk. Retrieved from Danylo Husar Struk, ed. *Encyclopedia of Ukraine, vol. 4*, Toronto: University of Toronto Press, 1993.
- Joseph Stalin, 1930-1936. Retrieved from Maksim Gorky, *The History of the Civil War in the USSR, Vol.1.* New York International Publishers, 1937.
- Leon Trotsky. Wikipedia.
- Beatrice & Sidney Webb. During their Trip to the Soviet Union in 1932. Library of the London School of Economics and Political Science, UK.

PART III

P. 134 – "Soup kitchen." Odesa. 1932-1933 archives, National Museum "Memorial to Holodomor Victims," Kyiv.

Pp. 138 to 142 – Student art provided by teacher Halia Sawycky-Dmytryshyn.

P. 143 – Jars for making butter. 2013. Halia Sawycky- Dmytryshyn.

P.161 – Book covers. Anatoliy Dimarov et al. *A Hunger Most Cruel: selected prose fiction.* Winnipeg: Language Lantern Publications, 2002; Marsha Forchuk Skrypuch, *Kobzar's Children.* Markham, ON: Fitzhenry & Whiteside, 2006.

P. 171 – "Ukrainian khata (house)." Ichnya, Chernihiv Oblast, 1977. Valentina Kuryliw.

P. 173 – Book covers. Ulas Samchuk, *Maria: A Chronicle of a Life,* Toronto: Language Lantern Publication, 2011; Olha Mak, *Stones Under the Scythe.* iUniverse Publication, 2011.

P. 178 – Drawing. "Despair in Ukraine." Anna Romaniak, 1998. Private collection.

P. 185 – "Hramota," (Soviet certificate for achievement in education for Olga Baranivska). Kyiv, 1930s. Ukrainian Canadian Research and Documentation Centre, Toronto.

P. 195 – "Empty khata (house)." Kharkiv Oblast, 1933. The Cardinal Theodore Innitzer collection, National Museum "Memorial to Holodomor Victims," Kyiv.

P. 213 – "Village home in Ukraine." Kyiv Oblast, 1932. National Museum "Memorial to Holodomor Victims," Kyiv.

P. 215 – "Confiscation of Kulak's property." Donetsk Oblast. 1932-1933 archives, National Museum "Memorial to Holodomor Victims," Kyiv.

P. 217 – Holodomor monument in Winnipeg, Manitoba. Roman Kowal, 1984. Photo by Norbert Iwan.

P. 238 – "Ukrainian village." Kyiv archives, 1929.

P. 240 – "Dead body in the streets of Kharkiv." Kharkiv Oblast, 1933. The Cardinal Theodor Innitzer Collection, National Museum "Memorial to Holodomor Victims," Kyiv.

PART IV

P. 266 – Holodomor monument in front of St. Michael's Cathedral, Kyiv. 80th Commemoration of the Holodomor, November 2013. Valentina Kuryliw.

Pp. 274 to 278 – Student art provided by teacher Halia Sawycky-Dmytryshyn.

P. 289 – "Harvest time for a Ukrainian farming family." *Selyanka Ukrainy* (The Ukrainian Villager), 1929, No. 11, p. 16.

P. 300 – "Euromaidan: Revolution of Dignity." Kyiv, December 1, 2013. Valentina Kuryliw.

(Inside back cover) Holodomor Mobile Classroom of the National Holodomor Awareness Tour, 2016. Valentina Kuryliw.